His
Tra
Gu
Flc

2nd Edit

Eliot K

Pineapple Press, Inc.
Sarasota, Florida

For Debra, my wife, who never stopped believing

Inquiries should be addressed to:
Pineapple Press, Inc.
P.O. Box 3889
Sarasota, Florida 34230

Library of Congress Cataloging-in-Publication Data

Kleinberg, Eliot.
    Historical traveler's guide to Florida / Eliot Kleinberg. -- 2nd ed.
        p. cm.
    Includes bibliographical references and index.
    ISBN-13: 978-1-56164-375-2 (pbk. : alk. paper)
    ISBN-10: 1-56164-375-0 (pbk. : alk. paper)
    1. Historic sites--Florida--Guidebooks. 2. Florida--Guidebooks.
I. Title.
F312.K57 2006
917.5904'44--dc22

                                        2006021055

Second Edition
10 9 8 7 6 5 4 3 2 1

Printed in the United States of America

Contents

Acknowledgments

The Palm Beach Post has granted permission for the adaptation and republication of "Florida Legacies." Post archives have provided many of the photographs contained here.

Most of the stories in this guide are adapted from the Florida Legacies columns that ran in *The Palm Beach Post*. Most contain additional material that had been cut from the original articles because of space limitations; all have been updated since they first appeared in *The Post*. Of course, all information, especially times and rates, is subject to change. And this is by no means a complete listing of historic sites in Florida, though in this second edition I've added 17 sites and updated each entry as needed.

Following are the sites added in this new edition: Panhandle — Florida Caverns State Park, Torrey State Park, and San Luís Talimali; North Florida — Fort Caroline, St. Augustine, Bulow Plantation, Cedar Key, Paynes Prairie, and Micanopy; Central Florida — Eatonville; Tampa Bay/Sarasota — Yulee Sugar Mill, Dade Battlefield, Tarpon Springs, Historic Spanish Point; South Florida — Boca Raton Resort & Club and Stranahan House; Keys — Monument to the Labor Day Storm. These were not published in The Post except for portions of the Eatonville, Tarpon Springs, and Boca Raton Resort entries and all of the Dade Battlefield entry.

Each site in this book presents a place in Florida where something happened. It may have been a major event or some obscure, yet fascinating, incident. In every case, we direct you to something you can see or a place you can tour. The book is assembled as a guide. Sites are split by regions. A cross-reference in the back lists sites by subject.

This book could not have been done without the support of The *Palm Beach Post*. Executive editor Edward Sears, managing editor Tom O'Hara, and associate managing editor Jan Tuckwood approved the series.

Travel editor Cheryl Blackerby approved topic selection, paid for required trips, decided when stories would run, and produced their publication. Photographers, artists, and copyeditors contributed to the final product. Library managers Mary Kate Leming and Michelle Quigley and their staff were talented and tireless resources.

The attractions, sites, parks, visitors' bureaus, chambers of commerce, museums, and libraries mentioned in this guide provided many of the pictures as well as comprehensive bibliographies. They painstakingly studied the text — pointing out errors, offering interpretation, adding information, and suggesting additional reading.

Of special help were the public libraries of Boca Raton and Delray Beach; Miami-Dade, Broward, and Palm Beach Counties; and Florida Atlantic University. The historical societies of Florida, South Florida, and Palm Beach County, and their staff and members, provided valuable information and guidance.

Introduction

I had gone to my college library with every intention of studying. But freshman fever had overtaken me, and my wanderings had led me to the newspaper microfilm room. The word "Richmond" topped the front page of the April 4, 1865, New York Times.

We all know Richmond fell. The history books tell it, often in dreary prose accompanied by insufferable analysis on how the end of the Civil War led to regional industrialization, westward expansion, and blah, blah, blah. But this wasn't some stuffy scholar's musings on long-dead people and long-ago events. These were eyewitness accounts of the death of a nation.

And a few years later, I found myself staring at the blood-stained wooden floor in the old U. S. Senate chambers. There, South Carolina U. S. Representative Preston Brooks — for whom Brooksville, Fla., is named — had conducted the near-fatal 1856 caning of a Northern senator who had insulted Brooks' uncle. I found myself wanting to shout, like Gene Wilder in Young Frankenstein, "It's alive! Alive!"

I had realized that history is blood and guts and laughter and tears — famous people and everyday people struggling to make a living and to cope with the dramatic events swirling around them. My love for history later became focused on the state where I was born. I learned it is more than wilderness and settlement, war and peace, boom and bust. It's former Governor Richard Keith Call furiously waving his cane at secessionists and grimly warning they were opening the gates of hell. It's Seminoles "mooning" soldiers to incense them into exhausting their ammunition. And it's gangster John Ashley placing a shiny bullet at the teller's window during a bank robbery to taunt the sheriff.

Florida is both the oldest state and the youngest. This was where Europeans first set foot on the North American continent five centuries ago, but its modern history mostly concerns this century. And while Florida has the most to tell, it tells the least. The average resident arrived six and a half years ago. Florida's public schools provide only a cursory curriculum in state history. And many journalists conduct ill-informed forays that unwittingly perpetuate myths and lies.

It is not so much that Floridians should be required to know their history. Apathy is not a character flaw; when people don't care, it's because no one has excited them. But knowing the past is crucial to understanding its impact on your life today. No discussion of Everglades cleanup, redistricting, or local civil rights can ignore history.

One of the few positive things to come out of a three-and-a-half-year exile in Texas was that I learned history storytelling at the feet of masters. It's not unusual for a Texan to be third-generation, and the state has no shortage of tales about the Wild West — many of them, surprisingly, true.

But I argue that Florida's past has more substance and more excitement. That's why I'm proud to have been born here, proud to have been in each of the state's 67 counties, and proud for the opportunity to share with you the tales, personalities, and events that have become like old friends.

Panhandle

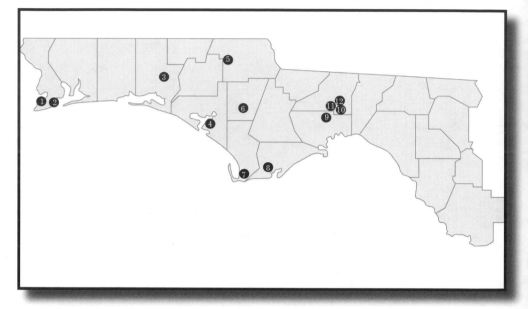

1. Fort Pickens, *Pensacola*
2. Historic Pensacola
3. DeFuniak Springs
4. Union Monument, *Lynn Haven*
5. Florida Caverns State Park, *Marianna*
6. Torreya State Park, *Bristol*
7. John Gorrie Museum, *Apalachicola*
8. Negro Fort/Fort Gadsden
9. Wakulla Springs
10. The Old Capitol, *Tallahassee*
11. San Luis de Talimali, *Tallahassee*
12. Natural Bridge Battlefield, *south of Tallahassee*

Fort Pickens

Pensacola

A monument to one man's anguish

The giant cannons of Fort Pickens, site of one of the first battles of the Civil War in Florida, stand silently, still pointing out to sea as a challenge to long-gone foes. Visitors can walk among the ruins of this installation, built to help protect Pensacola Bay, and explore the dark and damp hallways that sometimes lead to dead ends.

Fort Pickens is one of a string of forts lining the American coast rendered obsolete by the advent of air power. It's part of a triad built to protect Pensacola Bay; Barrancas is now on the grounds of Naval Air Station Pensacola, and McRee, built on the eastern side of Perdido Key, fell victim to Civil War bombardment, storms, and erosion.

Fort Pickens stands as a memorial to one man's great personal anguish. William Henry Chase, supervisor for the U. S. Army Corps of Engineers, built it between 1829 and 1834. He then liked the area so much he retired there.

In 1861, he volunteered to fight against the Union and for Florida. His first mission was to gain the surrender or destruction of the fort he had built. His troops confronted Fort Pickens, but when the Union soldiers inside refused to give up, tears welled in his eyes, and he turned away. He could not attack what he had created.

A compromise was later struck: the soldiers could stay as long as more troops were not sent. But President Abraham Lincoln later did just that; troops arrived a few hours after Fort Sumter came under attack in South Carolina. Chase was relieved of command, and General Braxton Bragg built up Confederate forces to about 10,000.

Finally, after a minor skirmish, the federal troops at the fortified Fort Pickens opened fire in November 1861 at rebels occupying Fort Barrancas and Fort McRee, and area residents watched cannonballs fly across the mile-wide strait. There was considerable damage. And the Civil War had come to Florida.

Fort Pickens, where the Civil War in Florida began. *Fort Pickens National Monument*

Fort Pickens is southeast of Pensacola. Follow U. S. 98 southeast across Pensacola Bay to Gulf Breeze. Take State Road 399 to Pensacola Beach, then west about nine miles. Visitors Centers and gift shops open May through September, 10:00 A.M. to 4:30 P.M. Self-guided tours are available daily. Guided tours available on weekends and holidays. Call (850) 954-2635. The museum was damaged by Hurricane Ivan in 2004 and storms in 2005 and was closed as of this printing. Please check to see if it has reopened before your visit.

Fort Barrancas is inside Pensacola Naval Air Station property. Follow Barrancas Avenue, then south on Navy Boulevard about one mile to the station entrance. Visitor Center open March through October, 9:00 A.M. to 5:00 P.M. and November through February, 8:30 A.M. to 4:00 P.M.. Closed Christmas Day. Call (850) 455-5167.

The fort is part of the **Gulf Islands National Seashore**. Write to 1801 Gulf Breeze Parkway, Gulf Breeze 32563. Call (863) 934-2600. Website: www.nps.gov/guis

Escambia County Tourism Department: Box 550, Pensacola 32593. (904) 438-4081.

Read More About It
Coleman, James C. and Irene S. *Guardians on the Gulf: Pensacola Fortifications, 1698–1980*. 1982, Pensacola, Pensacola Historical Society.

Historic Pensacola

Florida's other oldest city

The San Carlos came crashing down. The 83-year-old hotel, oozing history, had been abandoned since 1980. Several efforts to restore it failed, and no one was in a position to spend the money needed to fix it up or knew a way to make it profitable again. So down it came in pieces in April and May of 1993, to be replaced by a federal building.

Pensacola is the latest Florida city wrestling with the past and present. It was actually founded in 1559, before St. Augustine, America's oldest city, but was abandoned and resettled a half century later. Pensacola is a long way from much of Florida. But it may be the state's best secret.

Not everything has been peachy. A training-only aircraft carrier that had been in Pensacola for decades became a museum in Texas. And abortion clinic shootings in 1993 and 1994 brought the kind of national publicity the town didn't need.

Fiercely proud of its five-century history but eager to jump to the front of the growing list of bold new cities of the South, this town is spending millions of dollars to revitalize its historic areas. Downtown is where you'll find a restored historic village, a 10,500-seat arena, and a cemetery dating back to the 18th century — all within a few blocks.

Buildings and streets are being renovated and restored to their period look, often by removing façades to uncover the original turn-of-the-century fronts. The town's historic showcase is Historic Pensacola Village, a three-square-block area featuring restored period homes, an archaeological exhibit, and several museums. Nearby, the North

3

Tivoli High House, Historic Pensacola Village's information center and museum store.
Historic Pensacola Preservation Board

Hill Preservation district and Pensacola Historic District feature hundreds of restored homes.

Just as Jacksonville is in many ways more Georgia than Florida, Pensacola is often described as more related to the state next door; in fact, at least three times referenda have asked western Panhandle voters if they wanted to secede and join Alabama. But Pensacola's Florida roots are strong.

Pensacola was, after all, a capital of Florida — West Florida. The territory, later combined with East Florida and shrunk to its present borders, once spanned from the Apalachicola River to just east of New Orleans and included the southern parts of present-day Alabama and Mississippi.

When England was fighting the upstart colonists in the 1770s, the last thing it needed was a second front. But the governor of then-Spanish Louisiana saw a chance to take advantage of British vulnerability. His target: Pensacola, then capital of the territory of West Florida.

On March 8, 1781, armed with 64 ships and 4,000 soldiers, he arrived at Santa Rosa Island. For two months, bolstered by the arrival of fresh troops, the Spanish besieged Pensacola, finally overrunning its weary force of 2,000 Brits. West Florida was Spanish again. East Florida would soon follow. The leader of the siege of Pensacola, Bernardo de Galvez, was to later go to Texas, where Houston's beach city, Galveston, would be named for him.

A trip to the beach is mandatory here. There are two reasons. One is Fort Pickens, once one of America's great coastal forts when attacks from the sea were all the national defense Americans had to worry about. The fort was active up until World War II, and much of its building and armaments remain. The fort is part of the Gulf Islands National Seashore.

The second is the beaches. With sand so white, pure, and powdery it's used in construction work, they may be the finest in all of Florida.

Pensacola Historic Museum: 115 E. Zaragosa St. Call (850) 433-1559. Open Monday through Saturday 10 A.M. to 4:30 P.M. Free admission. Website: www.pensacolahistory.org

Pensacola Bay Area Chamber of Commerce: Box 550, Pensacola 32593. Call (850) 438-4081. Website: www.pensacolachamber.com

Pensacola Bay Area Convention & Visitors Bureau: 1401 E. Gregory St. 32502. Call (800) 874-1234. Website: www.visitpensacola. com

Read More About It
Bowden, Jessie Earle. *Pensacola: Florida's First Place City.* 1989, Norfolk, Va., Donning Co.

DeFuniak Springs

Where culture came to the Panhandle

No spot so sweet, no water half so blue
God's crowning circle wrought with compass true.

The streets of DeFuniak Springs radiate from the lake that is the town's physical and spiritual center. At the lake's edge is an ornate white building with hardwood and wooden decks that now houses Walton County's Chamber of Commerce.

Earlier this century, it was "the Hall of Brotherhood." This hub-shaped town was the unlikely hub for the winter meeting of the Chautauqua, a western New York gathering of intellectuals who discussed arts, sciences, history, politics, theology, and cooking.

The Chautauqua began as a Sunday school in 1874 at a Methodist camp on the shores of Lake Chautauqua, near Jamestown, New York. Within 30 years, more than 150 such societies, most not connected to the original Chautauqua Lake Association, had spread nationwide.

Association officials went south looking for a winter home for the gatherings. They ended up in DeFuniak Springs, a planned community set up in 1883 in central Walton County and named for an official of the Louisville & Nashville Railroad. It had been founded as a much-needed train stop, resort community, and county seat in the desolate Panhandle.

Founders built several structures, including the Hotel Chautauqua — rates were ten to fourteen dollars a week, with meals — but feared overflow attendance and even arranged for tent sites and for lumber to build temporary cottages. Admission to the month-long conference was twenty-five cents per event, one dollar for five days, or three

TOP: The Hotel Chautauqua boasts one thousand running feet of veranda.
CENTER: The former Chautauqua Hall of Brotherhood in DeFuniak Springs now houses the Walton County Chamber of Commerce. *Bob Shanley, Palm Beach Post*
BOTTOM: Florida Chautauqua map, DeFuniak Springs, 1884. *Florida Chautaqua, Inc.*

dollars for a full package. Eight schools offered lectures and classes on subjects as diverse as the art of roasting and life in Burma.

But only about 100 people attended the first gathering, and it collected only $400 in income against $11,000 in costs. Organizers bravely scheduled the second annual assembly. They also published a quarterly newspaper so successful it later went to a monthly schedule.

The Florida event was to last more than three decades, adding entertainment that included music and fireworks. DeFuniak Springs itself grew dramatically in population, and more structures were built.

The advent of newspapers and radio and the explosion of World War I left Chautauqua behind. Its 1920 session, its 36th, was its last, although the Florida version was believed to have operated into the late 1920s.

Many of the original buildings are now private homes. The centerpiece is the former 4,000-seat auditorium, built in 1909 for $28,000 and featuring 40 columns. Hurricane Eloise, in 1975, damaged much of the building. It now houses the Walton County Chamber of Commerce.

An annual festival that tries to recapture the heady days of the Chautauqua started up in 1978, and Florida Chautauqua, Inc., organized in 1993. It hosts a community theater, school programs, a speakers' bureau, and the Florida Chautauqua Institute, a center for learning and instruction in the arts.

The Chautauqua Festival is held in April in downtown DeFuniak Springs. The Chautauqua Auditorium is on the lake at West Avenue.

Take Interstate 10 to U. S. 331, then north about one mile to Live Oak Avenue; turn right and follow to the lake.

Brochures available for self-guided tour of historic downtown.

Florida Chautauqua, Inc.: Box 847, DeFuniak Springs 32433. Call (850) 892-7613. Website: www.florida-chautauqua-center.org

Walton County Chamber of Commerce: 95 Circle Drive, DeFuniak Springs 32433. Call (850) 892-3191. Website: www.waltoncounty chamber.com

Read More About It
McKinnon, John L. *History of Walton County.* 1911, Atlanta, Byrd Publishing.

Union
Monument

Lynn Haven

Yankee pride in the deep South

The statue of a mustachioed soldier stands with his rifle flush against his leg, facing north, toward the land for which he symbolically fought. What's wrong with this picture?

Here in what still passes for the deep South, Florida's Panhandle, he is one of the few monuments in the former Confederacy that honors the Grand Army of the Republic, the force that fought for the Union in the Civil War.

The memorial's been vandalized at times and sparks plenty of comment from people with long family memories on both sides of a struggle that ended more than a century ago.

The twenty-six-and-a-half-foot-high statue, down a side street in the downtown area of Lynn Haven, a Panama City suburb, was dedicated February 12, 1921 — Abraham Lincoln's birthday.

At the time, it was declared the southernmost Union monument.

"There it will stand, silently preaching 100 percent Americanism to those now living and to generations unborn for many years to come," the *Bay County Beacon-Tribune* wrote of the dedication.

Lynn Haven's founders — a Minnesota U.S. senator and the publisher of the official publication of the Grand Army — pitched the town heavily to Northerners. The local GAR post then coaxed members into donating part of their monthly pensions to pay for the monument. Spanish-American War veterans helped pay as well.

It was originally adorned with plaques on all sides of its ten-foot-square base, but vandals stole one during World War II, and

9

the other three were taken to the City Hall for safekeeping. The statue was rededicated in 1956 as a monument to all American war veterans.

Union monument, Lynn Haven.
Bob Shanley, Palm Beach Post

The Union Monument is on Eighth Street and Georgia Avenue in downtown Lynn Haven. Take State Road 77 north to Eighth Street, then west three blocks.

Bay County Chamber of Commerce: Box 1850, Panama City 32402. Call (850) 785-5206. Website: www.panamacity.org

Panama City Beach Convention and Visitors Bureau: 17001 Panama City Beach Parkway, Panama City Beach 32413. Call (800) PCBEACH (722-3224). Canada: (800) 553-1330. Website: www.thebeachloversbeach.com

Read More About It
Bell, Howard W. *Your 50 Years in Bay County, Florida.* 1967, Panama City, Boyd Brothers.

Florida Caverns State Park

near Marianna

Deep in Florida

Did Seminoles hide in the caves of Florida's Panhandle to escape the rampaging General Andrew Jackson? It's probably just legend, as are the tales of Confederates using the caves to hide ammunition and supplies from Union troops. They add to the mystery of these deep, dark holes in flat Florida, just about the last place you'd expect to find a subterranean cave.

Florida Caverns State Park is the only state park in Florida with cave tours. A guide walks you through about 1,600 feet of the primary cavern, explaining how acid in groundwater ate away at underground cavities, then drained.

You'll see limestone stalactites, hanging icicle-like formations made by dripping mineral-rich water; and stalagmites, formations on cave floors built up by dripping from above. You'll also see soda straws, thin and hollow stalactites; flowstone, coatings on rock cave walls caused by flowing water; and draperies, thin sheets of calcite hanging or projecting from cave walls.

In 1937, as Civilian Conservation Corps workers were doing the initial work on the park, developing its known caves for tours, a government surveyor was looking at a downed tree and saw the opening of a new cave. Workers enlarged the cave and made it accessible to the public. It and the park opened in 1942.

As is the case with many Florida state parks and other facilities, this one was built by the workers of the CCC, the federal program that was designed to find work — any work — for those who had none, leaving its legacy across the country.

11

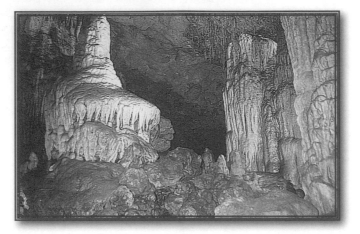

Stalactites in Florida Caverns State Park. *Doug Waitley*

Tours last about 45 minutes and the last one leaves the visitor center about 4 P.M. Tours regularly sell out. No smoking, food, drink, or flashlights. Flash photos OK.

The park also features camping, swimming, fishing, picnicking, canoeing, boating, hiking, bicycling, and horseback riding (bring your own steed, stables available). The visitor center features a walk-through museum and large-screen video tour of the caverns.

Florida Caverns State Park is three miles north of Marianna on State Road 166. From the east on I-10, take exit 142, then State Road 71 north to U.S. 90, then left, From the west on I-10, take exit 136, then U.S. 276 north to U.S. 90, then right. Follow brown park signs. Write 3345 Caverns Road, Marianna 32446. Call (850) 482-9598. Website: www.floridastateparks.org

The park is open 8 A.M. to sunset. The visitor center is open at 8:15 A.M.; an audiovisual tour is available. Fees: $4 per vehicle; $1 for bicyclists and pedestrians. Cave Tours: Every day except Thanksgiving and Christmas. Tour takes 45 minutes and is "moderately strenuous." Tour fees: 13 and older, $8; 3 to 12, $5; 2 and under free. Tours are limited to 25. Organized groups of 25 or more, $4 each prepaid with group reservations.

Read More About It

Baptist, Edward E. *Creating an Old South: Middle Florida's Plantation Frontier Before the Civil War*, 2001, Chapel Hill, University of North Carolina Press.

Torreya State Park

near Bristol

The Garden of Eden?

Only a pit remains where no fewer than six giant cannon once stood sentry on the high bluffs overlooking what was, during the Civil War, the most critical waterway in Florida.

The 90-mile-long Apalachicola River starts at Lake Seminole, at the confluence of the Chattahoochee and Flint Rivers and near where Alabama, Georgia, and Florida meet. Today, the river might be known to some mostly as the spot where Florida goes from the Central to the Eastern time zone. But through most of the twentieth century, in a period when the white population south of Ocala could be counted in the hundreds and interstate highways — or cars for that matter — were decades away, the Apalachicola was a major artery for commerce from the south to the Gulf of Mexico. More than 200 steamboats plied it.

When Florida broke away from the Union, the river became a strategic spot. Union gun boats patrolled it from its head to where it emptied into the Gulf of Mexico. Confederate leaders were determined to keep them away. No fewer than six cannon were lined up on these high bluffs to fire on the Union boats.

The bluffs, a Floridian-dizzying 150 feet high, are now known not for their military value but their beauty. And a rare type of the Torreya tree grows here. That gives the state park its name. The *Torreya taxifola* is found only here and in California and Japan. It's also known as the "stinking cedar" because a foul smell emerges if the bark is injured.

Torreya might be more than just a popular park. In 1971, lawyer and ordained preacher E. E. Callaway of nearby Bristol wrote a book called *In the Beginning* positing that the park was the site of no less

Florida Torreya tree.
Florida State Archives.

than the Garden of Eden. Callaway said the area matches the biblical description of the place and the rare Torreya is the gopher wood Noah used to build his ark.

Biblical significance notwithstanding, archaeologists have found many sites showing indigenous peoples lived in what is now the park.

During the First Seminole War in 1818, then-General Andrew Jackson — who would later be Florida governor, albeit briefly, and eventually president — brought his army into Spanish Florida to chase insurgents who were firing on American shipping. He crossed the Apalachicola at this spot.

Later, after Florida was a U.S. territory, the first government road across north Florida met the river here.

Across the water from the park, planter Jason Gregory built his plantation in 1849. Like many, it prospered on the backs of forced labor. The arrival of the Civil War, and the end of slavery, was bad for Gregory's business. The house stood empty for decades.

In 1935, the Civilian Conservation Corps workers building Torreya State Park took the Gregory House apart piece by piece and carted it across the river into the park boundaries. The house is fully furnished with period pieces and is open for tours every weekday morning and three times on weekends and holidays.

The 10,500-acre park features camping, hiking, picnicking, waterfalls, and bird watching; more than 100 species have been chronicled. Campers can stay in something called a YURT: Year-round Universal Recreational Tent. It's a tent with all the amenities of a cabin.

And, as hard as it is to believe, Florida actually has an autumn. The hardwood trees here will give you some of the state's best fall color sights, as limited and brief as they are.

Torreya State Park is off State Road 12 on County Road 1641, 13 miles north of Bristol. Write 2576 NW Torreya Park Road, Bristol 32321. Call (850) 643-2674. Website: www.floridastateparks.org

The park is open 8 A.M. to sunset. Fees: $2 per vehicle; $1 each for bicyclists and other individuals. Ranger-guided tours of Gregory House: 10 A.M. weekdays; 10 A.M., 2 P.M., and 4 P.M. on weekends and state holidays. Tours: adults $2, 12 and under $1.

Read More About It
Knetsch, Joe. *Florida's Seminole Wars, 1817-1858*, 2003. Charleston, SC, Arcadia Publishing.

John Gorrie Museum

Apalachicola

A cool place

Like Christopher Columbus, Dr. John Gorrie is both revered and reviled for his dramatic role in the development of Florida. Gorrie invented something without which Florida would still be, in the words of a nineteenth-century senator, "a land of swamps, of quagmires, of frogs, and alligators, and mosquitoes" that no one would want to emigrate to, even from hell.

He made the ice maker and led the way to that remarkable creation called air-conditioning. Without it, Florida would have far fewer people. That's why the merits of Gorrie's contributions will be debated forever.

Gorrie, born in 1803 in Charleston, South Carolina, first practiced medicine in nearby Abbeville, South Carolina, before coming to Apalachicola as a young man in 1833. It was the third largest port on the Gulf of Mexico. Gorrie was a mayor, postmaster, treasurer, council member, bank director and church founder.

In the 1830s, the town was plagued by malaria and yellow fever. Malaria struck its victims with shaking, violent chills, fever, and a drenching sweat. Yellow fever killed up to 70 percent of its victims. Shivering, high fever, thirst, headaches, and back and leg pains led to jaundice and vomiting of black blood. Your body temperature then dropped and your pulse faded; you often went into a coma. Within ten hours you were dead.

Terrified people buried victims quickly, quarantined areas, soaked handkerchiefs in vinegar and linens in camphor, placed garlic in shoes, burned sulfur and gunpowder, fired cannons. While quinine could treat malaria, there was no cure or vaccine for yellow fever.

Ignorant of the culprit that would be eventually identified — mosquitoes — most people believed the diseases were carried in vapors from coastal swamps, the kind that surrounded Apalachicola. Malaria is from the Italian for "evil air." Gorrie and other city leaders campaigned to drain swamps, clear weeds, and maintain clean food markets.

It was believed that cooling a room would improve or control the maladies. At the time, ice was cut from northern lakes in the winter, packed in sawdust and shipped around the Keys, to be sold on Apalachicola docks.

Gorrie rigged a machine to cool air and within a year had built a mechanism that produced eight to ten blocks of ice. His basic principle is still the one most often used today:

• Reduce the temperature of compressed air by injecting a small amount of water.

• Submerge the compressed air in coils surrounded by a circulating bath of cooling water.

• Condense the water out in a holding tank and release it into a tank of lower pressure containing brine. This lowers the brine's temperature to 26 degrees or less.

• Immerse drip-fed, brick-sized, oil-coated metal containers of rain water to make ice bricks.

• Release the cold air.

Gorrie got U.S. Patent 8080, the first ever for mechanical refrigeration, in May 1851, and one from London the year before.

But he was never able to market it, perhaps because the concept of artificially produced ice was too fantastic for investors. Northern business interests downplayed his accomplishments. He went from investor to investor but was continually met with skepticism.

A beaten Gorrie withdrew into seclusion, caught a fever himself and died in June 1855 in obscurity. His explanation of the remarkable machine was buried in a September 1849 issue of *Scientific American* and in the U. S. and British patent offices.

A half-century later, ice merchants came to realize Gorrie's contribution. In 1899, the Southern Ice Exchange in Apalachicola financed a monument to him.

In 1911, Florida leaders discovered to their embarrassment that an 1864 law had authorized statues of two heroes from each state in the U.S. Capitol's Statuary Hall in Washington; while most states had installed theirs, Florida had not. A hasty search settled on Edmund Kirby Smith, the last Confederate general to surrender in the Civil War, and John Gorrie.

Dr. John Gorrie's inventions led to the design of air conditioning.
John Gorrie State Museum/Bob Shanley, Palm Beach Post

Later a bridge over Apalachicola Bay was named for him and a state museum was set up in a small, red brick building in downtown Apalachicola. John Gorrie is buried in a small park across the street called Gorrie Square.

The John Gorrie State Museum is at Avenue D and Sixth Street in Apalachicola Take U. S. 319-98 into downtown Apalachicola, then go one block south to the museum. Write Box 267, Apalachicola 32329. Call (850)653-9347. Website: www.floridastateparks.org

The visitor center is open 9 A.M. to 12:00 P.M. and 1:00 P.M. to 5 P.M. except Tuesdays and Wednesdays and Thanksgiving, Christmas, and New Year's Day. Admission $1; kids 6 and under free.

Apalachicola Bay Chamber of Commerce: 122 Commerce Street, Apalachicola 32320. Call (850) 653-9419. Website: www. apalachicolabay.org

Read More About It
Becker, Raymond B. *John Gorrie, M.D.* 1972, New York, Carlton.
Sherlock, Vivian M. *The Fever Man.* 1982, Tallahassee, Medallion Press.

Negro Fort/ Fort Gadsden

A single shot brings catastrophe

Boom!

The red-hot cannonball, shot from the middle of the Apalachicola River, hit its target: a sprawling fort in Spanish Florida manned by Indians and runaway slaves.

The cannonball slammed into the ammunition pile. In a flash, 270 people died.

Today there's just a clearing here, dotted with puddles and swamps and frequented by big mosquitoes. But you can still look out from Prospect Bluff and see why the British fort, later Negro Fort, later Fort Gadsden, was put there in the first place.

The bluff, on a slow curve 25 miles north of the Gulf of Mexico, offers a clear view up the half-mile-wide, mist-covered Apalachicola River, a major artery through the South two centuries ago. Whoever commanded the bluff controlled all shipping along the river.

The tragedy of the Negro Fort stemmed from a multinational tug-of-war for the territories of West Florida and East Florida. They spanned the state's present boundaries plus parts of Alabama and Mississippi. Spain had possessed them since the sixteenth century, except for a 20-year British rule from 1763 to 1783. The Spanish were absentee owners, unable or unwilling to properly guard their sparsely populated possession.

During the War of 1812, the British, at war with America, boldly built a fort in Spanish territory to protect their interests. It went up inside a seven-acre rectangular fortification along the river. Bastions on the fort's eastern corners were 15 feet high and 18 feet thick. It was to be a base to recruit runaway slaves and Indians, including the Seminoles, who had recently migrated from Alabama.

A lucky cannon shot instantly killed 270 people at the Negro Fort.
Fort Gadsden State Historic Site

Three years later, the British abandoned the fort, leaving behind artillery and military supplies. Blacks and Indians stayed, living in the fort or in villages nearby. They fired at what few ships came down the river.

U.S. General Andrew Jackson wrote the Spanish governor, telling him to disperse the "banditti" or the Americans would do it for him. On July 17, 1816, Colonel Duncan Clinch and 116 men crossed into Spanish Florida.

The fort's leader, a black man known only as Garçon, had warned that the British had left him in charge and any American ship attempting to pass would be sunk. About 5 A.M. on July 27, Clinch's gunboats could see the Union Jack and a red flag called "the bloody flag" — a universal sign of no surrender.

From inside the fort, a 32-pound cannon shot flew toward the

Americans. Clinch returned fire. He launched four cannonballs and, having established his range, fired hot shots — cannonballs heated red hot for maximum carnage. The first one hit the ammunition pile.

"The explosion was awful and the scene horrible beyond description," Clinch wrote later. Only 30 of the fort's 300 inhabitants people were found alive; most of the fort was blown to pieces.

It was later rumored that spies had pinpointed for Clinch the location of the explosives. It's more likely his cataclysmic bull's-eye was just blind luck, says Dr. James W. Covington, a University of Tampa history professor who has written a book about the fort.

"That's all it can be," he says. "But, boy, what consequences."

Inside the ruins of the Negro Fort, the Americans found 10 cannons, 3,000 guns, and 500 swords, in addition to the 30 survivors. Clinch arrested Garçon and a Choctaw chief and had them executed on the spot. On August 3, the American troops burned down what was left of the fort and returned to New Orleans.

Jackson again went down the Apalachicola River on a search-and-destroy mission for Seminole villages that came to be known as the First Seminole War.

He instructed Lieutenant James Gadsden to build a fort where the former British fort had been. He named it for Gadsden, who is also the namesake for Florida's Gadsden County and the 1853 Gadsden Purchase in the southwestern United States.

Gadsden held the fort, despite Spanish protests, until Spain ceded Florida to the United States in 1821. It was mostly forgotten until the Civil War; Confederate troops occupied it until driven out by malaria.

The fort then fell to neglect. The state took charge of 78 acres in 1961 to create Fort Gadsden State Park. It still flies British and American flags. A marker may indicate where the bodies were buried, but rangers aren't sure. Grave robbers and wet acid soils have left little evidence of those who died so suddenly here.

Now even the fort built on their bodies has itself yielded to the elements and the surrounding Apalachicola National Forest. Only a few relics remain — and the view of the wide river that one day brought a flotilla of death.

Fort Gadsden is six miles southwest of Sumatra, 69 miles west of Tallahassee, and 24 miles north of Apalachicola. Write Box 157, Sumatra 32335. Call (850) 643-2282.

Take State Road 65 north from U. S. 98 in Apalachicola or south from State Road 20 in Tallahassee; follow signs. Open 8 A.M. to sunset. Admission is free.

Apalachicola Bay Chamber of Commerce: 45 Market St., Apalachicola 32320. Call (904) 654-9419. Website: www. apalachicolabay.org

Read More About It

Covington, James W. *The British Meet the Seminoles.* 1961, Gainesville, University of Florida Press.

Poe, Stephen R. *Archaeological Excavations at Fort Gadsden,* Florida. 1963, Tallahassee, Florida State University.

Thompson, Arthur William. *Jacksonian Democracy on the Florida Frontier.* 1961, Gainesville, University of Florida Press.

Wakulla Springs

A historic lodge and a beloved gator

The quaint state-operated Wakulla Lodge is the centerpiece of Wakulla Springs, a wilderness getaway about 15 miles south of downtown Tallahassee. Its checkerboard pink-and-beige marble floors, the arched doorway with its mosaic tile, and the ceiling beams with colorful designs recall an earlier time.

Bathing beauties with white toothy smiles from a long-gone era gaze out from giant photos. They were frozen in time in the pastel pictures, lounging on a dock or cruising in a canoe with a handsome companion. In other pictures, birds sun themselves and moss hangs from trees like musty tinsel.

The lodge, which overlooks the deep-water springs, is part of the 6,000-acre Edward Ball Wakulla Springs State park, one of the more popular sanctuaries for politicians and other residents of the capital city, not to mention people who converge on the wooded retreat from across the South.

The park, one of the few in the state featuring a hotel, sits on property once owned by north Florida financier Edward Ball. He built the lodge in 1937. The state bought the tract in 1986 from a trust set up after Ball's death.

The lodge's 27 rooms come in different sizes and styles; all have telephones but the only television is in the lobby, which also contains ornate lamps, marble checker tables, and a massive fireplace. You also can forget about radios, live bands, or a bar, and the ice cream counter is open only during the day.

The freshwater springs are among the world's largest and deepest; about 450,000 gallons flow each minute. Mastodon bones have been excavated from the cavern, which begins 120 feet below the surface. More than one headstrong diver has died in the labyrinth of underground caves.

The lagoon was used for several *Tarzan* movies and in the films *Airport '77* and *Creature from the Black Lagoon*.

The glass-bottom boats cruise the still waters, providing dramatic vistas of swarming fish and other aquatic life. Flatboat river cruisers glide past local and migratory birds and the numerous alligators who laze in the marshes; about 300 are believed to live in the springs, which stays at a cool 70 degrees year-round.

"Old Joe" was murdered in 1966.
Edward Ball Wakulla Springs State Park

The Death of Old Joe

Old Joe stares with lifeless eyes from his Plexiglas coffin.

He's been dead some four decades now. The outrage over his murder has all but faded. Now the corpse of Old Joe is a giant conversation piece in the lobby of the Wakulla Springs Lodge.

Old Joe wasn't just any alligator. He was 11 feet, 2 inches long and weighed 650 pounds. Locals said he was some 200 years old when he was found murdered August 1, 1966. (Alligators usually live 30 to 50 years, and the idea of a 200-year-old animal is folklore, game officials say.) Newspaper features said he had a ferocious grin but "a gentle nature" and was often mistaken for a stuffed or fake gator because of his lazy lifestyle.

One morning a boat operator found Joe's large body at the spring. He was believed to have been killed by a single shot behind the eyes, fired from a .22-caliber rifle. A sign inside the glass case calls it Joe's "first and only cage." The National Audubon Society and the Edward Ball Foundation set up a $5,000 reward for Joe's killer.

In 1984, a Tallahassee newspaper wondered what had happened to that reward. Leon County sheriff's Sergeant Keith Daws told the paper he knew who had killed Old Joe: Wilton Amos "Skebo" Ross, who had been charged in 1982 with bludgeoning his wife with a hammer and dumping her body in a lake. Daws says Ross told him he shot Joe by accident while hunting for younger alligators. Ross later said he'd never confessed.

Daws and another lawman said they didn't pass along the 1982 confession since it had been 16 years since Joe's death, and Ross could no longer be charged. The Edward Ball estate said the reward had been withdrawn before Ball died in 1981.

Wakulla Springs Lodge and State Park: From Tallahassee, take State Road 61 south, then go east on State Road 267 to the entrance.

Write 550 Wakulla Park Drive, Wakulla Springs 32327-0390. Call (850) 224-5950. Admission: $4 per vehicle, pedestrians, bicyclists, $1.00. Boat tours: Adults $6, 12 and under $4. Hours: 8 A.M. to sundown. Open 365 days a year. Website: www.floridastateparks.org

Wakulla County Chamber of Commerce: Box 598, Crawfordville 32327. Call (850) 926-1848. Website: www.wakullacounty.org

Tallahassee Area Convention and Visitors Bureau: (800) 628-2866. Website: www.seetallahassee.com

Read More About It

Revels, Tracy J. *Watery Eden: A History of Wakulla Springs.* 2002, Tallahassee, Sentry Press.

The Old Capitol

Tallahassee

Where Florida grew up

"The offices in the Basement of the Capitol are for rent," read the ad in the Jan. 15, 1848, *Tallahassee Floridian*.

Florida, a state for only three years, had only about 58,000 residents. Its government was so small — an oxymoron today — it sought private tenants to fill some of the offices in its new 23,000-square-foot, three-story capitol.

Now, Tallahassee boasts 28 major state buildings and a 22-story capitol tower. Nestled at the tower's base, making a stirring sight on the approach along Apalachee Parkway, is the Old Capitol. Saved from the wrecking ball when the new building opened in 1978 and restored to its 1902 appearance, it has been turned into a state historic museum that both displays and is part of the state's past.

The new capitol, parts of which are also open for tours, is the fourth such structure on the site. The territories of East and West Florida, with respective capitals in Pensacola and St. Augustine, once sprawled west almost to New Orleans and covered the southern halves of Alabama and Mississippi.

The borders were later shrunk to their current position, and in 1821, the territories went from Spanish colonies to American property and were combined. With virtually no population in the southern peninsula, Pensacola and St. Augustine were bookends.

Facing 400-mile, 20-day round trips between the two, legislators opted for a new central location. On March 4, 1824, they picked a cluster of seven hills halfway between the two former capitals. Local Indians called it "Tallahassee," Creek for "abandoned village" or "old fields."

The first statehouse, a log cabin, was replaced in 1826 by a two-story masonry building; it was never finished and its contractor went bankrupt. A state-of-the-art building, begun in 1839, opened in

Florida's old and new capitols.
Old Capitol Museum

1845, the year Florida became a state. The building was extensively damaged in an 1851 hurricane.

At the turn of the century, when Florida's population had grown to about a half million, the capitol — now featuring the luxuries of telephones and indoor plumbing — was expanded to 44,000 square feet, and the dome and north and south wings were added. It still held all of state government. East and west wings were built in 1923, and the north and south wings were expanded in 1936 and 1947.

Then Florida started to grow. At the end of World War II, it was ranked 27th in population. By 1960 it was tenth. In the 1960s, concluding the old edifice couldn't handle more additions, state officials began to build a brand-new capitol. It was dedicated March 1, 1978.

The old building was scheduled for the wrecking ball. But Florida Secretary of State Bruce Smathers gathered public support to save it. In 1982, the restored Old Capitol opened as a museum.

It had seen Florida grow from a backwater to an agricultural and trade giant, and a tourism and retirement mecca. Inside its walls, its leaders had embraced the United States, voted to leave it, suffered the humiliation of defeat and occupation, wrestled with booms, crashes, depressions and scandals, tried to ride herd on extraordinary growth, and anguished over a racial catharsis.

Now, visitors can walk through the restored Governor's Suite, rotunda, and halls, and chambers for the Supreme Court, House of Representatives, and Senate. Eight second-floor rooms have been filled with exhibits of photographs and artifacts interpreting Florida's history.

The Old Capitol Museum is directly east of the new capitol at 400 S. Monroe Street in Tallahassee.

The **Old Capitol** and **Florida Center of Political History and Governance** are at Monroe Street at Apalachee Parkway, Tallahassee, 32301. Call (850) 487-1902. Open for free, self-guided tours every day: 9 A.M. to 4:30 P.M. weekdays, 10 A.M. to 4:30 P.M. Saturdays, noon to 4:30 P.M. Sundays. Closed Thanksgiving and Christmas. Group introductions and paid programs available. Handicapped accessible. Website: www.flheritage.com/museum

Tallahassee Chamber of Commerce: Box 1639, Tallahassee 32302. Call (850) 224-8116. Website: www.talchamber.com

Tallahassee Area Convention and Visitors Bureau: Call (800) 628-2866. Website: www.seetallahassee.com

Read More About It

Ellis, Mary Louise and Rogers, William Warren. *Favored Land: Tallahassee: A History of Tallahassee and Leon County.* 1988, Norfolk, Va., Donning.

Miller, Sam. *Capitol: A Guide for Visitors.* Tallahassee, 1982, Historic Tallahassee Preservation Board.

San Luís de Talimali

Tallahassee

Religion and death

The irony is one that reverberates throughout the exploration of America. Europeans invaded Florida and inflicted slavery, disease, and massacres upon the local peoples, all while trying to bring them to God.

The Spanish, firmly ensconced in Florida after establishing St. Augustine in 1565, radiated out and began setting up both faith and commerce throughout the rest of Florida, which at the time extended throughout most of what is now the Southeast — and was all of North America they knew was there. Their motives were mixed: converted and stabilized natives were less of a threat, and the rich soils of the Florida panhandle became a source of badly needed grain for St. Augustine.

Some time between 1565 and 1585, they set up the San Luis townsite as the administrative center of the Apalache region. By 1675, at the height of the Spanish missions network, the 14 missions of Apalache hosted about 8,000 people, 1,400 of them in San Luís, making it one of the region's largest missions.

The San Luís settlement hosted a church complex, an Apalache council house, residential areas, and a large central plaza. It also had a full fort structure manned by a military garrison, including artillery. British traders, and eventually the empire's military, were encouraging local natives to attack missions, a strategy that eventually led to a full-scale assault on the Spanish mission network. The reinforcements could not come too soon.

While San Luís was one of the few to escape a direct attack, the Spanish decided themselves to raze it and abandon the region, fleeing to their territorial capitals at St. Augustine and Pensacola. They would not return to the area for a decade.

A reconstruction of a temple at the Mission of San Luís. *Doug Waitley*

Archaeologists began digging at the spot as far back as 1948. They have uncovered the fort's eastern moat and a post hole suggesting a wall of the blockhouse, and have found many artifacts.

The historic site was originally called San Luís de Apalache but has been renamed.

San Luís Archeological and Historic Site is about two miles west of downtown Tallahassee, just off U.S. 90 at Mission Rd. and Ocala Rd. Follow signs to the park. Call (904) 487-3711. Write 2020 W. Mission Rd., Tallahassee 32304.

The site is open Tuesday through Sunday, 10:00 A.M. to 4 P.M.. Closed Thanksgiving Day and Christmas Day.

Read More About It
Milanich, Jerald T. *Florida Indians and the Invasion from Europe.* 1998, Gainesville, University Press of Florida.

Natural Bridge Battlefield

South of Tallahassee

Where Florida held and boys became men

War, true to the adage, made old men young and turned boys into men in this quiet glen. Here, a river disappears underground and emerges 150 feet away. The span of land in between is a geographical oddity called a natural bridge.

On March 6, 1865, seasoned Union troops, most of them black, collided with Confederate defenders. Standing beside the rebel troops were local militia, wounded men rousted from their sickbeds, grizzled veterans, and teenage seminary cadets.

The dramatic call to arms established this skirmish as the most stirring in Florida's Civil War experience. The rebel victory that followed preserved Tallahassee as the only Confederate capital east of the Mississippi never to fall during the Civil War.

But even as the soldiers reveled, the end loomed. The Confederacy would last but a few more weeks. Florida's governor would soon end his life with a bullet to the head, unwilling to endure federal occupation. By the summer, Yankees would march unchallenged into proud Tallahassee.

Six acres of the 200-acre Civil War battlefield became a state park in 1922; the rest is on private land. A monument and three markers honor the soldiers.

"Never have people exhibited greater spirit . . ."
By early spring 1865, the Civil War was rushing toward climax. Sherman had finished his ruinous march to the sea and strategic Confederate port cities were falling to the Union like dominoes.

General John Newton, commanding Union-held Key West, launched a mission to north Florida. Some historians believe he concluded Florida was demoralized and emaciated and was ripe to fall.

But Bruce Graetz, a curator at the Florida Museum of Natural History, believes Tallahassee was never the goal. He believes Newton wanted to make an end-around and attack St. Marks, closing down still another blockade-running port and establishing a Union footing in the central Panhandle.

"At the time, the Tallahassee residents felt they were seriously being threatened," Graetz says. "There was a lot of legitimate drama in the city."

With most of Florida's and the Confederacy's soldiers off battling in the major theaters of war — Virginia, Mississippi, Tennessee, Georgia — Florida was left barely protected. A Union flotilla had arrived in Apalachicola Bay on February 28. Newton and a force of 900 landed at the St. Marks lighthouse with plans to push north toward the villages of Newport and St. Marks, destroying Confederate supplies and the railroad that linked St. Marks with the capital city. To do so, they had to cross from the east side of the river.

On March 3, 30 Union seamen surprised Confederate pickets and captured a bridge four miles north of the St. Marks lighthouse. On March 4, Navy gunboats ran aground in the shallows of the St. Marks River. They spent the next two days trying to get upstream, without success.

That delay gave just enough time for a Confederate scout to get to Tallahassee by 9 P.M. Saturday, March 4. A train sent from St. Marks blasted its whistle into the night air and cannons were fired.

"The alarm was given," the *Floridian and Journal of Tallahassee* later reported. "A unanimous and invincible response was made to the call. Every man and boy capable of bearing arms was at his post. Never, since the first commencement of the war, have the people exhibited a greater spirit."

Newton found out, writes historian Mark F. Boyd in a *Florida Historical Quarterly* account of the battle, "that he was poking a nest of hornets."

A Call to Arms

Volunteers rose to join the several hundred Confederate regulars scattered around the area: local home guard, volunteers from neighboring Jefferson County, wounded and sick Confederate soldiers recuperating at home.

Arriving by train from Quincy were the Gadsden Grays, a club whose members were residents of Gadsden County, west of Tallahassee, and who were all over 50. Their functions were usually limited to meetings and parades, where they proudly displayed their ribbons from the Seminole Wars and other assorted conflicts.

Whether they were thrilled at one last chance for glory or terrified that their boasts were finally being tested is lost to history. Governor John Milton himself called on the cadets. They were boys as young as 14 from West Florida Seminary, renamed in 1863 the Florida Military and Collegiate Institute. Their service had mostly been limited to guarding Union prisoners.

There's distinct disagreement on the number of cadets, with about two dozen the most agreed-upon number. None of the cadets were permitted into battle without their parents' permission. Distressed mothers and sisters accompanied the youngsters to the train station, where those under 12 were separated, and the rest were formally inducted into the Confederate army.

General William Miller gathered this raw assemblage and headed for Newport. Meanwhile, the Confederate 5th Cavalry had been driven back by Union troops. The 5th teamed up with the volunteers from Tallahassee.

After scouts revealed the Union troops were moving in the night, General Miller guessed the Union general's attempted surprise crossing and sent 700 men on their own overnight march to Newton's goal, the only place for several miles where troops could cross to the west side of the St. Marks without getting their feet wet: the natural bridge.

The Battle of Natural Bridge

In the pre-dawn hours, 500 to 700 Union soldiers, most of them troops from the 2nd and 99th Colored infantry with white officers, met the Confederates. The rebels had set up breastworks — earthen mounds used as shields — which still can be seen at the battlefield. They established a crescent to surround the Union troops and force them into a killing circle.

The crafty Confederate troops took advantage of their local knowledge to hide behind trees and bushes and in ponds, marshes, and thickets.

"For the most part, neither side saw the other real well or could

Florida Park Ranger Allen
Gerrell's ancestors fought each
other at Natural Bridge.
Bob Shanley, Palm Beach Post

get an idea of what numbers the other side had," Graetz says. "They'd
fire at puffs of smoke."

At the height of the battle, around midday, the Confederate line
consisted of the Gadsden Grays, another Gadsden County militia,
and an infantry unit from Milton. To the right was the 5th Florida
Cavalry, an artillery unit and a regiment of Florida reserves. In the
center, in front of the natural bridge, were the boys of the West Florida
Seminary. The 2nd Florida Cavalry arrived late and may have made
the difference in the battle of Natural Bridge.

Bennett Gerrell had signed up with the Confederates at the
start of the war but, at 14, was rejected as too young. The boy and
two other brothers later joined the 2nd Florida Union Cavalry, a
unit of Confederate deserters fighting for the North. One of the first
Confederate units to reach the battlefield had been the Kilcrease
Light Artillery. Among its members: their brother, George Edward
Gerrell.

"It was brother against brother," says park ranger Allen Gerrell,
who dresses in period garb about once every two months for events
such as the reenactment that takes place every March. He says he's
still trying to learn if his ancestors knew they were fighting each
other.

About two miles south of the battlefield, Lewis Franklin Hall,
a rebel soldier wounded at Gettysburg, had been home on sick leave
and unable to walk. Union troops discovered him and, fearing he
would warn the Confederates, loaded him onto the back of a wagon
and brought him to the rear of the battlefield. Hall, who watched

from a wagon, and George Gerrell, who fought his brothers, were ranger Allen Gerrell's great-great-grandfathers.

The Union's toll: 21 dead, 89 wounded or missing. Three rebels were killed. Remarkably, no cadets were hurt. The youngsters "behaved in the most gallant manner," the *Floridian and Journal* wrote. "Their praise is on the lips of all who took part in the fight."

Parade of the Victors

The victorious Confederate assemblage marched into Tallahassee to a hero's welcome. Residents met the train at one stop to provide refreshments and decorate the cadets with garlands.

Governor John Milton lauded the soldiers in the hall of the House of Representatives. A special company flag was crafted and presented to the youngsters.

The euphoria didn't last. In May, federal occupation troops in Tallahassee received the surrender of 8,000 rebel soldiers. Milton was already dead of a self-inflicted gunshot wound, finding death preferable to the humiliation of defeat and occupation. One of the early occupation commanders was John Newton — the general who had lost the Battle of Natural Bridge.

West Florida Seminary is now Florida State University. At its ROTC building, hanging among the flags representing its various units, is one for the brave group of youngsters who left their classroom and faced war and death.

The Natural Bridge Battlefield is about 20 miles south of Tallahassee. Follow Woodville Highway (State Road 363) south; turn left on Natural Bridge Road and go about six miles to the park. Open 8:00 A.M. to sunset. Free admission. Write 1022 Desoto Park Drive, Tallahassee 32301. Call (850) 922-6007. Website: www.floridastateparks.org

Tallahassee Chamber of Commerce: Box 1639, Tallahassee 32302. Call (850) 224-8116. Website: www.seetallahassee.com

Read More About It

Johns, John Edwin. *Florida During the Civil War.* 1963, Gainesville, University of Florida Press.

Schmidt, Lewis G. *Civil War in Florida: A Military History.* 1992, Allentown, Pa., L.G. Schmidt.

Taylor, Paul. *Discovering the Civil War in Florida: A Reader and Guide.* 2001, Sarasota, Pineapple Press.

North Florida

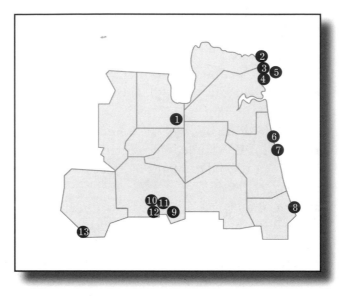

1. Olustee Battlefield, *Olustee*
2. Fort Clinch, *Amelia Island*
3. Fernandina Beach
4. Kingsley Plantation, *Fort George Island*
5. Fort Caroline, *east of Jacksonville*
6. St. Augustine
7. Castillo de San Marcos, *St. Augustine*
8. Bulow Plantation, *Flagler Beach*
9. Cross Creek
10. University of Florida, *Gainesville*
11. Paynes Prairie, *south of Gainesville*
12. Micanopy
13. Cedar Key

Olustee Battlefield

Olustee

Florida's great Civil War battlefield

The dead come to life every February in north Florida, as history buffs reenact the battle of Olustee. The curious come as well, many of them new Floridians who until recently may not have known so many died here in Florida's bloodiest Civil War battle, or even what side Florida fought on.

Winston Stephens was there the day blue and gray bled on North Florida's soil. "Never in my life have I seen such a distressing sight: Some men with their legs carried off, others with their brains out and mangled in every conceivable way," he wrote his wife Octavia. He told her he never wanted to see another battle. He got his wish. Within a fortnight, he was dead. In a span of five days, his wife lost a husband and a mother and bore a child.

"I have named my baby Winston, the sweet name of that dear lost one, my husband, almost my life. God grant that this son, whom he longed for but was not spared to see, may be like him."

The words are more than a century old, their authors long dead. But they still exude the hot blood of war; the sighing loneliness of separation and sting of sudden death; and the burning tears of humiliating military defeat, occupation, and financial devastation.

Florida was one of the first three states to leave the Union and is now perhaps the least Southern in the former Confederacy. But the Civil War in Florida has come alive in 33 diaries and about 600 letters written to and from members of a north Florida family. About 225 are between Confederate officer Winston Stephens and his young wife, Octavia.

The state's importance in the Confederacy hasn't received nearly enough attention, noted Civil War historian Shelby Foote says. "I'm

The bloody Battle of Olustee Battlefield turned the Union tide in Florida.
Palm Beach Post

glad of anything that comes along to help improve that," he says of the Stephens collection.

In a state where two in three residents are non-natives and the average resident arrived within about six and a half years, the letters provide a striking insight to everyday life into the frontier state during the country's greatest upheaval.

"My dear wife . . . Sometimes I know, my love, I write desponding letters, and I feel just as I write. Sometimes I am blue for truce and I can't see our way through this war. At other times I think that God will see fit to have it stopped at no distant day. . . . "

Winston Stephens

Winston Stephens was the son-in-law of James W. Bryant of Boston, who came to Florida about 1843, two years before it became a state. Seven years later Bryant founded the small town of Welaka, near Palatka. His daughter, Octavia, 14, developed an interest in Stephens, a nearby farmer 12 years older. To discourage the romance, her father sent "Tivie" to a Boston school, where she began keeping diaries.

Stephens, meanwhile, took part in the Third Seminole War. At its end, his beloved, now 18, returned from New England, and they married in 1859.

The winds of secession were swirling in Florida and throughout the South. While many Floridians openly opposed secession, the state, with more than 61,000 slaves — 40 percent of its population of 140,000 — voted to leave the Union.

A torchlight parade through the streets of Tallahassee wound to the home of former territorial governor Richard Keith Call. Call, who had agreed with the South's complaints but opposed secession as treason, grimly told them, "You have opened the gates of hell, from which shall flow the curses of the damned."

He was right. Before the war was over, Octavia Stephens, her family, and all of Florida would be materially and spiritually devastated. The state sent 15,000 soldiers, nearly one in 11 Floridians — the largest percentage of any Confederate state. That would be comparable to Florida sending about 1.4 million people to war today.

Rebel generals sent most to fronts far from Florida, leaving the frontier state ill-defended. Blockade ships formed an impenetrable gauntlet for nearly the entire peninsula, isolating it from commerce and supplies. Advancing armies of occupation trashed military and civilian property and at times controlled several north Florida cities.

The national rift separated the Stephens and Bryant families as well. Octavia's father, a Union sympathizer, sat out the war up north, while three of his sons fought for the rebels. A family gathering during the war had to be held under a flag of truce.

Early in the war, Stephens joined the volunteer St. Johns Rangers as a first lieutenant; the group later became Company B of the 2nd Florida Cavalry. Stephens, now a captain, fought battles along the St. Johns River and across north Florida.

His letters direct his wife's operation of his farm, where slaves raised cotton, livestock, and crops. When federal troops occupied North Florida, Octavia sold the 160-acre plantation for about $300, less than two dollars per acre. She fled with her family to Thomasville, Georgia, about 35 miles north of Tallahassee.

On February 20, 1864, Winston Stephens, 34, found himself in the small north Florida town of Olustee.

Olustee

The official reason Union General Truman Seymour advanced on this spot about 70 miles west of Jacksonville was to destroy a railroad crossing. But the Yankees' goals were far greater. President Lincoln wanted Florida back in the Union. In fact, he wanted the state, the third to secede in 1860, back in the fold by April, in time for people to vote for the great emancipator's reelection. A Union victory could lead to control of eastern Florida, east of the Suwannee River, spurring the state's many loyalists out of the shadows and leading to establishment of a provisional government by election time.

It didn't work. The resulting rout helped keep Tallahassee the only Confederate capital east of the Mississippi River never to fall during the war.

An inquiry after the battle indicated that Seymour had believed Florida was ready to reenter the Union, that he had not anticipated a large rebel force, and that he had believed destroying the crossing would keep rebels out of the state.

About 4,000 to 5,000 Union soldiers squared off with an equal number of Confederates. After about three and a half hours of battle — "during the whole time, there was not a moment's cessation of fire," one soldier wrote — the Union troops retreated into the dusk. They suffered 203 killed; the rebels lost 93. The federal defeat ended Lincoln's plans to make the first crack in the teetering Confederacy.

The next morning, Stephens surveyed the carnage, writing to his beloved of the horrible sights. Octavia wasn't sure where to send mail but wrote back anyway: "I have been anxious to see you. . . . God grant that your life may be spared and we united soon in health."

When her husband responded, the terrible images of battle and death at Olustee were fresh on his mind. " . . . to think of the loved ones at home who have been left lonely in this life by the loss of husband, son, or father, or some young lady who had been centered upon some dear one whose life is so suddenly cut off . . . "

And, he wrote, "God grant I may be spared to you. If not, grieve as little as you can for your lost husband and take consolation that I died a soldier defending a just cause."

"With a sad, sad heart . . . "

Days later, in what is now a western suburb of Jacksonville, an ambush made Octavia Stephens a widow at 22. Her brother gave grim details.

" . . . you know not the anguish of my heart when he was shot. We were side by side and tho' I was not looking at him when the fatal ball pierced him I heard it and turned. . . . That look, the last look was full of love. His lips moved but no word escaped. I see that look now and ever will."

The early days of March brought death and life to the lonely Stephens household. "With a sad, sad heart I begin another journal. On Friday March 4 . . . came news of the death of my dear, dear husband. He was killed in battle near Jacksonville on the first of March. Mother grew worse and on Sunday, March 6, she was taken from us between 12 and 1 o'clock. She passed quietly away (typhoid pneumonia). At 7 P.M. I gave birth to a dear little boy. . . ."

For Winston Stephens, the war was over. Within 13 months it would end for the Confederacy as well and leave Florida in shambles. A third of Florida's 15,000 rebel soldiers died in battle or from disease, the equivalent of Florida losing about 465,000 soldiers today. Their deaths left widows ill-equipped to manage farms. Most plantations lost their work force when the slaves were freed. In all, the state suffered the second-largest economic decline of all the Confederate states, behind only Virginia.

It would be three years before Octavia Stephens returned in 1868 to her family's north Florida home. Her own home had been trashed, as she had learned from her sister during the war. Octavia rebuilt as best she could. She never remarried. She saved the letters.

The Stephens Letters

Riviera Beach real estate agent Winston Stephens came to study his predecessor's collection, passed through generations, as a teenager in Maryland. Through it, he was introduced to the people he now knows intimately.

In 1975, Stephens donated the letters and diaries to the University of Florida. The collection was valued then at about $21,000 but bears inestimable significance to Florida history buffs and Civil War enthusiasts.

In Peabody, Massachusetts, Stephens's cousin, Ann Lainhart, painstakingly transcribed the handwritten words on fading paper into 2,000 pages of type. The book, *Rose Cottage Chronicles*, was published by University Press of Florida in 1998.

"It is not the typical Civil War story," UF history professor Fred Blakey says. "You don't have all the high-ranking politicians and military campaigns. . . . This is what it was like for literally millions of people on the Confederate home front."

The collection is one of the largest of its kind and is especially valuable because of the rarity of finding both sides of correspondence and because there are few Florida Civil War artifacts. Several collections of family correspondence and journals have come to light in recent years and gained national attention, but Auburn University history professor Frank Owsley, who read the Stephens collection, says, "I would rank this one about as good as any of them."

Octavia will be forever captured as she was then: young, newly widowed, facing a mountain. "I now begin as it were a new life and I pray that the Lord will give me strength to bear up under this great affliction and with His help . . . I may be enabled to do my duty in this life and be prepared when the Lord calls me to meet them in that better world, where there will be no parting and no more sorrow."

Olustee Battlefield State Historic Site is about 20 miles east of Lake City. Take Interstate 75 to Exit 45, follow U. S. 90 west about five miles. Interpretive museum. Battlefield site: P. O. Box 40, Olustee 32072. Call (386) 758-0400. Park hours: 8 A.M. to sunset. Center hours: 9 A.M. to 5 P.M. Free admission. The Olustee battle re-enactment is usually the second or third weekend in February. Website: www. floridastateparks.org

Olustee Battlefield Citizens Support Organization: Box 382, Glen St. Mary 32040. Call (386) 758-0400 or (877) 635-3655.

Lake City/Columbia County Chamber of Commerce: 162 S. Marion Ave., Lake City 32025. Call (850) 752-3690. Website: www. lakecitychamber.com

Read More About It
Keuchel, Edward F. *History of Columbia County.* 1981, Tallahassee, Sentry Press.
Johns, John Edwin. *Florida During the Civil War.* 1963, Gainesville, University of Florida Press.
Nulty, William. *Confederate Florida: The Road to Olustee.* 1990, Tuscaloosa, University of Alabama Press.
Schmidt, Lewis G. *Civil War in Florida: A Military History.* 1992, Allentown, Pa., L.G. Schmidt.
Taylor, Paul. *Discovering the Civil War in Florida: A Reader and Guide.* 2001, Sarasota, Pineapple Press.

Fort Clinch

Amelia Island

The loneliness of the Civil War

"I didn't join up in the Army to come into this infernal swamp to lay bricks," a scowling man in historic Union garb growls to a visitor. "I came here to fight rebs."

Fort Clinch, at the tip of Amelia Island, is as far north and east as you can get in Florida. Gaze north across Cumberland Sound, and you can see the wilds of Georgia's Cumberland Island. In the winter, the cold Atlantic Ocean winds are biting. In the summer, the heat and insects can be unbearable — especially "mosquitas: bayonet-bill gallon suckers," the soldier says.

The sentries grumble and complain as they walk aimlessly back and forth atop the fort parapet, inside the exposed 28-foot high brick walls. Be careful how you address these miserable soldiers. Walt Disney World? They've never heard of it. Ask who won the Civil War; they'll look at you cockeyed and ask how the heck are they supposed to know who won a war that ain't over yet. After all, it is 1864.

The sentries of Fort Clinch State Park are in character. The state park is one of three in Florida where employees and volunteers take part in "living history," dressing and acting in the period. The others are the Lake Kissimmee Cow Camp, near Lake Wales, and Fort Foster, near Tampa. Reenactors at Clinch walk sentry duty, maintain the fort, and cook meals.

Up to 40 volunteers are in character the first weekend of each month and up to 130 during the area's shrimp festival in May and a Confederate occupation reenactment in October. Replica cannons are fired each weekend and during encampments.

Not a shot was fired in anger from Fort Clinch during the Civil War. For the soldiers on both sides who inhabited it, the enemy was boredom, loneliness, illness, and the cold.

The fort is a brick wall frame surrounding an open area about

Corporal Timothy Matthews, a reenactor at Fort Clinch.
Bob Shanley, Palm Beach Post

100 by 100 yards. It was named for General Duncan Lamont Clinch, a leader of the Second Seminole War. Designed to house 550 soldiers, it was started in 1847, but only two of its five bastions were ever finished; bricks and mortar were diverted to strategic Fort Zachary Taylor in Key West.

Confederate troops occupied the unfinished, unoccupied fort when war broke out in 1861, but when the Union captured several Georgia and South Carolina coastal islands, Fernandina Beach was isolated. Robert E. Lee decided to abandon it, and rebels barely got out under heavy fire from Union gunboats on March 3, 1862. Yankees reoccupied Clinch three days later. A new effort to complete the fort began. But a new cannon design that could blast masonry walls with deadly power and accuracy rendered the fort obsolete. Some work continued through the end of the war and after, but it was finally halted in 1867. The garrison operation, greatly reduced after the war, was deactivated.

The fort was briefly reactivated in 1898 during the Spanish-American War, but inspections showed it had deteriorated dramatically during its dormancy. Its drawbridge was rotting. Sand blocked the entrance. There was no drinking water or sanitary toilets. The fort was auctioned off to private interests in 1926. The state bought the four-acre fort and 256 acres around it in 1935; the park, developed by the Civilian Conservation Corps, opened in 1938, and additional property was later acquired. It was activated once more, for coastal watches, during World War II. German U-Boats did their deadly work just offshore, sinking several ships, and Nazi saboteurs landed in Ponte Vedra Beach, south of Jacksonville.

The park property covers 1,153 acres at the northern tip of Amelia Island. It has 8,000 feet of shore facing Cumberland Sound, and 4,000 feet of Atlantic coastline to the east. The park's western portion is an estuary marsh.

Park rangers Corporal Timothy Matthews, Corporal Frank Ofeldt, Corporal Kevin Freeman, and Sargeant George Berninger reenact the daily grind of an 1864 occupation soldier. Matthews — he uses his real name in the reenactment — describes himself as a Michigander assigned to Company E, 1st New York Volunteers.

"All the reb sympathizers skedaddled when the rebs skedaddled in sixty-two," he says. "No matter how hard you try, you don't get to go home much."

Matthews says there's nothing to do, and the food's not too great; one local fish "has both eyes on the same side of its head." That line comes from a letter written by a Union soldier stationed in Jacksonville who apparently had never seen flounders.

But, Matthews says, "At least we ain't gettin' shot at."

Fort Clinch: Entrance just west of A1A, along Atlantic Avenue at the northern end of Fernandina Beach. Write 2601 Atlantic Ave., Fernandina Beach 32034. Park open 8 A.M. to sunset daily, including holidays. Fort and visitor center open 9 A.M. to 5 P.M. daily, including holidays. Admission: $2 for ages 6 and up, 5 and under free. Campgrounds available. Call (904) 277-7274. Website: www.floridastateparks.org

Amelia Island/Fernandina Beach/Yulee Chamber of Commerce: 961687 Gateway Blvd., Ste 101-G, Amelia Island, FL 32034. Call (904) 261-3248. Website: www.islandchamber.com

Read More About It

Johns, John Edwin. *Florida During the Civil War.* 1963, Gainesville, University of Florida Press.

Nolan, Terence H. *History of Fort Clinch,* Fernandina, Florida. 1974, Tallahassee, Florida Division of Archives.

Schmidt, Lewis G. *Civil War in Florida: A Military History.* 1992, Allentown, Pa., L.G. Schmidt.

Taylor, Paul. *Discovering the Civil War in Florida: A Reader and Guide.* 2001, Sarasota, Pineapple Press.

Fernandina Beach

Intrigue and mystery on Florida's coast

Smugglers, pirates, and mercenaries to rival any in the Caribbean moved in and out of the port town of Fernandina Beach with impunity. Far-off governments ruled it with a minimum of interest. A president called it "a festering fleshpot." It was North America's Casablanca.

On a fog-shrouded late afternoon, this village at Florida's northeast tip — about 35 miles north of Jacksonville and just across from southern Georgia, at the north end of Amelia Island — looks more like New England.

Trawlers are docked side by side. A monument declares this "the birthplace of the modern shrimp industry" because shrimpers first used the net-dragging boats here. The 52-block downtown area, much of it restored to its late nineteenth-century and early twentieth-century look, has been listed on the National Register of Historic Places.

Today's Fernandina Beach, where tourists stroll the quaint Centre Street to its dead end on the Amelia River, belies the tumultuous past of the town that claims to be the only one in America to have been under eight different flags. Five different nations have ruled it. Mercenaries twice "captured" it, only to later slink away. One group tried to start its own nation.

It is those eight flags that tell the town's story.

Crown and Cross

In 1513, Spain's Juan Ponce de León stepped ashore down the coast, claimed Florida in the name of crown and cross, then left. French settlers came ashore in 1562 and claimed the area for France. Three years later, the Spanish got word and reclaimed Florida, in the process

46

Fernandina Beach and its
Palace Saloon have seen war,
piracy, and intrigue.
Bob Shanley, Palm Beach Post

beheading most of the Frenchmen and establishing St. Augustine, the oldest continuously inhabited city in the United States.

Spain held this area, and the rest of Florida, for the next two centuries. Britain got it in 1763, then gave it back to Spain after the American revolution in 1783.

During the second Spanish occupation, Fernandina — "Beach" was added in 1951 — was an open city, famed for its lawlessness and intrigue. Goods and slaves were smuggled through the town and north into the new United States.

The U.S. government finally devised a plan to wrestle the area from Spain. It secretly backed a group of Americans living in Spanish Florida. They would seize St. Augustine, raise their flag, declare a new nation — then "surrender" to the United States and take a handsome finders' fee of sorts. But the "East Florida Patriots" were a little too successful. Spain complained so loudly that President James Madison pretended he'd never heard of the soldiers of fortune, and Spain regained northeast Florida once again.

Then "Sir General" Gregor MacGregor, a mercenary claiming five boats and a thousand men, seized Fernandina Beach without firing a shot and raised the Green Cross of Venezuela. He marched troops through the town bearing flags on tall poles — actually stalks of an odorous plant called dog fennel. MacGregor really had only 150 men. Like the East Florida Patriots, he'd planned to trade northeast Florida to the United States. When U.S. aid did not come, he slipped away.

Two henchmen left behind by MacGregor enlisted the help of "General" Luis Aury, a French privateer who frequented the area. Aury agreed to seize the town but demanded the raising of a new flag, that of Mexico; he had worked for those rebelling against Spanish authority in that country.

The United States then routed the privateers from what President James Monroe called "a festering fleshpot" and held Amelia Island for the Spanish until they finally gave Florida to America in 1821.

The Confederate flag flew briefly; Confederate forces controlled Amelia Island from secession in January 1861 to early March 1862, and the Union held northeast Florida during the rest of the Civil War. The Stars and Stripes has flown ever since.

Bordellos and Sailors

The centerpiece of Centre Street is the Palace Saloon, about two blocks from the harbor. Built in 1878 as a tie shop and converted in 1903, it is said to be Florida's oldest bar still operating under the same name. It stands as a drawback to the town's nineteenth-century heyday, when it was said to boast about 20 saloons and at least one bordello and thrived on brawling sailors and dock workers.

The dimly-lit bar is filled with folklore.

Sailors tossed coins over the back bar to assure a safe voyage; throwing one so it balanced on the bust of one of the bar's carved female figures established one as a great lover. But coins that fell into the narrow space behind the 13-foot-long bar couldn't be retrieved, and the structure has never been pulled away from the wall; no one knows how much money is back there.

One legend says the money is the property of "Uncle Charlie," the ghost of a bartender who had worked there since 1906 and died in an upstairs room in 1966. As the story goes, anyone who tries to recover Charlie's money will pay for their misdeed in the afterlife.

When nearby Cumberland Island, Georgia, became a playground for the rich and famous, the saloon became a popular getaway. When Prohibition loomed, the bar stocked up, and it was the last in Florida and one of the last in the nation to close. Cars backed up for miles on its last day, August 19, 1918; it rang up the then-astronomical figure of $60,000 in sales.

The saloon fell on hard times during the Depression and was sold in 1956 to a Fernandina Beach family for only $10,000. A series of individuals leased and operated the bar until 1991, when it was sold to a Miami-based investment group.

The walls of the Palace Saloon are covered with a series of murals drawn by artist Walter L. Kennard. Two portray figures from Shakespeare — Falstaff from *Henry IV, Henry V,* and *The Merry Wives of Windsor,* and Shylock and Portia from *The Merchant of Venice.* A third shows two British barristers arguing over a point of law. Another depicts Mr. Pickwick from Dickens' *The Pickwick Papers.*

Kennard drew a new one in 1959 to replace one that had faded. In an homage to Fernandina Beach's past, it shows a series of pirates, swords raised, and the legend, "Stand and Deliver."

Fernandina Beach is about 45 minutes north of Jacksonville. Take I-95 to exit 373 in Yulee, then A1A east about 15 miles

Amelia Island/Fernandina Beach/Yulee Chamber of Commerce: 961687 Gateway Blvd., Ste 101-G, Amelia Island, FL 32034. Call (904) 261-3248. Website: www.islandchamber.com

Read More About It

Jaccard, Deon L. *Clash of the Cultures: The Awakening of History for Amelia Island, Florida.* 1992, Fernandina Beach, Amelia Island Museum of History.

Litrico, Helen Gordon. *Centre Street: Fernandina Historic District.* 1976, Fernandina Beach, Amelia Island Fernandina Beach Restoration Foundation.

Smith, Joseph Burkholder. *The Plot to Steal Florida.* 1983, New York, Arbor House.

Kingsley Plantation

Fort George Island

Africa's legacy in north Florida

The plantation of Zephaniah Kingsley was not a place where blacks sang spirituals at revivals and in the fields. Kingsley's slaves were recent arrivals, and he allowed them to do tribal chants that bound them to their homeland. He had ripped out the grass around his home to protect it from brush fires. One could stand on Kingsley's porch and see the swirling dust and dancing flames of campfires as the drum beats and chants of the slaves echoed through the trees.

The home, which had been operated by the state, came under the National Park Service in 1991 after a large area northeast of Jacksonville became the Timucuan Ecological and Historic Preserve.

Visitors can see the Kingsley home, a kitchen house, the barn and the ruins of 25 tabby houses. Kingsley bought this two-and-a half-mile-long island near Jacksonville in 1817; its first owner received it under a grant from Spain. Kingsley bought slaves in Africa, where legend says he bought a tribal chief's vanquished enemies, allowing the chief to rid himself of them and make a profit at the same time. With 60 slaves, he produced Sea Island cotton, citrus, sugar cane, and corn. He eventually owned more than 32,000 acres, including four plantation complexes and more than 200 slaves.

Perhaps the most prominent figure in the Kingsley saga is his black wife, Anna Jai. She was from Senegal, and legend said she was the daughter of the African chief with whom Kingsley did business, and he married her according to tribal custom. But documents show he bought her in Cuba. She actively took part in running the plantation and had her own land and slaves when Kingsley freed her in 1811.

Kingsley's Florida was still part of the Spanish empire, whose

TOP: The home of north Florida planter Zephaniah Kingsley. *Eliot Kleinberg*
BOTTOM: Only 23 of 32 slave cabins at the Kingsley Plantation remain.
Timucuan Ecological and Historical Preserve

toehold in North America was dwindling. America badly wanted Florida, which Spain was finding as much a burden as a boon. There were foiled attempts to seize it, one backed clandestinely by the U.S. government.

Florida eventually joined the United States in 1821; Kingsley was recognized as one of its leaders and appointed to a special council to develop the new territory. But America's views on race and society jeopardized the lifestyle of Kingsley and his wife, not to mention the other two women who bore children of his and whom he had set up in plantations up and down the St. Johns River. America was less than tolerant of such relationships, and Kingsley feared the government would not recognize his mulatto children and could force them to leave the territory or even be sold back into slavery

Kingsley decided to sell his plantation in 1839 and set up Anna and her children in what is now the Dominican Republic. During a business trip to New York, he became ill and died in 1843. That sparked a decades-long estate battle between his descendants and his other relatives. One of the loudest voices of protest came from Kingsley's sister, Martha McNeill.

Kingsley's wives and descendants finally got some reward, although much of the estate was depleted by the cost of the lengthy court battle and years of political upheaval and corruption in Haiti. Anna returned to Jacksonville before the case was settled. She returned in 1846 to not only stay with her daughters, but to fight the court battle over the will, which, amazingly, she was able to win.

In the late 1850s, Martha's daughter, Anna McNeill Whistler, then living in New York, began taking lengthy visits to the Jacksonville plantation owned by her brother, Charles J. McNeill. It had been willed to him by Kingsley. In letters to her son, whom she called "Jemie," the woman wrote that she spent her days, "inhaling the sea breezes on the piazza, looking down the St. Johns two miles wide."

Anna McNeill later moved to London, and in 1872, when she was about 65 years old, her son "Jemie" painted a portrait of her that was to become of the world's most recognizable works of art. Anna McNeill Whistler was James Abbott McNeill Whistler's mother.

Kingsley Plantation is on Fort George Island, northeast of Jacksonville. Take Heckscher Road (Florida 105) east almost to the beach to the turn off to Kingsley Plantation, 1/2 mile north of the St. Johns River Ferry Landing. Or take the Mayport Ferry north; follow signs about three miles. Turn right, or east, and follow directions. Open daily 9 A.M. to 5 P.M. except Thanksgiving, Christmas, and New Year's Day. Visitor center. Tours available. Admission free. Write Kingsley Plantation, 11676 Palmetto Ave., Jacksonville 32226. Call (904) 251-3537.

Jacksonville Convention and Visitors Bureau: 550 Water St., Suite 1000, Jacksonville, 32202. Call (904) 353-9736 or (800) 733-2668. Website: www.jaxcvb.com.

Read More About It

Corse, Carita Doggett. *The Key to the Golden Islands*. 1931, Chapel Hill, University of North Carolina Press.

Fretwell, Jacqueline K. *Kingsley Beatty Gibbs and His Journal of 1840–1843*. 1984, St. Augustine, Jacqueline Fretwell.

Kingsley, Zephaniah. *A Treatise on the Patriarchal, or Cooperative System of Slavery As It Exists in Some Governments Under The Name of Slavery*. 1829, New York.

Schaefer, Daniel L. *Anna Kingsley*. 1994, St. Augustine, Daniel Schaefer.

Fort Caroline

east of Jacksonville

A failed French foothold

When Juan Ponce de León claimed La Florida for Spain in 1513, he took one look at the inhospitable swampland, then turned around and went back to Puerto Rico. Spain didn't return to colonize the place for a half century. What brought them back? Other Europeans. Not just any — these were French. This was intolerable for the Spaniards. They massacred the Huguenots and ended the French enterprise, or else Miami might have a little Le Havre instead of Little Havana.

What's left of France's efforts to grab a piece of the newly encountered Americas can be seen at Fort Caroline. La Caroline, near the mouth of the St. Johns River not far from present-day Jacksonville, was the first French attempt at settlement in North America. The venture was to be strictly business. But back in France, Protestants — Huguenots — were being persecuted. They petitioned the crown to let them leave the mother country and set up a colony in the New World. An expedition lead by explorer Jean Ribault landed May 1, 1562; he named the waterway Rivière de Mai.

By 1564, a settlement of 200 stood on a bluff on the south bank. They named it La Caroline for King Charles IX. Tensions with local Timucua and lack of food sparked two mutinies, and defecting settlers tipped the Spanish that their historical nemeses were just up the coast.

In August 1565, just as the French were about to abandon the place, Ribault showed up with relief supplies and another 600 settlers. But the Spanish now knew about La Caroline.

Admiral Pedro Menéndez de Aviles sailed from the islands and established St. Augustine in 1565. Ribault went south, looking for the Spaniards, but was hammered by a hurricane.

Fort Caroline. *Florida State Archives*

Menéndez, meanwhile, came to Fort Caroline, where his forces were able to overwhelm the garrison in a little more than an hour. They executed some 140 soldiers and settlers, sparing only 60 women and children. The fort was christened San Mateo, a name that survives in an area neighborhood.

Menéndez then headed back south and found Ribault and his crew, who surrendered, at an inlet near present-day St. Augustine called Matanzas   Spanish for slaughter. And that's what Menéndez did to Ribault and about 350 colleagues, seen as heretics and enemies of Spain.

Perhaps it was the admiral's way of showing the local savages how civilized nations act, but it did assure that, centuries later, Florida would be awash in café con leche rather than café du monde.

One lasting legacy of the ill-fated La Caroline: French artist Jacques le Moyne de Morgues came with the 1564 expedition and painted many images of the landscape, vegetation, and most importantly, inhabitants of this new land. He escaped the Spanish slaughter and got back to France with his drawings.

Anthropologists estimate as many as half a million indigenous people inhabited Florida at the time of the Europeans' arrival. Within two centuries they were extinct, doomed by slavery, massacres, and mainly European diseases to which they had never been exposed and so were defenseless. Le Moyne's images provide an invaluable snapshot of peoples now lost to history.

At Fort Caroline's visitors center, exhibits portray both Fort Caroline and the Timucua. "Where the Waters Meet" shows the plant and animal life that inhabit the wetlands and salt marshes at the confluence of the St. Johns and the Atlantic Ocean. Maps show the New World as the sixteenth-century Europeans saw it, long before aerial photography, radar and satellites gave us a more accurate picture. The center also displays many Le Moyne drawings.

Behind the visitor center you can overlook the St. Johns and see how, while development has altered the view, much of the area still looks as it would have to Jean Ribault. A replica of Fort Caroline, much smaller than the original, was based on Le Moyne's images. A reproduction of a Timucua hut shows how the civilizations survived for hundreds, perhaps thousands, of years before the Europeans drove them out of existence.

Fort Caroline is about 14 miles east of downtown Jacksonville. Take Interstate 95 to exit 340, Southside Boulevard. Take the Southside Connector to Merrill Road. Turn right. Merrill Road merges with Fort Caroline Road; continue about 4 1/2 miles and follow brown National Park Service signs. The entrance is on your left.

Fort Caroline National Memorial is part of the **Timucuan Ecological & Historic Preserve**, established in 1988, which also includes the Kingsley Plantation. Call (904) 641-7155. Write 12713 Fort Caroline Rd., Jacksonville 32225. Website: www.nps.gov/foca

Visitor center and grounds open 9 A.M. to 4:45 P.M. daily except Thanksgiving, Christmas, and New Year's Day.

Read More About It
Bennett, Charles E. *Fort Caroline and its Leader*. 1976, Gainesville, University Press of Florida.

St. Augustine

The oldest city

It's 1740. This outpost of the Spanish empire is locked tight and armed to the teeth. Already more than one opportunist has tried to seize it and its treasures. At nightfall, soldiers gather at Government House. They salute their flag and king. Torches lit, they march through the town as residents and visitors look on. At the Castillo de San Marcos, the great fort that has warded off many an attempted invader, cannons fire in homage. At the City Gate, the guard changes, followed by a volley of ceremonial musket fire.

Some American history books, often written by Northerners, would have you believe the modern history of North America began with Plymouth Rock in 1620. By then, St. Augustine had been around for 55 years.

It was on August 28, the feast day of the fifth-century philosopher St. Augustine, of the year 1565 when Admiral Don Pedro Menéndez de Aviles first sighted the coast of Florida. Twelve days later, on September 8, he came ashore with 600 soldiers and settlers. The place he established claims to be America's oldest continuously inhabited European-settled city.

St. Augustine went from Spanish to British to Spanish again, and finally, became part of the United States in 1821. The Americans found a city that had gone to seed, stagnated by lame-duck Spanish apathy and local economic ills. Speculators rushed in, but a yellow fever outbreak the same year wiped out many of them.

The town's malaise and remoteness meant it was mostly unchanged and mostly left alone. But the Second Seminole War came to its doorstep; some captured Seminole leaders were held in the Castillo de San Marcos and some escaped.

The Civil War found a city with a large colony of snowbirds, who

Casa Monica Hotel. *Doug Waitley*

got out of town until conditions changed. Union troops blockaded the city in 1862 and occupied it for the duration of the war. Like the rest of Florida, St. Augustine was economically devastated after Appomattox. Fires in 1887 and 1914 didn't help.

But as in the rest of the Florida, salvation came via tourism. Soon came Henry Flagler and his railroad and hotels. For a while, St. Augustine was America's Riviera, until Flagler was persuaded to continue south. The city's prosperity came at the price of some historic buildings. But it has saved many and built several structures with a Spanish colonial look.

A city this old boasts several historic neighborhoods, covering 144 blocks, with 33 individual buildings recognized by the National Register of Historic Places.

The 22-block "Old City" includes the 1808 City Gate. It's also home to Flagler College — at Henry Flagler's former Hotel Ponce de Leon — as well as the Florida School for the Deaf and the Blind, the headquarters for the Florida National Guard, and a national cemetery. And the Old City hosts a cathedral, four churches, a monastery, and a convent.

Old St. Augustine Village is a collection of nine historic houses showing St. Augustine from 1790 to 1910. They sit on a city block that can be found in the town's plans as far back as 1572. Markers show where a hospital, a cemetery, a defensive line, and a bridge once stood.

At the Colonial Spanish Quarter, reenactors in period costume portray St. Augustine in 1740, when the city had already been a Spanish outpost for nearly two centuries. The interpreters actually conduct their crafts, working as blacksmiths, carpenters, leather workers, and candle makers.

One thing you will not find here: the "Slave Market." Historians say some slave auctions might have taken place, but the market was primarily for the sale of meat, fish, and produce. It was only after the Civil War, historians say, that a huckster came up with the "slave market" legend to sell photographs.

St. Augustine Visitor Center: 25 Castillo Drive. Open daily 8:30 A.M. to 5: 30 P.M. CALL (904) 825-1000. Website: www.historicstaugustine. com

St. Augustine, Ponte Vedra & The Beaches Visitors & Convention Bureau: 88 Riberia St. Suite 400, St. Augustine 32084. Call (800) 653-2489. Website: wwwvisitoldcity.com

Read More About It
Harvey, Karen G. *St. Augustine and St. Johns County: a Pictorial History.* 1979, Virginia Beach, Donning Co.

Castillo de San Marcos

St. Augustine

The old fort

In a state that embodies transience, Castillo de San Marcos, America's oldest masonry fort and the only seventeenth-century fort still standing, wears its age proudly. Up to a million people a year cross its drawbridge without incident. But over three centuries, raiders tried, and failed, to take the four-sided fort on Matanzas Bay.

Sir Francis Drake torched the Spanish city in 1586, but it wasn't until the British sacked the town again in 1668 that leaders decided their wooden forts were inadequate to protect them from freelancing pirates or the British tormenting them from their base in Charleston, South Carolina.

Work started October 2, 1672; it took two decades to build the structure, mostly with coquina blocks — compressed mixtures of oyster shells, sand, and lime mined from adjacent Anastasia Island. Up to 150 men would work at a time; they were a diverse crew of white artisans, black slaves and freedmen, convict laborers and Indians.

The incomplete fort survived assaults in 1683 and 1686 and was finished August 31, 1695, in time for two British sieges, of 50 days in 1702 and 27 days in 1740. It was renovated from 1738 to 1740 and from 1745 to 1756.

The fort is a classic star design: a nearly square central hollow body with a series of storage rooms around a central courtyard with diamond-shaped bastions at each corner. Its angled walls range in thickness from nine to 19 feet. Three sides are surrounded by a moat; the fourth was filled in for a battery. About 40 cannons ring the fort, and you can still see the hot shot oven, where cannonballs were made red hot to set ships afire on impact.

Ironically, nature is slowly doing what raiders could not; sun,

The Castillo de San Marcos has protected St. Augustine for more than three centuries. *Palm Beach Post*

sand, waves, and wind are eating away at the fort. Officials are studying ways to shore it up but say it is in no immediate danger.

When the British took Florida in 1763, the bastion was Anglicized as Fort St. Marks. It was a base for raids against rebels in Georgia and South Carolina and a prisoner-of-war stockade. During the American Revolution, three South Carolinians infuriated their captors as their stirring refrain wafted out from the prison at Castillo de San Marcos.

America's oldest city was at the time part of the Territory of East Florida, then the fourteenth colony of British America. Its residents had been subjects of the crown for a little more than a decade and had no gripe with the king. They had no patience with rebels. So when the three were captured by Redcoats in Charleston in 1780, they found no friends in St. Augustine.

On the Fourth of July, 1781, they showed their impudence by changing the words to "God Save the King," instead singing "God Save the Thirteen States." All three later became South Carolina legislators; one was also a governor of the state, and one a member of the Continental Congress. What made these men famous was the simple scrawling of their names on a declaration in which they pledged their lives, their fortunes, and their sacred honor. More than two centuries later, the document, one of the most cherished in the world, still bears their signatures — or if you will, their John Hancocks. They were Arthur Middleton, Edward Rutledge, and Thomas Heyward Jr., signers of the Declaration of Independence.

When Spain regained Florida in 1783, Fort St. Marks regained its original name. After Florida became a U.S. possession, it was named Fort Marion from 1825 to 1942. It held Indians in the Seminole wars, was briefly occupied by Confederates in the Civil War, and was a military prison in the Spanish-American War. The fort became a national monument in 1924 and regained its original name in 1942.

Castillo de San Marcos is along State Road A1A at the north end of the Old City area in downtown St. Augustine. Open 8:45 A.M. to 5:15 P.M. Ticket booth closes at 4:45 P.M. Closed Christmas. Adults $6; 15 and under free. Write 1 South Castillo Drive, St. Augustine 32084. Call (904) 829-6506. Website: www.nps.gov/casa

St. Augustine & St. Johns County Chamber of Commerce: One Riberia St., St. Augustine 32084. Call (904) 829-5681. Website: www. staugustinechamber.com

Read More About It

Arana, Luis and Albert Manucy, *The Building of the Castillo de San Marcos*. 1977, St. Augustine, National Park and Monument Association for Castillo de San Marcos National Monument.

Arnade, Charles W. *The Siege of St. Augustine in 1702*. 1959, Gainesville, University of Florida Press.

Waterbury, Jean. *Oldest City: St. Augustine: Saga of Survival*. 1983, St. Augustine, St. Augustine Historical Society.

Bulow
Plantation

Flagler Beach

Short and sweet

The Bulow sugar plantation operated for only 15 years before war ended its enterprise.

Florida's entry into the United States in 1821 brought the promise of prosperity for Major Charles Wilhelm Bulow. At a spot between Jacksonville and Daytona Beach, the German immigrant acquired 4,675 acres — about seven square miles — of untamed land bearing a creek that would be named for him. Bulow worked slaves to clear 2,200 acres of the property. He planted sugar cane, cotton, rice, and indigo, a plant used to make dye.

But just two years later, Bulow died at age 44. Everything fell to his son, John Joachim Bulow. John was all of 17.

For young Mr. Bulow, the transition from cosmopolitan Paris to the wilds of Florida must have been difficult. But he soon made a go of it and impressed a figure no less prominent than famed naturalist John James Audubon, who guested at Bulowville during Christmas week in 1831.

"Mr. J.J. Bulow, a rich planter, at whose home myself and party have been for a whole week under the most hospitable and welcome treatment is now erecting some extensive buildings for a sugar house," Audubon wrote on New Year's Eve.

The "sugar house" was the centerpiece of Bulow's spread. Built of local coquina, a mix of shells and sand, it was the largest mill in east Florida. At boat slips, workers loaded barrels of raw sugar and molasses onto flatboats that were floated down Bulow Creek to be shipped north. Bulow's enterprise ended abruptly when the Second Seminole War broke out in December 1835.

Bulow opposed the exiling of Seminoles to the American west, to the point of firing cannon at American soldiers. Ironically, it was

The ruins of John Bulow's sugar mill. *Doug Waitley*

he who fell victim to Seminoles who were infuriated by the American military and took out their rage on one of the few people who sympathized with them. In January 1836, a band of Seminoles looted and burned the plantation. Bulow never rebuilt. He returned to Paris and died later that year at only 26.

Eventually the sugar plantations of north Florida would fade. It would be a century before, to the south, the muck east of Lake Okeechobee produced an industry that accounts for about half of America's cane sugar.

Only the coquina walls and chimneys of the mill remain. You can also see a "spring house," a building that covered a freshwater spring, as well as several other wells and the foundations of the plantation house and slave cabins.

Bulow Plantation Ruins Historic State Park is 3 miles west of Flagler Beach off County Road 2001 (Old King's Road), between State Road

100 and Old Dixie Highway. Call (386) 517-2084. Write Box 655, Bunnell 32110. Website: www.floridastateparks.org

Open 9 A.M. to 5 P.M. daily. Fees: $3 per vehicle for up to 8 people. Pedestrians, bicyclists, and other individuals $1. The park features boating, canoeing, kayaking, and hiking. On the self-guided walking tour, interpretive signs explain the sugar-making process. An interpretive kiosk tells the plantation's history.

Read More About It

Clegg, John A. *The History of Flagler County.* 1976, Bunnell, John Clegg.

Cross Creek

An author's solace

Beloved Florida author Marjorie Kinnan Rawlings made her home in this settlement of 800 about 20 miles southeast of Gainesville, and immortalized it in many of her nine books — eight of them about Florida.

The creek runs a few hundred yards from where Rawlings sat on her porch and created stories that captivated the world. Rawlings probably would laugh to see herself become a demigod of Florida folklore, and the wooden green and white "cracker" house, complete with cat napping on the porch and blackbirds circling a feeder, made into a shrine.

The house is set up so that you can see into most of it from the outside. When you take a tour, guides dressed in period clothing take you through the various rooms. On the porch is a typewriter very much like Rawlings', with copies of her original drafts of *The Yearling*. It tells of a young boy's friendship with a fawn, his wonderment at the beauty around him, his relationship with his earthy parents and neighbors as they fought each other or banded together to fight the hazards of nature, and his coming of age as he confronted the dilemma of his once-wild pet.

The book was published worldwide, in dozens of languages, and won a Pulitzer Prize in 1939. It later became a film that was shot on location in Cross Creek. It wasn't long before Rawlings, who continued to write until her death at age 57 in 1953, had become a state literary treasure, providing Americans a glimpse of a Florida far from the beaches and resort hotels — a place that surprised and intrigued readers everywhere.

Today, Cross Creek welcomes visitors with the same pristine landscape that greeted Rawlings in the 1930s. The dramatic combination of creeks, forests, swamps, and lakes remains, vastly different from the big cities of New York and Washington, where Rawlings had lived.

Behind her home, blue herons still step gingerly through dark water, reflections shimmering. The water still dissolves through the grasses into the nearby lake and beyond it, into the horizon.

A Wave of Interest

In 1983, *Cross Creek*, a film based on Rawlings' memoirs spurred a wave of interest. The film, and the books on which it was based, featured composite characters representing the many real and fictional people who made Rawlings' home what is was. They were fishermen, hunters, farmers, poor, uneducated black sharecroppers and servants, white landowners and squatters, all struggling to stay fed and free from disease and injury.

They were rough and unrefined, but carried a sense of loyalty, family, and honor that was reflected in Rawlings' writings. So was her personal fight to preserve the land, which she held in awe and respect.

After the movie, attendance at Cross Creek jumped from 15,000 a year to 45,000, then leveled off at 30,000. In 1988, a squabble among residents over development led to a plan designed to protect the pristine area. Rawlings had bequeathed her home to the University of Florida, where she had lectured. The university gave it to the state in 1968 as a historic site.

Lacking the literary aristocracy of other states, Florida has come to cherish Rawlings. Widower Norton Baskin, then 86 and living in St. Augustine, said in a 1988 interview that annual sales of her books continue to generate an income equal to one New York Times bestseller.

"I practically know them by heart," said Baskin, a former hotel manager who continued to operate her estate. "Her books are more or less timeless. She did not want to be regional. She thought the things she said were universal. Especially the environmental things, love of the land. That's the same everywhere. Everything she ever wrote was as a conservationist. I don't want one memory to go, good or bad. Her writings were not the biggest thing in my memory of her. Our life was very hectic and very wonderful."

A typewriter contains early drafts of her classic *The Yearling*.
Marjorie Kinnan Rawlings State Historic Site

Who Owns Cross Creek?

"Who owns Cross Creek?" Rawlings wrote at the end of her memoir. "The red-birds, I think, more than I, for they will have their nests even in the face of delinquent mortgages. And after I am dead, who am childless, the human ownership of grove and field and hammock is hypothetical. But a long line of red-birds and whippoorwills and blue-jays and ground doves will descend from the present owners of nests in the orange trees, and their claim will be less subject to dispute than that of any human heirs. Houses are individual and can be owned, like nests, and fought for. But what of the land? It seems to me that the earth may be borrowed but not bought. It may be used, but not owned. It gives itself in response to love and tending, offers its seasonal flowering and fruiting. But we are tenants and not possessors, lovers and masters. Cross Creek belongs to the wind and the rain, to the sun and the seasons, to the cosmic secrecy of seeds, and beyond all, to time."

The Marjorie Kinnan Rawlings Historic State Park is in Cross Creek. Take I-75 to Micanopy Exit, go east into Micanopy and take County Road 346 east to County Road 325, then south to Cross Creek. Cross the bridge and follow County Road 325 to the right. The house is one-half mile from the bridge on the right.

Write 18700 S. County Road 325, Cross Creek 32640. Call (352) 466-3672. Park open daily. Admission: $2 per car. Hours: 9 A.M. to 5 P.M. Except for Christmas and Thanksgiving, tours are offered at 10 A.M. and 11 A.M. and 1 P.M. to 4 P.M., Oct. 1 through July 31; hourly the rest of the year. Tours: adults $3, kids 6-12 $2. Groups of 10 to 45 can be reserved well ahead of time on Tuesdays and Wednesdays. Website: www.floridastateparks.org

Read More About It

Acton, Patricia Nassif. *Invasion of Privacy: The Cross Creek Trial of Marjorie Kinnan Rawlings*. 1988, Gainesville, University of Florida Press.

Bigelow, Gordon, and Laura V. Monti, eds. *The Selected Letters of Marjorie Kinnan Rawlings*. 1988, Gainesville, University of Florida Press.

Bigelow, Gordon E. and Laura V. Monti, *Frontier Eden: The Literary Career of Marjorie Kinnan Rawlings*. 1966, Gainesville, University of Florida Press.

Glisson, J. W. *The Creek*. 1993, Gainesville, University of Florida Press.

Parker, Idella. *Idella, Marjorie Kinnan Rawlings' "Perfect Maid."* 1992, Gainesville, University Press of Florida.

Rawlings, Marjorie Kinnan. *Cross Creek*, 1942, New York, Scribner.

Rawlings, Marjorie Kinnan. *The Yearling*, 1938, New York, Scribner.

Silverthorne, Elizabeth. *Marjorie Kinnan Rawlings, Sojourner at Cross Creek*. 1990 (reprint edition), Overlook TP.

Tarr, Rodger, ed. *Max and Marjorie*. 1999, Gainesville, Unversity Press of Florida.

University of Florida

Gainesville

Florida's higher education legacy

The University of Florida is famous for a lot of things, from academics to parties to football. But the state's premier university is also historic.

Twenty-one buildings constructed between 1906 and 1939 have been grouped into a historic district that in 1989 was put on the National Register of Historic Places. Now the University of Florida is the flagship of ten state universities — including Florida Gulf Coast University, which opened in Fort Myers in 1997 — and 28 junior and community colleges.

Its start was far more humble — and even the facts of that start are in dispute. While UF officially opened in 1905, it attributes its origins to the East Florida Seminary, a small academy in Ocala that the state took over in 1853. Critics disagree. On January 3, 1853, a tiny, private academy in Ocala agreed to turn over the three small wooden buildings, land, and equipment, and $1,600 in cash if the state would run it. It was renamed the East Florida State Seminary. None of its first class of students was older than 14. After the Civil War, the seminary was moved up the road to Gainesville. And in 1884, the Florida Agricultural College was opened in Lake City.

By the turn of the century, higher learning in Florida was a loose confederation of eight different provincial state-supported institutions. Everything changed with the Buckman Act in 1905. The Legislature, concluding the existing setup guaranteed mediocrity, created a state university system. The act scrapped the eight schools and created three. Two were established in Tallahassee: Florida Female College, later Florida State College for Women; and the Negro Normal and Industrial School, later Florida Agricultural and Mechanical University, primarily for blacks. The third was the

70

flagship, the University of the State of Florida, which was primarily for white men.

Lake City was confident it would get UF. Critics said Gainesville was a backwater town with poor transportation. But Gainesville offered the state 517 acres, free water, and $70,000 in cash. A civil engineer laid out the University of Florida campus, planting a row of oaks on either side of a curving road at what is now the college's northeast corner. Architects proposed an ambitious plan of 44 buildings. They selected a style of architecture called Collegiate Gothic: masonry construction, red brick with molded stone or glazed terra cotta trim, and gabled roofs with intricate carvings. They decorated buildings with brickwork patterns, plaques, even gargoyles. Two of the early buildings have not survived; one was torn down in 1960, another burned in 1987.

When UF opened in 1906, tuition was free to Florida residents; out-of-state students paid $20 a year. Dormitory rent was $2.50 a month. The first year's enrollment was 102. The first graduating class, in 1907, numbered four.

In 1925, the university invited the noted landscape architect Frederick Law Olmstead Jr., son of the man who designed Central Park in New York. Olmstead set up a plan of native trees and plants. The campus green was dedicated in 1931 as the Plaza of the Americas, during the first meeting of the Institute of Inter-American Affairs. Twenty-one live oaks were planted, one for each of the American nations in existence at the time.

Smathers Library. *University of Florida*

While the campus originally sported only three buildings, it hosted 20 major buildings by 1938. By the end of World War II, enrollment in 1945–1946 was 3,216; a year later it had more than doubled, to 7,373. The university, which had let in a scattering of women since 1924, opened up in 1947. Up the road in Tallahassee, the Florida State College for Women began admitting men and became Florida State University. The first black student at UF entered the law school in 1957, and the full campus was opened to African Americans five years later. Enrollment continued to grow; it crossed the 10,000 mark in the 1960s, 20,000 in the early 1970s, and 30,000 in the late 1970s.

What started as a tiny academy is now one of the five largest universities in America, with more than 49,000 students. Its budget of $39,192 in 1906 now wouldn't even pay a year's salary for many of its professors; its current budget is $1.9 billion. And it now has more than 900 buildings.

But as new buildings went up, many were built as close as possible to the old style. Some are connected to the old buildings via shared arcades or courtyards. The concept is so successful the campus has become the site for various film and commercial projects; producers can approximate an Ivy League look and still shoot in the winter. The college says it wants to present UF as a modern university that hasn't forgotten its humble past.

The University of Florida is in Gainesville. Take Interstate 75 to Williston Road (S.R. 331), Archer Road (S. R. 24), or University Avenue (S.R. 26) and head east to the campus.

Visitors may make self-guided walking tours; pick up a campus map at the visitors entrance on SW 13 Street, about one block south of University Avenue, next to Tigert Hall. Parking is available on campus.

Brochure and map of historic district are available at UF Bookstore and Welcome Center on Museum Road, University of Florida, Gainesville 32611. Call (352) 392-0194. By mail: send self-addressed, stamped envelope. Website: www.ufl.edu

Alachua County Visitors and Convention Bureau: Call (352) 374-5260/374-5231. Website: www.visitgainesville.net

Read More About It

Proctor, Samuel, and Wright Langley. *Gator History*. 1986, Gainesville, South Star.

Paynes Prairie

south of Gainesville

Where the buffalo roam

Buffalo roam on Paynes Prairie. That's not the strangest part. At least once, Paynes Prairie turned into Paynes Lake.

Actually, it was called Alachua Lake. After two years of heavy rains, a sink that funnels water down to the Floridan aquifer plugged up in 1873 and the prairie filled to three to five feet in depth. It stayed that way for 18 years. Steamers crossed it to haul lumber, citrus, and passengers.

The sink eventually opened and the water slowly dropped over a couple of years, then drained in just ten days. Locals held fish fries to handle the sudden glut of seafood, but couldn't keep up and the restored prairie was a stinky place as thousands of dead fish rotted in the sun.

It's believed humans have occupied the area for 12,000 years. In the late 1600s, the largest cattle ranch in Spanish Florida operated here. In 1774, William Bartram described the basin as "the Great Alachua Savannah." The prairie is believed to have been named for King Payne, a Seminole leader, and several skirmishes took place there during the Second Seminole War.

Buffalo — actually American Bison — were found in Florida until the early 1800s. They were reintroduced to Paynes Prairie from Oklahoma in the mid-1970s as part of the Florida Park Service's goal to restore parks to the way they looked before the arrival of Europeans. The half-ton animals roam more than 6,000 acres, so you might not see them.

A herd of about 18 wild Spanish horses can often be seen from the visitor center's observation tower. Sandhill cranes are common during the winter, and alligators are hard to spot during what's been a long-term drought in the region.

Paynes Prairie. *Doug Waitley*

Paynes Prairie became Florida's first state preserve in 1971 and is now designated as a National Natural Landmark.

Exhibits and an audio-visual program at the visitor center explain the area's natural and cultural history. A 50-foot-high observation tower near the center provides a panoramic view of the preserve. Eight trails offer hiking, horseback riding, and bicycling. Ranger-led activities are offered on weekends, November through April.

Paynes Prairie State Preserve is on U.S. 441, 10 miles south of Gainesville. From I-75, take exit 374, for Micanopy, and turn east on County Road 234. Go 1½ miles to 441, then south about a half mile. Write 100 Savannah Blvd., Micanopy 32667. Call (352) 466-3397. Website: www.floridastateparks.org

Open 8 A.M. to sundown every day. Admission: $4 per vehicle, up to 8 passengers. Solo driver or motorcycle: $3. Pedestrians, bicyclists, and other individuals: $1.

Read More About It
Andersen, Lars. *Paynes Prairie: A History of the Great Savanna.* 2001, Sarasota, Pineapple Press.

Micanopy

Oldest inland city

This tiny village of fewer than 1,000 people, south of Gainesville, founded in 1821, holds the claim of Florida's oldest inland town. So it's not surprising that its primary industry is antiques.

Micanopy is believed to have started centuries ago as a settlement of Timucua, one of several indigenous groups wiped out by European diseases by the time the Seminoles migrated south into Florida in the 1700s. Naturalist William Bartram identified a Seminole settlement called Cuscowilla in the area in 1774 during his famed travels. In 1817, Spain's King Ferdinand VII made a grant of land to Don Fernando de la Maza Arredondo of Havana and St. Augustine.

Just a few years later, Florida became a U.S. territory. A man named Edward Wanton was hired to promote settlement and established a trading post. The first post office, in 1826, was named Wanton, but many were already calling the town "Micanope" for a local Seminole leader. Fort Defiance was built in 1835 but burned; Fort Micanopy went up the following year and was active until the end of the Second Seminole War in 1842.

The historic district, placed on the National Register of Historic Places in 1983, covers only a few blocks, mostly along Cholokka Boulevard, but contains no fewer than 39 sites listed on the register. Former stores, warehouses, and homes have been converted to antique shops and art galleries, along with cafes and restaurants.

Thrasher Warehouse is home of the Micanopy Historical Society Museum. It contributes to the kitschy atmosphere of the antiques mecca with a giant Coca-Cola sign painted in the 1930s. The warehouse, built in the 1890s, and the nearby Thrasher Store, built in 1923, were part of one of the area's largest general stores.

The Dailey building, built in 1925, housed a drug store and

Micanopy has become famous for its antiques. *Doug Waitley*

doctor's office and hosted a hotel on the second floor. The town hall and public library are in the Old Brick School House. Built in 1895, it at one time educated children from Paynes Prairie down to the Marion County line. And the Herlong Mansion has been converted to a bed-and-breakfast.

Parts of the film *Cross Creek*, the story of beloved author Marjorie Kinnan Rawlings and her rural home not far from Micanopy, were filmed in the town, as were parts of the Michael J. Fox film *Doc Hollywood*.

Micanopy is about 11 miles south of Gainesville. Take U.S. 441 to County Road 234, then turn right at the blinking light. Follow signs into town.

Micanopy Historical Society Museum is at Cholokka Boulevard and Early Street. Open 1 P.M. to 4 P.M. daily. Suggested $2 donation. Call (352) 466-3200. Write Box 462, Micanopy 32267. Website: www.afn. org/~micanopy/

Read More About It
Watkins, Caroline B. *The Story of Historic Micanopy*. 1996, Micanopy, Micanopy Historical Society.

Cedar Key

Salt and pencils

This charming village of about 800 near Florida's inside elbow owes much of its legacy to two humble products: salt and pencils.

Settled in the early 1840s, Cedar Key was the terminus of the Cross Florida Railroad, built by David Levy Yulee, Florida's first U.S. Senator. The railroad ran diagonally across what was then most of Florida, connecting to Fernandina Beach, north of Jacksonville at the state's northeast corner. It carried lumber, turpentine, cotton, seafood products, and passengers. By the start of the Civil War, Cedar Key's bustling population of about 2,000 made it Florida's second largest city.

When war broke out, Confederate blockade runners continued to bring in supplies for distribution through the South. The town had another strategic asset: salt. In a time before refrigeration, salt was the critical ingredient for preserving meat. Large kettle and boiler operations, including one at Cedar Key, boiled sea water down to the sea salt. That made them important targets for the North. In 1862, a Union party attacked the city by sea, destroying the salt works. It then occupied Cedar Key until just before the end of the war.

Later, the lumber industry began to prosper again. The area produced pine and cypress, and cedar, which was used for making pencils. Seventeen mills cut cedar boards and the town shipped a million cubic feet a year. The Eagle and Eberhard Faber companies put tiny Cedar Key, Florida, on the map. Steamers brought passengers to and from Havana, New Orleans, Tampa, and Key West.

Lumber dwindled in the late 1800s, and residents turned to the sea. Fishing produced up to a million pounds a year of seafood and shellfish. The area also became a center for shipbuilding.

When the fish schools and oyster beds were all but fished out and

The Dock Street Pier in Cedar Key. *Bruce Hunt*

the shipbuilding industry fell victim to new materials that replaced wood, the town began turning palm fiber into brushes and brooms — but plastics killed that. Cedar Key had lost its importance as a commercial center. But its obscurity would later benefit it, as it became a popular destination for people searching for a little piece of old Florida. Artists and craftsmen set up shop, and former business hotels were converted to bed-and-breakfast inns.

At the town's historical museum, exhibits include the fishing and lumber industry, fiber and brush manufacturing, the railroad, the Civil War period, and information on the history of Cedar Key. Cedar Key Museum State Park includes the former St. Clair Whitman house, which has been restored to its 1920s look, and focuses on the life of St. Clair Whitman and his collections of natural items. Part of the collection has sea shells and Indian artifacts collected by Whitman, founder of the town's first museum.

Three reserves — one federal, two state — are nearby for enjoying the abundant beauty of nature around Cedar Key.

Cedar Key is about an hour's drive southwest of Gainesville on State Road 24 (Archer Road).

Cedar Key Historical Society Museum is in the historic Lutterloh Building at Second (Main) Street. The historic Andrews home was moved to the museum property in 1995. Write Box 222, Cedar Key 32625. Call (352) 543-5549. Open Sunday through Friday 1 P.M. to 4 P.M. and 11 A.M. to 5 P.M. on Saturday. Admission: Adults, $1; kids under 12, 50 cents. Website: www.cedarkeymuseum.org

Cedar Key Museum State Park is off State Road 24 in Cedar Key. Follow signs to museum. Write 12231 SW 166th Court, Cedar Key 32625. Call (352) 543-5350. Museum open from 9 A.M. to 5 P.M. Thursday through Monday except. Christmas. Admission: $1 per person; under 6 free. Website: www.floridastateparks.org

Waccasassa Bay Preserve State Park comprises 34,000 acres of limited-access wetlands. It is accessible only by boat from town.

Cedar Key Scrub State Reserve, six miles northeast of Cedar Key on State Road 24, has about 5,000 acres of salt marsh, pine flatwoods, and sand pine scrub, and offers eight different nature trails. Open 9 A.M. to sundown. No admission fee. Write Box 187, Cedar Key 32625. Call (352) 543-5567. Website: www.floridastateparks.org

Cedar Keys National Wildlife Refuge encompasses 13 offshore islands totaling 762 acres. It is accessible only by boat from Cedar Key or nearby towns. Write 16450 NW 31st Place, Cedar Key 32626. Call (352) 493-0238. Website: http://www.fws.gov/cedarkeys/

Read More About It
Fishburne, Charles C. Jr. *The Cedar Keys in the 19th Century*. 1997, Cedar Key, Cedar Key Historical Society.

Central Florida

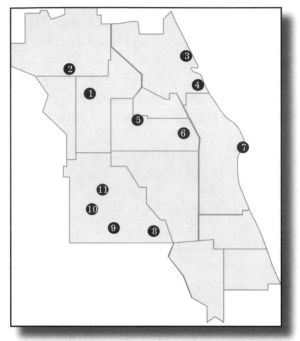

1. Mount Dora
2. Barker House, *Ocklawaha*
3. The Batista Collection, *Daytona Beach*
4. Charles Dummett's Grave, *New Smyrna Beach*
5. Eatonville
6. Christmas
7. Kennedy Space Center, *Cocoa Beach*
8. Lake Kissimmee Cow Camp, *east of Lake Wales*
9. Bok Tower, *Lake Wales*
10. Florida Southern College, *Lakeland*
11. Cypress Gardens, *Winter Haven*

Mount Dora

A bit of New England in Central Florida

This hidden treasure about 20 miles north of Orlando still honors the spirit of its namesake, 1840s homesteader Dora Ann Drawdy. The town struggles to maintain its character even as the rest of Central Florida has become an endless sprawl.

In the 1950s, Mount Dora was given the option of having U.S. 441, a key highway in the time before Florida's Turnpike, come through the 3.6-square-mile town. Mount Dora declined; the highway was routed around it toward Eustis and Tavares, the remainder of Lake County's "Golden Triangle."

Mount Dora's not so hidden any more; in 1994, *Money* magazine named it Florida's favorite retirement spot and rated it third in the country.

At a dizzying 184 feet above sea level — thus the town's ambitious name — the countryside is actually hilly, offering a refreshing change of pace from pancake-flat South Florida.

It counts only 8,000 permanent residents, but a multitude of part-timers and weekend visitors. Festivals draw more than 750,000 people a year. Every February, more than 200,000 pour in for the town's weekend arts festival. The calendar also includes a powerboat race, sailing regatta, bicycle festival, antique car show, crafts fair, and "art in the park" weekend.

December features the town's Christmas walk and the lighting of the city, when 80,000 lights sparkle in the Annie E. Donnelly downtown park. The main streets of the 20-square-block downtown are packed with early-century buildings housing dozens of shops, many of them antique stores.

Royellou

A three-mile historic tour of downtown features 29 buildings offering a spectrum of architecture from the late 1800s to the 1920s. They include the 1913 train depot, in use until 1950; the 1912 yacht club, oldest inland yacht club in Florida; the 1920s City Hall; and the town's oldest church building, Community Congregational, which dates to 1887.

A former town jail houses the Royellou Historical Museum. Royellou was the town's first name, honoring the 1880s postmaster's three children, Roy, Ella, and Louis. The Ice House Theater, started in 1948 in a converted ice plant, was moved ten years later to a 280-seat playhouse. It hosts a thriving community ensemble. Mount Dora's residential area is also becoming a favorite of refugees from Orlando, who seek solace in its tree-lined streets and expensive lakeside homes.

Downtown's jewel is the Lakeside Inn, an institution at the south end for more than a century. Its quaint charm and down-home feel symbolize Central Florida in the 1930s, a wide-open, rural region of orange groves and pasture land when Walt Disney was first getting started. The 87-room inn, established in 1883, is one of five Florida lodges named "historic hotel of America" by the National Trust for Historic Preservation. It is also listed on the National Register of Historic Places. It underwent a $500,000 renovation from 1985 to 1987.

Lake Dora, one of 1,400 in Lake County, is 7 1/2 miles by 11 1/2

A panoramic sunset at Mount Dora's Lake Dora. *Eliot Kleinberg*

miles with its own 35-foot-high miniature lighthouse. Its lakeside boardwalk, running for a quarter of a mile, is the longest in the state. The lake provides the highlight of a day at Mount Dora — a dazzling sunset that seems to set the surface on fire as it melts into the surrounding hillside.

Mount Dora is north of Orlando Take Florida's Turnpike to exit 267, State Road 429 north (toll road). Follow 429 to its end at U.S. 441 north. Turn north (left) on U.S. 441 and follow about 12 miles to Mount Dora.

    Lakeside Inn: 100 N. Alexander St., Mount Dora 32757, at the south end of downtown. Call (800) 556-5016 or (352) 383-4101. Website: www.lakeside-inn.com

    Mount Dora Chamber of Commerce: Box 196, Mount Dora 32757. Call (352) 383-2165. Website: www.mountdora.com

Read More About It

Archer, Ron and Karl Meek. *Mount Dora, 1880–1980.* 1990, Mount Dora, Community Broadcasting, Inc.

Kennedy, William T. *History of Lake County, Florida.* 1988, Tavares, Lake County Historical Society.

Longstreet, Rupert. *The Story of Mount Dora, Florida.* 1960, Mount Dora, Mount Dora Historical Society.

Barker House

Ocklawaha

Ma Barker's last stand

There should be bullet holes. Why aren't there bullet holes? After all, the two-story, 100-year-old green wooden home with white trim was reportedly punctured about 1,500 times during a six-hour gun battle the morning of January 16, 1935 — the day the feds caught up with Ma Barker and her son, Fred.

The "Belle Air," connected by a 100-yard boardwalk with a boathouse on the shores of Lake Weir, is set back several yards from County Road 25 in this lakefront town of Ocklawaha, about 17 miles south of Ocala. The house, built in 1893, sports a screened porch that faces the lake. Weeping willows and other trees partially block it from the busy road. It looks virtually the same as it did in 1935. The house, which has changed hands over the years, isn't open to visitors.

The Chamber of Commerce throws a "Ma Barker Day" every January. The Marion County Sheriff's SWAT team, dressed as period FBI agents and riding a 1930s cruiser seized in a drug raid, squares off with chamber officials posing as the Barkers. The event is accompanied by food, refreshments, music, and entertainment.

In 1985, on the 50th anniversary, the owner allowed an open house. He later said that was a monumental mistake. About 3,000 people came to the celebration, and many of them traipsed through Belle Air.

A Big Red Circle

The 25-member Barker gang, once considered the nation's most clever and dangerous, terrorized much of the Midwest. It was blamed for at least three kidnappings and ten murders and for robbing or stealing between $1 million and $3 million.

Its leader was Ozark Mountain daredevil Arizona Kate Donnie

Up to 1,500 bullet holes reportedly pierced the Barker gang hideout near Ocala. *Bob Shanley, Palm Beach Post*

Clark Barker; the papers liked to call the Missouri native "Machine Gun Kate" but most people just called her "Ma." With her were sons Arthur ("Doc"), Lloyd ("Red"), Herman, and Fred, along with co-leader Alvin "Creepy" Karpis. Father George Barker had fled his family in 1927, fearing for his life.

When the gang made the mistake of kidnapping a Minnesota banker whose father was a friend of Franklin Roosevelt, the president of the United States ordered the federal law enforcement community to bear down on Ma and her gang.

Herman had killed himself in a 1928 shootout. Red was at the federal prison in Leavenworth, Kansas. Doc decided to take his chances in Chicago. The rest of the gang came to south Florida.

They checked into downtown Miami's deluxe El Commodore hotel, a popular hangout for the area's power elite. The head of the Biscayne Kennel Club dog track was impressed by "Mrs. T.C. Blackburn," and when the gracious, heavyset mystery woman, then 63, said she needed a quiet retreat, he recommended his place on Lake Weir. In November 1934, the gang moved in, paying $75 a month.

Back in Chicago, the FBI swooped down on Doc and some other gang members. In the hideout, the feds found a road map of

Florida. Someone had drawn a red circle around the town of Ocala. The agency kept the Chicago raid a secret and tracked the Barkers down to Ocklawaha. Fifteen agents showed up in the town of 300 — little more than a post office, a service station, and some vacation bungalows. Armed with fishing poles, they split up and posed as separate groups of vacationers.

Finally, Fred Barker, 32, had a passing chat with one of the disguised agents on a dock, and the FBI had its positive identification.

At 5:30 A.M. on January 16, the feds descended on the Belle Air.

Shooting at Nothing

Retired Ocala police chief Lee McGehee, whose father worked at the funeral parlor, has become captivated by the event. He talked to two of the agents who were there that day. Here's what they said happened:

Chief Agent C. E. Connally knocked on the porch screen door and backed away. Ma came to the home's front door. Connally identified himself and said he had arrest warrants.

Ma said something like, "Wait a minute, let's see what Freddy says," in a tone that hinted the gang would surrender. She shut the door. After a few minutes, Fred Barker appeared at an upstairs window. He fired a round at Connally, who dove for cover behind a tree. The battle was on.

Willie Woodberry, a local cook hired by the gang — he later refused interviews unless he was paid and died in the late 1980s — recalled hiding under a bed in the adjacent workers' quarters during the long barrage of bullets and tear gas. Neighbors converged on the yard, only to duck flying bullets; one split his pants in the process.

The agents told McGehee that gunfire was furious for the first 45 minutes, then slacked off.

"It would get very quiet," McGehee explained. "An agent would see something — a shadow, a curtain blowing." Then, the feds would begin a new barrage.

The shooting finally stopped about 11:30 A.M. — around six hours after Fred first leaned out the upstairs window. Agents asked the cook to go inside. There he found Fred, hit by about 11 bullets, including a row raked across his chest. Ma had about four bullet wounds, including one in her head.

Funeral home workers, including McGehee's father, said the two had been dead several hours. McGehee now believes the Barkers were killed in the first 45-minute barrage and that jumpy agents later shot any time something moved.

A search of the house uncovered a stash of weapons and ammunition, bulletproof vests, jewelry, and more than $14,000 in cash. Agents later learned Karpis and other gang members and friends had left three days before the shootout; Karpis was caught 17 months later in New Orleans.

After Ma's estate was finally settled, her husband, George, claimed the bodies. The two are buried in a family plot in Welch, Oklahoma. Shortly after the shooting, the house was patched up. All the bullet holes were filled in. Now you'd never know it's the house where the Barkers met their bloody deaths.

The Barker House is closed to the public but can be seen from the road. Ocklawaha-area residents conduct a one-day reenactment festival every January. Lake Weir is about 17 miles southeast of Ocala. Take Interstate 75 to the Dunnellon/Belleview exit (County Road 484). Head east into Belleview, then east on County Road 25 into Ocklawaha.

Lake Weir Chamber of Commerce: Box 817, Ocklawaha 32183. Call (352) 288-3751.

Read More About It
Nash, Robert Jay. *Bloodletters and Badmen.* 1972, New York, Lippincott.

The Batista Collection

Daytona Beach

Legacy or booty?

T he painting shows a woman, dressed in black, smiling and holding a small book and a rosary. It's called "On The Way To Mass." It hangs in a corner of a gallery at the Museum of Arts and Sciences, in the very un-Latin north Florida tourist town of Daytona Beach — an unlikely place for the largest collection of Cuban art outside the island nation.

Every once in a while, someone at the gallery will stop cold at the painting. Some will stare at it for several minutes. Some will weep. Perhaps they cry for their own mama; perhaps for their mother country. For many, both are long gone.

The painting once hung in the National Gallery, before Fidel Castro changed Cuba forever. It is part of the 350-piece Cuban Foundation Collection, the core of it donated by the family of the man Castro overthrew: Fulgencio Batista.

"The strongman of Cuba," who had adopted Daytona Beach as a vacation home, fled in great drama in the early hours of New Year's Day, 1959. As with most historical figures, he is remembered either as a saint or a sinner, just as Castro is either Cuba's salvation or ruin.

Batista is credited with upgrading his nation's educational and medical systems and labor conditions. But he was also described as a dictator for whom bribery and corruption were policy. Some reports said he took as much as $700 million from the nation's treasury. Castro would later claim Batista had presided over a reign of terror and killed more than 20,000 Cubans.

Batista, father of eight from two marriages, died in 1973 of a heart attack.

This painting at the Museum of Arts and Sciences in Daytona Beach is a poignant reminder of old Cuba. *Museum of Arts and Sciences*

Controversial Collection

When Batista, who was divorced, remarried Marta Fernandez de Batista, he became a patron of the arts and built a national gallery in Havana. Spurred by his wife's interest, Batista began gathering colonial-era paintings and artifacts and modern paintings. Museum officials insist his trove, which comprises about a fifth of the museum's total Cuban collection, is not booty looted from Cuba. But the Cuban government says Batista both stole art and bought works with money he plundered from the nation's treasury. The museum says Castro destroyed much of the nation's Spanish art. Cuba says it has never destroyed art; it is now restoring historic sections of Havana and it would not ignore any of its history, good or bad.

Cuba's government has challenged the museum's ownership and suggested the gallery is concealing expensive art. The museum has loaned materials to many museums in Florida and the United States but canceled one exhibit of photos after radical exiles bombed the Cuban Museum of Art and Culture in Miami, which had displayed work of artists who had stayed in Cuba under Castro.

The six-sided, 3,000-square-foot wing in Daytona Beach,

housing the Cuban art, was established in 1981. Exiles and non-Cuban owners of Cuban art continue to add to the collection.

The collection features paintings, woodcarvings, glass and jewels, murals, and rare photographs of life in pre-Castro Cuba: sugar fields, workers relaxing on plantation porches, Havana city life.

Twelve pieces are beautiful pastel lithographs showing scenes of sugar fields and rolling hills. They date back to a time when much of Cuban sugar companies' stock was held in Spain; the lithographs would be gifts to stockholders that accompanied financial reports.

The "Mass" painting spurs the strongest reaction. One Cuban woman who visited in 1990 with her teenage children suddenly ran to the painting and broke down in tears, saying she remembered seeing the work as a child in Havana.

The Strongman of Cuba

Batista, born in 1901 — a year before Cuba's independence — worked as a stenographer, railway brakeman, grocery clerk, barber, carpenter, tailor, and sugar mill timekeeper. He worked his way up the military ranks and first came to power in 1933 when, as an army sergeant, he took part in a coup that ousted Gerardo Machado and, three weeks later, a provisional government.

Six years later he was elected president outright. In 1944, a term limitation forced him to leave office. For the next four years he lived off and on in Daytona Beach, establishing himself as a civic benefactor. In 1948, he returned to Cuba and was elected senator.

Batista had gone shopping for a Florida getaway. His first stop was Palm Beach. But town fathers weren't keen on Batista, who reportedly had Spanish, Black, Indian, and Chinese ancestry.

Batista and his wife rented a car and headed north up U.S. 1. The end of the day found them in Daytona Beach. They pulled off for the night. They were amazed at how well they were treated, and the Halifax River and acres of pines reminded Batista of his homeland. The next day he found a realtor and bought a large riverfront home.

Batista would often tool around in his big yellow convertible. Once, after taking a friend to the train station, he was approached by two arriving passengers who thought he was a cabby. The world leader gave the two a ride.

In 1952, three months ahead of scheduled elections, Batista ousted President Carlos Prio Socarras in a coup that lasted less than

80 minutes. Two years later, Batista was reelected in a landslide. As many as 50,000 people reportedly attended a "Batista Day" parade that year during one of Batista's visits to Daytona Beach.

In 1955, Batista tried to show he was not a dictator by pardoning several political prisoners, including a young man named Fidel Castro. A year later, Castro took to the hills to begin his revolution.

A Midnight Move

On December 30, 1958, Batista went to the National Gallery and removed any personal art he had loaned it. He sent Marta and the children to Daytona Beach.

In the Cuban tradition, the approaching revolutionary had sent word to Batista that he would offer him "a bridge of silver," giving him advance warning so he and his family could prepare for their flight to exile. That night, Batista had aides begin calling the 40 top officials on a list he had dictated ten days earlier. After a buffet dinner of chicken and rice — Batista ate standing up — the dictator, two weeks short of his 58th birthday, announced he was stepping down to avoid a bloodbath. A few minutes after midnight, Batista and 100 top officials and their families boarded three airplanes at Havana's José Martí Airport. One plane carrying 47 people, including Batista's brother, flew to Palm Beach International Airport. From his suite at the Palm Beach Biltmore, Batista promised his family would be back in power "after the trouble is over."

Although Batista maintained good relations with the United States, then-president Dwight Eisenhower wouldn't let Batista in. He fled to the Dominican Republic, then to Spain, where dictator Francisco Franco also denied him sanctuary. He ended up in Portugal and later made his way into Spain.

Later, Batista deeded the Daytona Beach home and his collection to the city. The house was briefly a museum before being sold in 1971 to become St. Demetrios Greek Orthodox church. Proceeds helped pay for the 90-acre museum complex and park that now houses the collection of artifacts from a Cuba that has passed into history.

The Cuban Museum is part of the Museum of Arts and Sciences, 352 South Nova Rd., Daytona Beach 32114. Call (386)-255-0285. Take Interstate 95 to Highway 400 (Beville Road), then east to Nova Road, then north. Open 9 A.M. to 5 P.M. Monday through Saturday, 11 A.M. to

5 P.M. on Sundays. Adults $12.95; students and children over 6 $6.95. Website: www.moas.org

Daytona Beach Area Chamber of Commerce: Box 2475, Daytona Beach 32015. Call (386) 255-0981. Website: www.daytonachamber. com

Daytona Beach Area Convention and Visitors Bureau: Call (800) 854-1234. Website: www.daytonabeach.com

Read More About It

Batista, Fulgencio. *Betrayed*. 1962, New York, Vantage Press.

Farber, Samuel. *Revolution and Reaction in Cuba, 1933–1960: A political sociology from Machado to Castro*. 1976, Middletown, CT, Wesleyan University Press.

Gold, Pleasant Daniel. *History of Volusia County, Florida*. 1928, St. Augustine, Record Co.

Charles Dummett's Grave

New Smyrna Beach

Monument to a father's sorrow

Young Charles Dummett probably deserved better. Killed in a hunting accident, the 16-year-old was buried by his grief-stricken father in the quiet glen where he had fallen. When development caught up, it was forced to go around Charles' final resting place. But time and vandals have taken their toll.

Canova Drive is a quiet road one block east of the Intracoastal Waterway east of downtown New Smyrna Beach. Smack in the middle of the street stands Dummett's tomb, positioned at an awkward angle almost perpendicular to the street. No guided tours visit it.

"Most people don't know about it," says Gary Luther, a local historian and publisher. "You're off the main thoroughfare. Here you are in a residential community, and you wouldn't expect to find a grave in the middle of the street."

The 30-foot-square concrete monument is cracked and covered in ivy. Flowers and plants surrounding it are maintained by the city's parks department; a lone sprinkler head emits a mist. You can barely read the inscription:

"Sacred to the memory of CHARLES DUMMETT. Born August 18, 1844. Died April 23, 1860."

The tomb has been so defiled that Luther believes Charles isn't even there any more.

Charles's grandfather, Thomas Henry Dummett, was an officer in the British Marines and a planter in the West Indies. He fled Barbados in 1807 during a rebellion and secured land grants on the Tomoka River north of Daytona Beach for a sugar plantation. Legend says he was a "remittance man" — a black sheep of the family who was paid

Young Charles Dummett's grave stands in the middle of a quiet New Smyrna Beach street. *Bob Shanley, Palm Beach Post*

to leave his native Britain.

Charles's father, Douglas Dummett, commanded a group of volunteer soldiers in the Second Seminole War (1835–1842) and ran sugar and citrus groves. His research is credited with leading to the Indian River citrus industry. When his wife, daughter of a socially prominent family, deserted him for another Army officer, he built a home on an Indian mound and called it Mount Pleasant. Gary Luther says Dummett then married a slave and had three daughters and a son — Charles.

Charles was sent to a northern school and was home on break when he went hunting with a friend. He tripped and his gun went off, killing him instantly. Twelve years after his son's death, Douglas Dummett fell ill and went to nearby Merritt Island for treatment. He died there and was buried in an unmarked grave.

There are the usual legends: Young Charles actually committed suicide because he learned he was part black. His friend accidentally shot him. The grave was used by Prohibition-era rumrunners to hide liquor.

Around the 1940s, film star and Jacksonville native Judy Canova sent her brother to the area to search for real estate investments. The city refused her plans to set up a trailer park. The street eventually became residential Canova Drive.

In the 1960s, Mt. Pleasant was bulldozed for development. The legal complexities of moving Dummett's grave led developers to leave it where it was.

Charles Dummett's Grave is on Canova Drive in New Smyrna Beach, just south of Daytona Beach. From Interstate 95, take State Road 44 east, which becomes the South Causeway, and across the Intracoastal Waterway. Turn north on South Peninsular Avenue and go about a mile to Canova Drive, then left.

    Southeast Volusia Chamber of Commerce: 115 Canal St., New Smyrna Beach 32168. Call (877) 460-8410 or (386) 428-2449. Website: www.sevchamber.com

    Daytona Beach Area Convention and Visitors Bureau: (800) 854-1234. Website: www.daytonabeach.com

Read More About It

Hebel, Ianthe Bond. *The Dummetts of Northeast Florida.* 1968, Daytona Beach, Hebel.

Luther, Gary. *History of New Smyrna, East Florida.* 1987, New Smyrna Beach, G. Luther.

Eatonville

A racial haven

When Eatonville, claimed as America's oldest incorporated black municipality, celebrated its centennial in 1987, the estimated 10,000 onlookers included two members of the Ku Klux Klan. The men told reporters they wanted to laud the town just north of Orlando for its racial separation. As usual, the Klansmen didn't get it, local officials said: Eatonville is about 90 percent black but has several white-owned businesses and is open to everyone. City leaders say the primary color in Eatonville is the green they hope will continue to bring prosperity to the town.

Of course, the town's founding was necessitated because it came at a time when too many people thought like the Klan members. The two-square-mile city of about 2,500 is one of about 100 nationwide that were founded by former slaves as all-black towns between the Civil War and the turn of the twentieth century. Only a dozen remain.

Following the war, recently freed slaves moved to central Florida in search of work. They cleared land and planted vegetables and citrus groves, built houses, worked on central Florida's first railroad, and were domestics in wealthy families' homes. The black workers built shanties for housing. None of this sat well with the nineteenth-century white Floridians. Leaders came up with the idea of letting blacks buy land a few miles from Maitland and set up their own town.

This didn't work at first; white landowners didn't want to sell a large tract for a black town. Finally, some whites sold 112 acres. They included Maitland's mayor, Captain Josiah Eaton. On Aug. 15, 1887, with slavery out of business for only two decades, 27 black men met and voted the town into being, naming it Eatonville for the generous Maitland mayor.

Zora Neale Hurston.
Florida State Archives

While Eatonville denizens include Hall of Fame football player Deacon Jones, and former Florida A&M president Benjamin Perry, the most famous is probably Zora Neale Hurston. Zora, who saw only modest attention in life and was buried in a pauper's grave in Fort Pierce, has since become a towering literary figure. Born in Alabama, she grew up in Eatonville, and her experiences in a black town in the Deep South — her father was an early mayor — influenced much of her writing. Eatonville is one of the main settings for her classic *Their Eyes Were Watching God*, its climax based on the great 1928 Lake Okeechobee hurricane, which drowned 2,500 to 3,000people, most of them black.

Early each year since 1990, the town grows tenfold as it hosts about 25,000 for the Zora Neale Hurston Festival of the Arts and Humanities. And in January 2005, the town dedicated a children's library, part of the Orange County library system: Eatonville Branch Library at Zora Neale Hurston Square.

Eatonville is about 10 miles north of Orlando and 2½ miles north of Winter Park. Follow Interstate 4 to Lee Road, then right, then north on Wymore Road to Kennedy Boulevard, then east into town. Write: Town of Eatonville, 307 E. Kennedy Blvd., Eatonville 32751. Call (407) 623–1313. Website: www.townofeatonville.org/

Zora Neale Hurston Festival of the Arts and Humanities: Write 227 E. Kennedy Blvd., Eatonville 32751. Call (407) 599-9930. Website: www.zoranealehurstonfestival.com/

Read More About It
Otey, Frank M. *Eatonville, Florida: A Brief History of One of America's First Freedmen's Towns*. 1989, Winter Park, Four-G Publishing.
Glassman, Steve, and Kathryn Lee Seidel, eds. *Zora in Florida*. 1991, Gainesville, University Press of Florida.

Christmas

Florida yule

The town of Christmas, Florida, cynics will speculate, was built in two weeks by clever hucksters to sell trinkets to Disney-goers on the way out of nearby Orlando. For once, they'll be wrong.

The unincorporated settlement of 4,000 is one of only four in America named for the holiday, according to the U. S. Geological Survey. Another five have Christmas in their name, like Christmasland.

Christmas, Florida's name is easily explained. During the Seminole Wars, soldiers stopped here — about halfway between Orlando and the Space Coast — and built a fort. Since it was around the Christmas season, that's what they called the encampment.

But that hasn't stopped the town of Christmas — or at least its post office — from cashing in. As many as 150,000 people visit every Christmas season, and people send in bundles of mail, all just to get that one-of-a-kind postmark. In 1993, the post office was selected for the "first day of issue" cancellation of that season's contemporary Christmas stamps. And there are the sacks of mail from youngsters that are addressed simply: "Santa Claus, Christmas, Florida."

A permanently decorated 35-foot evergreen and a statue of Santa in his sleigh catch the eyes of motorists on State Road 50. Nearby, an altar of ceramic tile, hand-painted signs, and Bible scenes inside glass boxes are mounted along the path of a "peace garden."

"The permanent Christmas tree at Christmas, Florida, is the symbol of love and good will; the Christmas spirit every day of the year," a sign reads.

A tiny three-room building next to the Peace Garden that had been the Post Office is still jammed with hundreds of artifacts sent from all over the world: plastic reindeer, holiday coffee cups, stockings,

Thousands arrange for their holiday mail to be postmarked at the Christmas, Florida, post office. *Florida Development Commission*

ceramic Madonnas, a life-size picture of Jesus Christ created from rows of stamps, and, of course, hundreds of Santas. Plans are to move the items to Fort Christmas. A "cracker Christmas" event the first weekend in December includes a tree-lighting ceremony and caroling.

Juanita Tucker, postmaster for four decades before retiring in 1974, is the town's curator of sorts and was the guiding force behind the holiday theme. The post office was established in 1892. Troops came through in December 1837 and built a fort in three days, starting Christmas Day. The complex — two 20-foot-square blockhouses surrounded by a pine picket — was a supply depot for about 2,000 soldiers working the nearby countryside; about 75 soldiers actually lived there. The fort never saw battle; it was abandoned three months after it was built, and finally fell victim to deterioration and fire. Nothing remains.

With area Seminoles routed, cattle ranchers and farmers — some of them former soldiers from the fort — began to homestead the area. Many current residents are their descendants.

In 1975, Orange County commissioned a $100,000 reconstruction about a mile south of the original fort site. The replica, dedicated two years later, houses a museum showing the life of early area settlers. Tourists can see the full-dress garb of a U. S. soldier and a Seminole, along with swords, guns, and other artifacts.

Christmas is about 25 miles east of Orlando on State Road 50.

Christmas Post Office is on SR 50 just west of County Road 420; 23580 E. Colonial Drive, Christmas 32709-9998. Call (407) 568-2941. Open regular business hours only. Guided group tours by arrangement.

Fort Christmas is north about two miles on CR 420 at 1300 Fort Christmas Road, Christmas 32709-9427. Call (407) 568-4149. Open all year except county holidays, 8 A.M. to 8 P.M. The museum is open 10 A.M. to 5 P.M., closed Monday. Guided group tours by arrangement. "Living history" reenactments two weekends a year.

East Orange Chamber of Commerce: 10111 E. Colonial Drive, Orlando 32817. Call (407) 277-5951. Website: www.eocc.org

Orlando/Orange County Convention and Visitors Bureau: Call (800) 972-3304 or (407) 363-5872. Website: www.orlandoinfo.com

Read More About It
Mahon, John. *History of the Second Seminole War, 1835–1842.* 1968, Gainesville, University of Florida Press.

Kennedy Space Center

Cocoa Beach

Where we touch the stars

Perhaps nowhere else is Florida's historical paradox more clear. Not far from here, Juan Ponce de León is believed to have launched Florida's modern history when he claimed, for cross and crown, a new land he called Florida. And here is where mankind is reaching for the stars.

Of course, the Kennedy Space Center is still making history. Anywhere from 15,000 to 500,000 people swarm roads and beaches to see the sky brightly lit and the ground rumble as a space shuttle or one of the smaller unmanned spacecraft rides a tower of flame into the heavens.

Visitors to America's launching pad can view the dramatic story of America's space era. Their initial feeling is one of size and its extremes. The center itself covers 140,000 acres — nearly 219 square miles.

Its most formidable structure is the 525-foot high, 716-foot long, 518-foot wide vehicle assembly building. Some say clouds have formed inside and dropped rain. The building contains four bays, each with its own door 456 feet high. They're the world's largest doors.

At a *Saturn V* center, about a mile away, is a full assembly of one of the *Saturn V* rockets, the 363-foot-long mammoths that seemed to crawl into the sky, sending men to the moon. At its top is the command module. It's about the size of the inside of a van. Astronauts squeezed into it for days on courageous treks to the moon, all the while separated only by a few inches of steel from the instant cold death of space.

In the near distance, the space shuttle, a sporty coupe to the lumbering *Saturn* bus, leaps into the sky, awing people as the space

Launch pads at Kennedy Space Center. *U.S. Air Force*

program has for nearly half a century.

To see a launch up close, go online to www.kennedyspacecenter. com or check at the visitors center to try to obtain one of about 5,000 passes that will get you closer to the launch pad.

The first stop for the Kennedy Space Center narrated bus tour is the LC-39 Observation Gantry, which offers a panoramic view of Kennedy Space Center and the Space Shuttle launch pads, as well as the rocket launch pads at Cape Canaveral Air Force Station. A short film and interactive displays show how the pad is built and how a shuttle is launched. Buses then go by the Vehicle Assembly Building (VAB), where the Space Shuttle is stacked for launch and where the *Apollo/Saturn V* rockets were once assembled, as well as the Orbiter Processing Facility, where the orbiter is examined and maintained after each mission.

The second stop is the *Apollo/Saturn V* Center, where multi-media shows and hands-on displays provide a look into America's guest for the moon. You can relive the launch of *Apollo 8* at the Firing Room Theater and see a 363-foot-long *Saturn V* moon rocket, one of only three in existence. The Lunar Theater provides a rare look at the final moments before man landed on the moon.

Six miles west of the main Visitor Complex is the Astronaut Hall of Fame, Kennedy Space Center's newest attraction. The Hall of Fame features the world's largest collection of personal astronaut mementos, plus historic spacecrafts, hands-on activities, and astronaut training simulators. Sit at a mission control console or take a virtual moonwalk and feel the pull of 4 G's in the G-Force Simulator.

Start your visit at Spaceport USA, the visitors center, packed with space artifacts and equipment. They include a replica of the lunar rover astronauts used to race across the moon at ten mph, a moon rock brought back in 1972, a space suit worn by James Lovell during the ill-fated *Apollo 13* mission in 1970, a full-scale orbiter and booster rockets, and a launch status center.

The IMAX movies *Magnificent Desolation: Walking on the Moon 3D* and *International Space Station in 3D,* filmed by astronauts, provide magnificent views of space and the good Earth. Spaceport is also the site of the stirring space mirror, a monument to astronauts who died during the brief but momentous history of space exploration.

From the Earth to the Moon

Space travel from Florida dates all the way back to legendary French author Jules Verne. From across the peninsula, in Tampa, he sent a team of fictional nineteenth-century astronauts *From the Earth to the Moon.* While there is no evidence Verne visited Florida, NASA officials say Verne was right in placing his site between the equator and the 28th parallel to afford the best angle for a moon launch. Cape Canaveral is at latitude 28.5 degrees north.

America's sprawling space center had a more inauspicious beginning. The Long Range proving ground, created by President Harry Truman on May 11, 1949, later became nearby Patrick Air Force Base. Fourteen months later, on July 24, 1950, just up the road, a German V-2 became the first rocket ever launched by the United States. For the next decade, the space program would moved toward its goal of manned flight, a goal sped up when the Soviets did it first.

On May 5, 1961, Alan B. Shepard Jr. lifted off and became the first American in space. On July 20, 1962, John Glenn was the first American in orbit.

Then, John F. Kennedy, who had thrown the space program into overdrive and brashly promised a man on the moon by the end of the decade, was slain. Six days after his assassination, the space center area was renamed, from Cape Canaveral to Cape Kennedy. While a well-meaning gesture, the move was not popular. Historians decried the loss of one of Florida's oldest continuous place names, and by the end of the decade, the region was again called Cape Canaveral, with the facility on it called the Kennedy Space Center.

By the late 1960s, the eyes of the world were on what was now being called Florida's Space Coast. Man was going to the moon. And people were moving in droves to the once-sleepy region.

But nothing comes easy. On January 27, 1967, in a flash of only a few seconds, a fire incinerated the three-man crew of *Apollo 1* as they sat helplessly on the launch pad. NASA officials feared the tragedy would deal a major setback to John Kennedy's lofty goal. But they quickly recovered, and only two and a half years later, a rocket the size of an office building lumbered into the skies. Four days later, man was on the moon.

Exuberant legislators named the moonstone Florida's official state gem, even though the stone is not naturally found in Florida or on the moon. More moon missions followed — including unlucky *Apollo 13*, which left Cape Kennedy on April 11, 1970. Man's third attempt to land on the moon was aborted in open space when an oxygen tank exploded. The three-man crew crawled into the lunar landing module and rode the crippled craft home. The saga sparked a 1995 film.

By the mid-1970s, a lull in the space program took its toll on the Space Coast. But the end of the decade brought a new program: the space shuttle. *Columbia* shot off the pad April 12, 1981, starting a string of dozens of shuttle missions. NASA wanted space travel to become workaday. But America grew too used to it.

That complacency was jolted on January 28, 1986, when *Challenger* exploded 74 seconds after takeoff, killing seven astronauts. They died one day shy of 19 years from the *Apollo 1* disaster, less than a mile away. NASA reeled from the *Challenger* catastrophe, and some feared the space program would not recover. It would be 32 months before Americans returned to space.

A gigantic space mirror was paid for with money raised by a *Challenger* license plate, the first specialty plate in Florida and the most popular. It has sold nearly 60,000 and raised more than $27 million. The plate had to be redesigned in 2003. On Feb. 1 of that year, *Columbia*, the fleet's flagship and first vehicle, disintegrated on reentry. The loss was yet another blow for the agency, and the shuttle would not fly for two and a half years.

The space mirror stands as a monument to the Challenger and Columbia astronauts and all who died reaching for the stars.

Kennedy Space Center Visitor Complex is 45 minutes east of Orlando on State Road 405, six miles inside the Kennedy Space Center entrance. From Orlando, take State Road 528 east and follow the signs to Kennedy Space Center. From Interstate 95, take exit 212 northbound or exit 215 southbound. Call (321) 449-4444. Website: www.kennedyspacecenter.com

Open daily, except Christmas and some launch days, 9 A.M. TO 6 P.M. Admission: adults $38, kids 3–11 $28. Admission includes KSC tour, interactive space-flight simulators, space films, and Astronaut Hall of Fame.

Florida's Space Coast Office of Tourism: 2725 Judge Fran Jamieson Way, #B-105, Viera 32940. Call (321) 637-5483 or (800) 936-2326. Website: www.space-coast.com.

Read More About It

Carr, Harriett. *Cape Canaveral.* 1974, St. Petersburg, Valkyrie Press.

Scarborough, C.W. and Stephen B. Milner. *Liftoff: The Story of America's Spaceport.* 1966, Pioneer, Little Rock, Ark.

Wolfe, Tom. *The Right Stuff.* 1979, New York, Farrar, Straus, Giroux.

Lake Kissimmee Cow Camp

east of Lake Wales

Cowboys and dogies

The guys in chaps and boots are pretending to be nineteenth-century cow hunters. The cows are the real thing.

The cow camp living history program at this park on the shore of Lake Kissimmee, about 20 miles east of Lake Wales, portrays a time when cattle were hunted, gathered, and moved across the state to market. The small herd kept at the park is composed of the rare Andalusia cattle, first introduced by Spanish explorers more than four centuries ago but now almost gone.

Every weekend, visitors see a re-creation of an 1876 encampment for the hunters who herded as many as 1,000 cattle across the Kissimmee River Valley in an arduous 45-day journey from Okeechobee to Paynes Prairie, south of Gainesville. From there, cows were fattened before being loaded onto trains for slaughterhouses in Georgia. Other cowboys drove cattle down to the docks at Punta Rassa, north of Fort Myers, where boats shipped them to Cuba.

Florida is the nation's sixteenth-biggest cattle state, with more than 1.7 million head, and the biggest beef cattle state east of the Mississippi.

The characters at Lake Kissimmee, with names like Rooster and Cooter, eat, tell stories, crack whips, even let kids hold the heavy guns. The idea is to dispel their images of an easy and excitement-filled life as a cowboy. The painstakingly recreated 1870s frontier cow hunter camp portrays a time when cattle roamed the open range, and hunters

A cowboy reenactor at Lake Kissimee State Park.
Florida State Parks

had to comb woods and fields to round them up. Wearing jeans and a shirt, cowboys drink black coffee from a tin cup, pump water by hand, stretch out in rope-and-log beds, whine about their $1.50-a-day pay, and show off their cracking 13-foot buckskin whips.

While the living history is staged only on weekends and holidays, except Christmas, the park, a 5,030-acre preserve along the giant lake, is open all week. It offers shaded campsites, 13 miles of hiking trails, an observation tower, and a marina.

The camp is also a working 200-acre ranch for two herds, about 25 head each, of the moderate-sized "scrub cows" that the Spanish brought to Florida. They average 400 to 800 pounds; more traditional cows can range from 1,000 pounds to a ton. The Andalusia cattle, named for the Spanish state of their origin, are the same ones that pursue matadors in that nation's bull rings. The herds basically run wild, although the camp workers do patrol them on horses called "marshtackies." They, too, were bred in Spain to be lean and sure-footed to track the cows through the brush, and they have also become rare.

In recent years, the Lake Kissimmee herds, which had suffered from crossbreeding, have been mated with other, more pure Andalusia herds to maintain genetic integrity and keep the historic animals around for future generations.

Lake Kissimmee State Park is 15 miles east of Lake Wales at 14248 Camp Mack Road, Lake Wales 33853. Call (863) 696-1112. Website: www.floridastateparks.org

Take State Road 60 to Boy Scout Road, north to Camp Mack Road, then east six miles.

The park is open 8 A.M. to sunset every day. The cow camp is open 9:30 A.M. to 4:30 P.M. Saturdays, Sundays, and major holidays, except Christmas. Admission: $4 per vehicle, $1 for pedestrian or cyclist, $3 solo. Campsites available.

Lake Wales Area Chamber of Commerce: 340 W. Central Ave., Lake Wales 33859. Call (863) 676-3445

Polk County Tourist Development Council. Call (800) 828-7655.

Read More About It

Akerman, Joe A. Jr. *Florida Cowman: A History of Florida Cattle Raising*. 1976, Madison, Florida Cattleman's Association.

Brown, Canter. *Florida's Peace River Frontier*. 1991, Gainesville, University of Florida Press.

Smith, Patrick. *A Land Remembered*. 1984, Sarasota, Pineapple Press.

Taylor, Robert A. *Rebel Storehouse: Florida in the Confederate Economy*. 1995, Tuscaloosa, AL, University of Alabama Press.

Bok Tower

Lake Wales

One man's quest for beauty

From a hidden place inside Bok Tower, the music flows over the lush foliage, the sidewalks, the still ponds, the fearless squirrels, and the hushed visitors.

Sanctuary.

This was Edward Bok's idea. And despite the overwhelming growth of surrounding Central Florida, the process still works.

"Make you the world a bit better or more beautiful because you have lived in it," reads a marker. Bok said it often; it was one of his grandmother's favorite phrases. The words are on one of several markers posted around the gardens that surround the 205-foot tower, one of the tallest structures in central Florida and one of only four carillon towers in Florida.

The gardens went on the National Register of Historic Places in 1972. In April 1993, it became one of about three dozen in Florida to be named a national historic landmark by the U.S. Department of the Interior.

The tower and gardens were built by Dutch-born publisher and Pulitzer Prize–winning author Edward Bok in 1929 in gratitude to his adopted land. Bok would say he built the tower and gardens "to preach the gospel of beauty and to provide a quiet glade where travelers could rest or meditate awhile, listen to the blended music of bells and birdsong, and go on their way, refreshed in spirit."

Bok, who immigrated at six and started as a Western Union office boy, ran *The Ladies' Home Journal*, the first magazine to obtain one million subscribers, for 30 years. He retired in 1919.

Bok wrote his autobiography and a dozen other books, created three different awards to encourage excellence and an endowment at Princeton University, and founded a speaker's forum in his hometown of Philadelphia.

Bok was inspired to create his tower and gardens by his grandfather, who helped convert a desert island in the North Sea into a haven of vegetation. He bought the first of several pieces of land in 1922. Seven years later, President Calvin Coolidge dedicated the gardens and tower. Bok died nearby less than a year later and is buried at the foot of the tower.

60 Bells

The attraction is operated by a nonprofit organization. In its first 50 years, it had only two directors, three horticulturists, and two carillon players. About 100 acres of the property has been set aside as a nature reserve, 60 acres are in the historic garden, and the sanctuary encompasses nearly 250 total acres of gardens and grounds. The squirrels have become completely unafraid of people, and small children might be startled when one crashes unseen through the brush or suddenly pops onto a walkway, although managers say kids love watching the animals scurry.

The tower, rising atop a nearly 300-foot hill that is the highest

Bok Tower's carillons send music wafting through the countryside. *Bok Tower Gardens*

point on the peninsula, is made of pink and gray northern Georgia marble and tan St. Augustine coquina limestone, with a mixture of coral and shell. The tower is 51 feet wide at the base and 37 feet at the top, and is square up to 150 feet, then octagonal. It is closed to the public and surrounded by a moat. Designed by architect Milton Medary, the tower's finely detailed artwork represents the work of three artists and hundreds of craftsmen. It shows a young man feeding birds and watering plants, and eagles, doves, hens, palms, and roses. A sundial is on the south wall.

The carillon is a musical instrument comprising 60 bells, ranging in weight from 16 pounds to nearly 12 tons, and played from a keyboard. The bells don't swing; they play when the operator strikes wooden keys with the hands and pedals with the feet. Each key then pulls a wire which draws the clapper onto the bell. Recorded selections are played on the half hour and hour, and recitals take place at 1 P.M. and 3 P.M. daily. Live performances take place daily from December 1 to April 30.

Bok Tower is three miles north of downtown Lake Wales (1151 Tower Blvd., 33853). Call (863) 676-1408. Take State Road 60 to Lake Wales; turn north on Buck Moore Road (State Road 17B), then left on Burns Avenue (State Road 17A). Entrance is on the right. Open 8 A.M. to 6 P.M. every day, last admission is at 5 P.M. Adults, $10; children 5–12, $3. Free under age 5. Memberships available. Guided tours available.

The nearby **Pinewood House**, a 20-room Mediterranean Revival mansion restored to its 1930s look, is open for guided tours daily at 12:00 P.M. and 2:00 P.M. Guided tours are limited to 16 people. Adults, $6; children 5 to 12, $4. Free under age 5. Tour tickets available at Bok visitor center.

Lake Wales Area Chamber of Commerce: 340 W. Central Ave., Lake Wales 33859. Call (863) 676-3445. Website: www.lakewaleschamber. com

Central Florida Visitor and Convention Bureau: Call (800) 828-7655 or (863) 534-2500. Website: www.sunsational.org

Read More About It

Bok, Edward. *Americanization of Edward Bok*. 1920, New York, Scribner's.

Frisbie, Louise. *Yesterday's Polk County*. 1976, Miami, Seeman Publishing.

Florida Southern College

Lakeland

Frank Lloyd Wright's gift

Florida Southern College is a hidden treasure. In this region noted more for orange trees and phosphate pits, finding the 1,500-student school requires turning out of downtown Lakeland and negotiating a residential neighborhood. But you soon see that mixed among the more traditional brick edifices on the 52-building, 100-acre lakefront school are dramatic, daring, and visionary structures. Their designer: Frank Lloyd Wright.

The "Child of the Sun Collection" that the aging architect — already a luminary — designed in the heart of the Depression for the Methodist institute represents the largest concentration of his works at one spot in the world. The 12 structures completed out of Wright's original 18 designs underwent a $2 million restoration in the mid-1980s, financed mostly by alumni and trustees.

The school, founded in 1885 in Orlando and moved several times before settling in Lakeland in 1922, was an obscure and financially strapped institution with only four buildings in 1936 when its president, Ludd M. Spivey, mulled the bold plan of hiring Frank Lloyd Wright, then in his late 60s, to create "a great education temple in Florida."

Wright was given free rein to design the campus. Florida Southern gave him $13,000 for his master plan and eventually paid $100,000 for the project, raising the money bit by bit. Students actually constructed three of the buildings. In the height of the Depression, it was an ambitious gamble for the small school.

Construction began with the chapel in 1938. It would be two

113

LEFT: Eminent architect Frank Lloyd Wright made tiny Florida Southern College a showcase. *Worldwide Photo*

BOTTOM: Twelve Frank Lloyd Wright structures highlight Florida Southern College. *Florida Southern College*

decades before the twelfth building, the science center with its white-domed planetarium, was finished in 1958 — the year before Wright died.

"Child of the Sun"

According to college literature, Wright envisioned the campus as "a child of the sun." Its buildings were to be in harmony with surroundings and incorporate Florida aspects. He designed open courtyards, lush gardens, pools, and glass skylights. Look for triangles inside triangles, sharp angles, flat roofs, and low overhangs that seem to lack support.

The architect used only six materials: copper, concrete, steel, wood, aluminum, and glass. He employed native material, including beach sand and crushed seashells, to give the concrete-block buildings their cream color. Woodwork featured red cypress.

Wright spent a lot of time on campus early on, then made numerous visits over the two-decade span of the project. With his white hair, cane, and mink-collared cape, he could be found sitting under an orange tree talking with students or luring them to a nearby tavern, much to the chagrin of the Methodist college's leaders.

Published reports say that once, furious that a bougainvillea had crawled up one of his creations, he tore the offending vine down with his cane, bemoaning the crime of covering "the most beautiful buildings in the world . . . with 15 cents' worth of seeds." Another time, at a dinner, he saw waiters bringing ice cream and declared it "the worst thing you could eat on a full stomach." Of course, his voice carried perfectly in the hall he had designed so well.

He designed the library for natural light, and the school later had to install desk lamps for night work, which they hid every time Wright visited. He didn't want the intricate administration building cluttered with bathrooms; administrators must still walk next door.

By their nature, his designs caused maintenance problems; leaking roofs and skylights led to the 1980s renovation project.

Today 15,000 to 20,000 people visit the campus each year just to view the legacy of Frank Lloyd Wright.

Florida Southern College is at 111 Lake Hollingsworth Drive, Lakeland 33801-5698. Call (863) 680-4110. Take Florida Avenue in downtown Lakeland to about 10 blocks south of Main Street, then east on McDonald Street about five blocks to campus. Frank Lloyd Wright Visitor Center open 10 A.M. to 4 P.M. Monday–Friday, 10 A.M. to 2 P.M. Saturday, 2 P.M. to 4 P.M. Sunday. A marker and an information center with free maps and brochures for self-guided walking tours are on the Johnson Street (west) side of the campus.

Guided tours for large groups available by arrangement; $5 per person. Please call ahead.

Lakeland Area Chamber of Commerce: Box 3538, Lakeland 33802. Call (863) 688-8551. Website: www.lakelandchamber.com

Central Florida Visitor and Convention Bureau: (800) 828-7655 or (863) 534-2500. Website: www.sunsational.org

Read More About It

Florida Southern College. *The Frank Lloyd Wright Campus.* 1953, Lakeland, Florida Southern College.

Frisbie, Louise. *Yesterday's Polk County.* 1976, Miami, Seemann Publishing.

Haggard, Theodore M. *Florida Southern College, Lakeland, Florida: The First 100 Years.* 1985, Lakeland, Florida Southern College.

Secrest, Meryle. *Frank Lloyd Wright.* 1992, New York, Alfred A. Knopf.

Cypress Gardens

Winter Haven

Where Florida tourism was born

This is how family summer vacations worked in Florida in 1961. Leaving our South Dade home before dawn, we worked our way up U.S. 27. Sugar fields gave way to the rolling hills of central Florida. Two 20-somethings and four kids — ages 7, 5, 2, and 9 months — piled into the Lake Roy Lodge, a complex lining one of the area's many lakes.

As we bobbed in the calm waters in bright orange life jackets almost bigger than our bodies, our young parents zipped around on water skis. We remember meeting a not-yet-famous comedienne named Carol Burnett. But the highlight was our trek next door — we could actually boat through connecting canals and tie up at the entrance — to watch the pros ski at Cypress Gardens. When Walt Disney's empire was only a little mouse with big black eyes cavorting on celluloid, Dick Pope was birthing Florida's modern tourism industry on 16 acres of swamp.

The park's "Cypress Roots" historical museum tells the story, in pictures, displays, and memorabilia, of the man who would be called an "aquatic Barnum." He was called worse by naysayers when he opened Cypress Gardens, Florida's first theme park, on January 2, 1936. At 25 cents a head, his first day's take was $38 — meaning he saw, at most, 152 people. The original 16-acre garden is still there. But Cypress Gardens now covers 150 acres. It attracted more than 1 million visitors in 2005, after undergoing a $70 million renovation.

Spreading from a giant lake where ski shows go on, rain or shine, the park features the original gardens with more than 8,000 varieties of plants and flowers from 90 countries, a 5,500-square-foot conservatory housing about 1,000 butterflies, a 153-foot high "Sunshine Sky Adventure" revolving platform that provides a view of the countryside, museums, shops, restaurants, and rides and games. It is a fraction the size of Disney World but a sight bigger than the old alligator farms and orange stands that once were its only competition for tourists.

Pope had moved his family from his native Iowa in 1908, drawn by Florida's land booms. When the bust wiped him out, he drove to Wisconsin to work for the fledgling Johnson outboard motor company, stopping along the way to send telegrams heralding the arrival of "the world's greatest publicity man." Later, after reading an article about a man in South Carolina who earned $36,000 in three months simply by charging people to view his estate, Pope had his idea.

"Punch-drunk with beauty . . . "

Pope built Cypress Gardens not just as a moneymaker itself, but also as a come-on.

"When people came out of the gardens punch-drunk with beauty," Pope would say years later in an newspaper interview, "they might say something like 'This is a beautiful spot. I sure would like to buy a little piece of land here.' To which I would say, 'It just so happens . . .'"

Pope and a partner, John Snively, paid $500 down and took a three-year note from the city of Winter Haven and a local canal commission for $1,800 in cash and in "man days" from the Florida Emergency Relief Association, a local branch of the Works Progress Administration. Later, the other groups pulled out, saying the property would never be more than swamp; they dubbed Pope "Swami of the Swamp" and "Maestro of the Muck." Pope and his partner went on alone. They hired about 30 men for $1 a day. Later they were forced to pay in scrip good at the neighborhood grocery store. That store grew into the Publix empire.

For five months, workers toiled with buckets and shovels. Pope got building materials from a cypress growers' association in exchange for naming his park after their product. He laid rye grass and $300 worth of azaleas and camellias.

Pope soon saw the attraction could be more than a salesman's bait. America was fascinated with tropical Florida, and the camera would let Pope bring it to them. Pope built the gardens — and put Florida as a major destination on the map — with photography. Over the years, he sent magazines and newsreel outfits thousands of still

Cypress Gardens has lured nature lovers for six decades. *Cypress Gardens*

photographs and small reels of film the size of coasters.

Freezing Northerners devoured the lush images of orange blossoms, swimsuit-clad maidens, even a swimming pool in the shape of Florida. The attraction graced hundreds of magazine covers. Feature films were shot there. *Life* called it "photographer's paradise." The press also loved the water skiing stunts. One magazine spread showed Pope sitting at a boat pulled grand piano; it also showed the contraption flipping over.

60,000 Shows

During World War II, soldiers from nearby bases began showing up, wanting to know where they could see the stunt shows featured in print and film. The Popes were in a jam.

Pope's wife Julie wrote the *Orlando Sentinel*, promising a show. Three soldiers came. The next day it was 400. Pope began working the bases and ran weekly beauty contests with GIs as judges. Many of those soldiers went home after the war, then put Cypress Gardens on their family vacation list. Since then, the place has run about 60,000 shows and set more than 50 world skiing records. Pope was credited with the first ramp jump and the first kite flying on skis; his first attempt ended with a 50-foot fall and a black eye.

Pope even turned misfortune into a tradition that continues

today. In the 1940s, after a freeze, the Popes feared the dead flame vines lining the entrance would scare off tourists, even though the vegetation inside had been saved by smudge pots. Julie Pope placed women in hoop skirts out front to greet visitors — and block their view of dead vegetation.

After Walt Disney opened his first park in California, Pope invited him to Florida. Disney stood at the entrance with a counter and clicked off customers as they came in. He was impressed. Disney World opened in 1971. Even Pope saw it would grow to dwarf Cypress Gardens, but he believed it would bring tourists to him as well. He bought a full-page newspaper ad welcoming Disney and was awarded the park's first lifetime pass.

Meanwhile, Pope diversified, putting about two-thirds of the company's business in the attraction and a third in making water skiing and water sports products. He retired in the early 1980s and died at age 87 in 1988.

Cypress Gardens underwent a $5.5 million renovation and expansion in 1980. The Harcourt Brace Jovanovich publishing and entertainment empire bought it in 1985 and sold it four years later to the Anheuser-Busch conglomerate, making the theme park one of ten in the country — four in Florida — owned by the beer giant. Senior management bought out the park in 1995.

All seemed lost in April 2003, when the park closed suddenly, citing low attendance due to, among other things, the drop in tourism following the September 11, 2001, terrorist attacks. Both employees and regular customers begged for help in saving the attraction. Kent Buescher, who had bought a 100-acre southern Georgia horse farm in Valdosta, Georgia, in 1991 and turned it into Wild Adventures Theme Park, worked with state and local governments in Florida and the Trust For Public Land to strike a deal to rescue Cypress Gardens. Work revitalizing and restoring the park began immediately and Cypress Gardens Adventure Park was reborn in 2004, the Splash Island Water Park opening two years later.

Cypress Gardens is in Winter Haven. Write 6000 Cypress Gardens Blvd. Winter Haven 33884. Call (863) 324-2111. Take U. S. 27 to State Road 540, then west to the entrance. Open every day at 10 A.M.; closing times vary by the season. Adults $39.95 plus tax; children 3–9 and seniors 55 and over $34.95 plus tax; 2 and under free. Splash

Island included in admission. Annual passes available. Website: www. cypressgardens.com

Winter Haven Area Chamber of Commerce: 401 Ave B NW, Winter Haven 33881. Call (863) 293-2138. Web page: www.winterhavenfl. com

Read More About It

Burr, Josephine. *History of Winter Haven, Florida.* 1974, Winter Haven, J. Burr.

Florida Cypress Gardens: Guide to America's Tropical Wonderland. 1949, Chicago, Curt Teich and Co.

Frisbie, Louise. *Yesterday's Polk County.* 1976, Miami, Seeman Publishing.

Tampa Bay/Sarasota

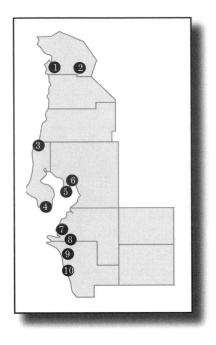

1. Yulee Sugar Mill Ruins Historic State Park, *Homosassa*
2. Dade Battlefield, *Bushnell*
3. Tarpon Springs
4. The Don CeSar, *St. Petersburg Beach*
5. University of Tampa, *Tampa*
6. Ybor City, *Tampa*
7. De Soto Memorial, *Bradenton*
8. Gamble Mansion, *Ellenton*
9. Ringling Museum and Home, *Sarasota*
10. Historic Spanish Point, *Osprey*

Yulee Sugar Mill Ruins Historic State Park

Homosassa

Attack on Marguerita

David Levy Yulee was a businessman, entrepreneur, trailblazer, and politician. He was the state's first U.S. senator and built the Cross Florida Railroad, the first into peninsular Florida. And he owned a prosperous west central Florida sugar plantation, now a state park.

Yulee, born in St. Thomas, in what is now the U.S. Virgin Islands, descended from a line of Jewish courtiers to Morocco's sultans. He grew up with his mother but moved to Florida when his father, Moses Levy, bought 100,000 acres near present-day Gainesville. While Moses Levy proposed making Florida a refuge for the world's scattered Jews, his son was more secular, and Moses Levy disowned him. David later took his mother's maiden name, calling himself David Levy Yulee.

David Levy later became a lawyer, took part in negotiations preceding the Second Seminole War, and was elected to the Territorial Senate, where he pushed for statehood. When Florida became a state in 1845, he became Florida's first U.S. senator. Soon after that, he married the daughter of a former Kentucky governor.

Narrowly defeated in his reelection bid, he took on the plan for the railroad, obtaining federal and state grants and selling corporate stock. Meanwhile, he was returned to the Senate in 1855, where, conflict of interest notwithstanding, he helped push through a bill

David Yulee. *Florida State Archives*

that gave more federal land to three railroads, including 500,000 acres for his own.

Building conditions were brutal; the first 10 miles of the 155-mile line took nearly a year. The first train arrived in Cedar Key on March 1, 1861. But the Civil War broke out only six weeks later. Levy left the Senate and returned to Florida.

His sugar plantation, Marguerita, stood on 5,100 acres north of Tampa. The plantation house and a small settlement stood on Tiger Tail Island, about four miles down the Homosassa River. Historians aren't sure of the exact location of Yulee's cane fields but speculate they were planted in the rich wet soil of hundreds of acres in the Homosassa River area and many of the nearby coastal marsh islands. Yulee also grew cotton and oranges and developed a hybrid orange called the Homosassa sweet that's still an industry staple.

Slaves ran the steam-powered mill, squeezing the cane juice and turning it into sugar in large cooking kettles brought down from New

York. The finished product was put onto boats and hauled to Cedar Key, where it was loaded on railroad cars for Fernandina. The refining process also produced molasses, which was shipped to the Caribbean to make rum.

The mill operated from 1851 to 1864, those last few years tumultuous ones. Yulee, a reluctant supporter of the Confederacy, supplied sugar products to rebel troops. On May 29, 1864, Union troops came up the river on a mission to destroy Yulee's enterprise. They burned the stockpile supplies and lumber near the plantation house; the flames quickly spread, burning the house to the ground. While the invaders never did find the mill, the operation never recovered.

Levy, who had built a second home on his Cotton Wood plantation in Archer, near Gainesville, was in that area at the time and escaped the attack. A year later, his problems would continue; he served ten months in prison on a treason charge dating back to secession. Yulee returned to Washington in 1881 and died of pneumonia five years later.

At the ruins of the sugar mill, you can still see the steam boiler, an iron press, a 40-foot limestone masonry chimney, the well, and the foundation. A small oval pathway around the ruins has interpretive markers.

Yulee Sugar Mill Ruins Historic State Park is in Homosassa, about 60 miles northwest of Tampa. Take U.S. Highway 19 to Homosassa Springs, then west on County Road 490 West (Yulee Drive) about 2½ miles. Brown and white highway signs will lead you to the park. Write 3400 N. Museum Pointe, Crystal River 34428. Call (352) 795-3817. Website: www.floridastateparks.org

The park is open 8 A.M. to sunset every day. No entrance fee. Ruins of the mill are within five feet of the road and can be easily seen. Ask about available tours.

Read More About It
Sweet, Frank W. *Yulee's Railroad.* 2000, Palm Coast, Backintyme.

Dade
Battlefield

Bushnell

"Our difficulties are over now."

One-two, one-two, one-two. Hut, hut. Through the low grass they marched, two abreast, in the December chill, weighed down with heavy woolen uniforms and bulky firearms. Fort Brooke lay five days' march behind them; Fort King, another five days ahead. Christmas had come and gone during the march, and the soldiers were hungry, weary, filthy, and a long way from home.

"Have a good heart; our difficulties and dangers are over now, and as soon as we arrive at Fort King you'll have three days to rest and keep Christmas gaily," their leader consoled them as they approached a stand of pine.

Soon their troubles were indeed over. Within three minutes Brevet Maj. Francis Langhorne Dade would be dead. Only two of his 107 troops survived. For the rest of the Florida and the nation, the trouble was just starting. One of the deadliest and most controversial wars in American history was under way.

The war, second of three called "Seminole Wars," would last seven years, kill 1,500 Americans and countless Seminoles, and end inconclusively. Years later, historians draw many parallels between Vietnam and the nineteenth-century conflict that was the most unpopular of its time. Americans criticized a war with vague goals against locals who knew the territory and had been driven to desperation. They wondered why they were sending their brave men into a worthless swamp where disease killed three for every one who died in battle.

Seminoles called the event of December 28, 1835, a great victory in their decades-long battle to keep the white man from killing or exiling them. White America long called it the Dade Massacre. It earned posthumous fame for Dade, for whom Florida's most famous county is named.

The 80-acre site features a visitor center containing memorabilia, artifacts and exhibits about the battle. Three obelisks on the grounds bear the phrases, "Dade fell here," "Mudge fell here," "Fraser fell here." Dade's is farthest from the front; he fell first, dropping from his horse. Capt. Upton Sinclair Fraser and Lt. Robert Rich Mudge followed within seconds. To the southeast, across from the visitors center, is the field, privately owned and fenced off, where the soldiers had been marching in the open, making them easy pickings for the Seminoles who lay in wait.

Some Seminole leaders had signed treaties under duress that called for removal to the West, but most leaders had ignored the agreements. They gathered arms and organized resistance. At Fort Brooke, now Tampa, the army sent a troop of 100 enlisted men across a gash through the wilderness to reinforce Fort King, now Ocala. They were led by eight officers. At the front was Dade. The Virginia native had arrived at Fort Brooke from Key West on December 21, and Miami might find itself in Gardiner County if Capt. George Washington Gardiner had not been delayed to tend to his ill wife. Instead Major Dade was sent to lead the fatal mission.

On December 27, Dade and his men crossed the Little Withlacoochee and camped on a knoll. The next morning they began marching before sunup. The Seminoles, believed to number about 180, watched from the woods as the men walked in plain sight in their bright blue garb. Historians believe the soldiers were betrayed by a black slave who spoke the Seminole language. His owner had hired him out to the Army and sent him to catch up with Dade. However, Frank Laumer, who wrote *Dade's Last Command,* the definitive book on the battle, says he doesn't think anyone betrayed Dade.

"They were marching for five days in full uniform in broad daylight right through the Seminole nation," Laumer said in a telephone interview from his home in Dade City, not far from the

Traces of the old military trail still remain at the place where Seminole warriors ambushed Major Dade's command in 1835. *Doug Waitley*

battlefield park. He said that Seminoles told interviewers after the battle, "We had scouts out and they watched the command day by day."

The first volley dropped Dade and half the soldiers. One officer, possibly Gardiner, led the survivors as they gathered behind trees. They fired the cannon they had lugged from Tampa, holding the Seminoles off for 45 minutes so the soldiers could set up a barricade of logs. According to the Seminole plan, they were to be satisfied with taking out two-thirds of the command and scattering the rest. But when the soldiers erected the flimsy Swiss-cheese logworks they became easy pickings.

When Gardiner fell, Lt. William Elon Basinger looked at the dozen or so men still alive and able to shoot. "I am the only officer left, boys; we must do the best we can," he said grimly. Soon he, too, would go down. Two years later, Fort Basinger would be built in Highlands County, across the Kissimmee River from the present-day town of Basinger in northern Okeechobee County.

Two soldiers crawled away. One was discovered by Seminoles and finished off; the other, Joseph Sprague, somehow got to Fort Brooke and recovered, but for some reason there are no recorded interviews with him, Laumer says. A third, Ransome Clarke, was found amid the dead and left to succumb but managed to stay alive and crawl off and reach Fort Brooke.

But it would be almost two months before soldiers got to the battle site. They arrived February 20, 1836, and found the decomposed remains. Cold air had left their skin dried and hard, making identification easier. Nearly 100 soldiers were interred with military honors in two mass graves inside the barricade. Another grave outside the barricade held the fallen officers.

Dade Battlefield Historic State Park is in Bushnell, about 4 1/2 hours north of West Palm Beach, about an hour's drive north of Tampa. From I-75 take the Bushnell exit, which is County Road 48. Go east about a half-mile and turn right at the sign onto Battlefield Parkway, then about a mile to the park.

Open 8 A.M. to sunset year-round. Museum open 9 to 5 daily. Free organized talk and tour on request. Admission: $2 per vehicle or $1 for a pedestrian or bicyclist. Write 7200 CR 603 S. Battlefield Drive, Bushnell 33513. Call (352) 793-4781. Website: www.dadebattlefield.

The **Dade Battlefield Society** works to preserve the battlefield site. **The Seminole War Foundation** works to preserve all sites and memorabilia of the three Seminole wars. Write to 35247 Reynolds Road, Dade City 33523. Call (352) 583-2974.

Read More About It

Laumer, Frank. *Dade's Last Command*. 1995, Gainesville, University Press of Florida.

Mahon, John K. *History of the Second Seminole War, 1835–1842*. 1991, Gainesville, University Press of Florida.

Meltzer, Milton. *Hunted Like a Wolf*. 2004, Sarasota, Pineapple Press.

Tarpon
Springs

A taste of Greece

E very Epiphany Day, January 6, boys dive into an inlet of the Gulf of Mexico at Tarpon Springs. The first one to surface with a white cross that had been tossed into the water earns good luck for a year. About one in ten of the city's population of about 25,000 claims Greek ancestry.

Tarpon Springs rings with Greek tradition, culture, and — good news for everyone—food. The downtown sports more than 100 antique shops, art galleries, specialty shops and 15 restaurants and bakeries, most of them Greek. Favorite eats include the famed gyro, marinated meat in pita slathered with tzaziki sauce, and pastitso, or pastitsio, a version of white lasagna dripping with cheese. Greece is a land of islands, and seafood also figures heavily in Tarpon Springs' cuisine.

Visitors can take a sightseeing cruise down the Anclote River or go deep sea fishing or for a lunch or dinner cruise. There's also a live sponge-diving exhibition. Attractions include a 120,000-gallon saltwater aquarium and the sponge museum.

The community, about 45 minutes' drive north of St. Petersburg, was settled just after the Civil War. The arrival of the railroad in 1887 helped establish the town. Sponges were found in the Keys during the 1820s and around Tarpon Springs in 1872. By 1905, more than 500 divers had been brought over from the thriving sponge industry in Greece. Soon Tarpon Springs was the nation's largest sponge port and looked more like a Mediterranean city than anything else in early twentieth-century Florida. The local industry has dealt with blights, red tide, and the advent of synthetic sponges, but still brings in about

Sponge boats still operate out of Tarpon Springs' harbor. *Doug Waitley*

$2 million a year. A life-size bronze statue of a sponge diver stands at the harbor.

The downtown area, about a mile south of the sponge docks, is listed in the National Register of Historic Places. In its cultural center is St. Nicholas Greek Orthodox Cathedral, a replica of the St. Sophia Cathedral in Constantinople, now Istanbul. The cathedral is open daily to visitors and worshipers.

Tarpon Springs is about 30 miles north of St. Petersburg via U.S. 19.

Chamber of Commerce: Write 11 East Orange Street, Tarpon Springs 34689. Call (727) 937-6109. Website: www.tarponsprings. com

City of Tarpon Springs: Write 324 E. Pine Street, Tarpon Springs 34689. Call (727) 938-3711. Website: www.ci-tarponsprings.fl.us

Read More About It
Kilgo, Dolores Ann. *Tarpon Springs*. 2002, Charleston, S.C., Arcadia
    Publishing.

The
Don CeSar

St. Petersburg Beach

St. Pete Beach's boom hotel

As you drive down the southern stretch of Gulf Boulevard, the beach road along the Pinellas barrier islands, you pass under a giant ramp that leads from a parking lot to the front doors of the Don CeSar, as much a monument to Florida's 1930s art deco heydays as Miami Beach's South Beach.

The hotel is, of course, flamingo pink.

Like many of the great boom hotels, "The Don," built in 1928 for $1.5 million, came close to the wrecking ball. It was instead rescued and has undergone more than $50 million in renovations. It is one of only eight Florida hotels in the National Trust for Historic Preservation's Historic Hotels of America program. The 277-room, ten-story hotel approximates a giant Moorish wedding cake, with its four side towers and the center two-tower structure rising above the beach.

Land developer Thomas J. Rowe named his subdivision for his favorite opera, *Maritana*, and his hotel for its hero, Don Caesar de Bazan. On opening night, January 16, 1928, about 1,500 paid $2.50 each to sup in the fifth-floor dining hall and to dance to a five-piece orchestra.

Rowe saw the Don Ce-Sar (it later lost the hyphen) as a gleaming mecca to draw tourists and potential investors to the booming Tampa Bay area. Gangsters, royalty, and the New York Yankees were among its guests. Writer F. Scott Fitzgerald called it "the hotel in an island wilderness."

Guests dressed formally. Men even wore white flannel pants and sports jackets to the beach, where they could enjoy a lunch delivered by a waiter who also brought an umbrella and table. Cost: 25 cents.

When a miniature golf course was rendered useless by mosquitoes, Rowe used his own money to start the county's first Mosquito Control Board.

Fleeting Glory

The glory days would last only two seasons. The hotel was clobbered by the Crash and the Depression. Rowe was appointed his own receiver to try to pull The Don out of debt. The famous still came; names like Gimbel, Bloomingdale, Clarence Darrow, Franklin Roosevelt. But, after a 1931 bank failure, Rowe's savings were gone, and he couldn't finance the next season. Colonel Jacob Ruppert saved the day by signing a three-year contract to house his Yankees for spring training. Rowe also began offering the hotel to tour groups for summer weekend vacations. In 1933, another bank failure left him with $100 in the till. The next year he was forced to cut staff salaries in half, but was able to pay his bills and restore back pay by the end of the season.

Rowe finally got the hotel out of debt. He died in 1940 and his estranged wife took over. But the hotel again fell into financial trouble. Then came December 7, 1941. With a world war now underway, cancellations poured in, and the hotel staggered through the 1941–1942 season. It was revived when the federal government bought it for $440,000 as a hospital. It was later a rehabilitation center for soldiers.

From 1945 to 1969, it was the regional office of the U.S. Veterans Administration. The interiors were stripped to the bare walls and painted government green. Furnishings were packed up and trucked away. The fountain was demolished. Then, facing an estimated $3 million restoration cost, the Veterans Administration took a pass and moved out. The once-grand edifice, now padlocked, became a target for vandalism and graffiti. The county made plans to level it for a park.

But local residents formed a "Save the Don" group and convinced hotelier William Bowman Jr. to buy the Don Ce-Sar in 1972. He eliminated the hyphen and began rebuilding it. Workers shoveled out tons of debris, tore down doors and partitions, and painstakingly replaced 13,000 panes of glass. They also created a new entrance at the second-floor lobby with a 152-foot vehicle ramp that angled over

The Don CeSar, the Gulf Coast's art deco monument. *Don CeSar*

Gulf Boulevard. The original wide, wooden staircase, which led from a downstairs ice cream parlor to the main lobby, was covered up.

Restored to its early elegance, the hotel reopened in November 1973. In 1975, it went on the National Register of Historic Places. That year, the company that would become CIGNA Insurance took over The Don.

A dramatic 16-month refurbishing from 1985 to 1987 replaced the old Spanish interior, with its terra cotta tile floors, for a lighter and brighter European look: marble, light-toned wood, and soft pastel colors.

Balconies offer a spectacular view of the Gulf's sunsets. The rooms, halls, and restaurants feature elegant marble, lavish art and architecture, and glittering chandeliers. Visitors can take advantage of the golf course or pools, sail, parasail, or fish.

The Don CeSar Beach Resort and Spa is at 3400 Gulf Blvd., St. Pete Beach 33706. Call (866) 728-2206 or (727) 360-1881. Website: www.doncesar.com

Take Interstate 275 across St. Petersburg, south to Pinellas Bayway, west to Gulf Boulevard. Or take Interstate 75 to I-275, north across Sunshine Skyway to Pinellas Bayway, then west.

St. Pete Beach Area Chamber of Commerce: Box 66375, St. Pete Beach 33736. Call (727) 360-6957. Website: www.tampabaybeaches. com

St. Petersburg/Clearwater Convention and Visitors Bureau: Call (877) 352-3224. Website: www.floridasbeach.com

Read More About It

Hurley, June. *The Don Ce-Sar Story*. 1974, St. Petersburg, Partnership Press.

Hurley, Frank T. Surf, *Sand and Post Card Sunsets: A History of Pass-a-Grille and the Gulf Beaches*. 1977, St. Petersburg, Hurley.

University of Tampa

Tampa

Henry Plant's jewel

The Moorish-style, minaret-topped spires of the University of Tampa rise from the downtown Tampa skyline like a mirage. The private school, with about 5,000 students, is also a national historic landmark, now gleaming after an eight-year, $6 million restoration and millions in improvements since. It was once the Tampa Bay Hotel, the exotic vision of turn-of-the-century pioneer Henry Bradley Plant, Tampa Bay's counterpart to Henry Flagler. Plant, like Flagler, was encouraged by the state to bring his railroad down the peninsula from Jacksonville. While Flagler moved down the east coast, Plant angled across to the Tampa Bay frontier.

He built his hotel for the then-outrageous cost of $2 million, designing it to exploit America's fascination with "Moorish revival" architecture. He topped each of the 13 minarets, cupolas, and domes with a crescent moon. His wife traveled the world and spent another $1 million on furnishings; her purchases filled 80 boxcars.

The hotel opened in April 1891, nearly three years before Flagler's Royal Poinciana put Palm Beach on the map. Some 2,000 of the cream of society came. And, like its east coast counterpart, the Tampa Bay hotel provided them with the luxuries they demanded: a grand salon, two ballrooms, two reading rooms, a billiard room, a "gentleman's bar," grand dining rooms, and sitting rooms. Each of its 511 rooms had electricity and phones, a rarity at that time.

The grounds sprawled with a golf course, race tracks, tennis courts, and sidings for six private railroad cars at a time. A casino built across from the hotel was used for various events until it burned down in 1941.

University of Tampa at night. *University of Tampa*

In 1898, the hotel was selected as a military headquarters and press center for the Spanish-American War. For a month, Teddy Roosevelt and his Rough Riders drilled west of the campus and impatiently waited for the order to head for Cuba and destiny.

After Plant died in 1899, the hotel went through several managers before Plant's family sold it to the city in 1905 for $125,000. It became a center for weddings, balls, and other events. When baseball spring training came to Florida, the hotel housed the Chicago Cubs. Babe Ruth lounged in its lavish rooms; he signed his first baseball contract in its grand dining room and hit what was believed to be his longest home run in a spring training game at a diamond on the hotel grounds.

The collapse of Florida's real estate boom gave Florida a head start on the Depression. In 1931, a group of businessmen and community leaders put together a private college to fill a higher-learning vacuum in the area and to try to keep local youngsters at home. Two years later, when it outgrew Plant High School, the city leased out the former resort for $1 a year.

The historic centerpiece of the university, which hosts about 50,000 visitors a year, is its main academic building, Plant Hall. An adjacent ballroom has floor-to-ceiling windows. Administrative offices lining the 900-foot main hallway still contain finely carved fireplaces. Plant Hall's south wing houses the Henry B. Plant Museum, featuring furniture and fine art from the original resort.

The University of Tampa is along the Hillsborough River just west of downtown Tampa, at 401 W. Kennedy Blvd. 33606-1490. Call (813) 253-3333. The visitors center is just west of the river; the first right if you're coming from the west. Tours of Plant Hall are available upon request. Website: www.utampa.edu

Nearby is the **Plant Museum** which is open year-round, 10 A.M. through 4 P.M. Tuesday through Saturday and noon to 4 P.M. Sunday; a $5 donation for adults and $2 for children is requested. Call (813) 254-1891. Website: www.plantmuseum.com

Tampa Convention and Visitors Bureau: 400 N. Tampa St., Suite 2800, Tampa 33602. Call (813) 223-1111. Website: www.visittampabay. com

Read More About It

Covington, James W., and C. Herbert Laub. *The Story of the University of Tampa*. 1955, Tampa, University of Tampa Press.

Mullen, Harris W. *A History of the Tampa Bay Hotel*. 1966, Tampa, University of Tampa Foundation.

Ybor City

Tampa

Cigars and history

Italian immigrants and Cubans fleeing the Spanish colony of Cuba created the thriving community of Ybor City, adjacent to downtown Tampa. Settled in 1885 by Cuban cigar-maker Vincente Martinez y Bor, the city has cobblestone streets and Spanish-style architecture — featuring wrought iron balconies — that appear much as they were then. The Ybor City Historic District, a national historic landmark district, stretches 11 blocks by three blocks, just east of downtown. Free walking tours are offered three times a week.

The Ybor City State Museum features the history of the neighborhood and displays workers' tools and a large mural portraying an early factory. La Casita is a tiny three-room cigar workers' home restored to its turn-of-the-century appearance.

Visitors can treat themselves to Cuban and Italian cuisine, read *La Gaceta,* claimed to be the nation's only trilingual newspaper (English, Spanish, Italian), or watch the Italian lawn bowling game of boccie, in which players compete to roll heavy wooden balls near a target ball.

Restaurants still draw in the curious with their exotic and enticing aromas — fresh bread, robust coffee and, of course, cigars. Chief among them: the Columbia. A century old —a Methuselah by Florida eatery standards — the place that claims to be the world's largest Spanish restaurant started as a corner café, and now covers

El Sol Cigars, Tampa's oldest cigar store. *VISIT FLORIDA*

indignities for a clock: it stopped. It stood dormant for a half century, its hands gone, its face withered by wind and rain, its machinery rusting. The clock was recently repaired and began pealing again in October 2002. But many of the factories are closed now, torn down, or turned into quaint tourist attractions and malls of crafts and souvenir shops that capitalize on their storied pasts.

The cigar workers would busy themselves with the frenzied, but nearly silent, work of rolling and cutting cigars while a man on a high chair — *El Lector* — read them the day's newspaper or a book. Sometimes they heard talks and speeches while they worked. One stirred them to make the giant halls ring as they noisily banged their tools on their wooden worktables, cheering a young man who would become a legend.

José Martí, then only 38, arrived at Ybor City's little railroad station in a driving rain on November 27, 1891. His homeland had been devastated by a ten-year war to end Spanish colonial rule. Martí had emerged as an expatriate fighter for the cause, organizing Freedom Clubs from New York to Key West to raise money for the continuation of the *Cuba libre* — free Cuba — effort. Tampa's expatriates were among the most tenacious supporters. The next night, in a jammed hall, he presented his memorable *nuevo piños* speech, telling workers that even as the Spaniards were cutting down the patriots of Cuba, more would rise like new pines.

On January 10, 1895, Martí and others loaded three boats in Florida for an incursion into Cuba. The boats were seized by U. S. officials, who feared allowing a revolt against a friendly nation to start on their soil. Martí later sneaked into Cuba, where he died in battle May 19, 1895. But many others rose like new pines, and when the sinking of the *Maine* brought America to war, Cuba's dream of independence was realized.

Ybor City is just south of downtown Tampa, bordered on the north by Interstate 4 and on the west by I-275.

Ybor City Chamber of Commerce: 1800 E. Ninth Ave., Tampa 33605. Call (813) 248-3712. Website: www.ybor.org

Tampa Convention and Visitors Bureau: 400 N. Tampa St., Suite 2800, Tampa 33602. Call (813) 223-1111. Website: www.visittampabay.com

Read More About It

Mormino, Gary R., and George E. Pozzetta. *The Immigrant World of Ybor City: Italians and Their Latin Neighbors in Tampa, 1885–1985*. 1987, Champaign, Ill., University of Illinois Press.

Pacheco, Ferdie. *Ybor City Chronicle: A Memoir*. 1994, Gainesville, University Press of Florida.

Pizzo, Tony. *Tampa Town: The Cracker Village with a Latin Accent*. 1968, Coconut Grove, Hurricane Press.

Turton, Peter. *José Martí*. 1986, London, Zed.

De Soto National Memorial

Bradenton

Did de Soto land here?

The problem with the De Soto National Memorial: everyone agrees Hernando de Soto came to Florida — but not necessarily that he came there. The federal historic site and park sits on a spit of land providing a majestic view of the mouth of giant Tampa Bay. It's a monument to the historic moment when the Spanish explorer came ashore on May 30, 1539, and started his four-year trek across the continent. But some argue the actual landfall was at Charlotte Harbor, about 100 miles south, or the Little Manatee River, a little to the north.

At the De Soto Memorial, you will find a gathering of thatch huts, a visitors center, and walkways with bayfront plaques describing the expedition. From late December to early April, park rangers dressed in period costume portray life as it may have been in De Soto's base camp. Their special programs include demonstrations of sixteenth-century Spanish weapons.

A nature trail follows a half-mile loop through mangroves and beach. A visitors center displays samples of period armor and weapons. Other materials show the culture of the natives who inhabited Florida before the Europeans but were extinct within two centuries of their arrival.

Earlier, in 1513, Juan Ponce de León had planted the cross and the flag of Spain on Florida's east coast. Spain hadn't a clue of how far *La Florida* went, so the king sent De Soto to inspect the property. The explorer, only 39, was already wealthy from having helped plunder Peru and hoped for more loot in this terra incognita, this dark continent to the north:

"Some old men of authority . . . say that . . . two days journey beyond is another town called Ocale . . . that there are many traders among them . . . and abundance of gold and silver and many pearls; . . . Glory be to God . . . it seems He has a special care that this be for His service," De Soto wrote.

"Black Legend"

Some people were already inhabiting North America, but no matter. Europeans considered them savages. The "black legend" of Spanish atrocities in the Americas includes De Soto's first encounters with Indians, many of whom he slaughtered or enslaved.

De Soto began his mission with more than 600 men and 223 horses, pigs, and dogs. Indians were enslaved and brought along; the number grew at times to more than 1,000. The group first wintered at a site near Florida's present capital, Tallahassee. There, they probably spent North America's first Christmas before continuing inland, heading through the southern interior of the continent. The expedition wandered through what is now Arkansas; on June 20, 1542, De Soto was felled by a fever and a broken heart. He was buried in the Mississippi River, his dream of riches unfulfilled.

The rest — discouraged, hungry, and frightened — decided the glorious mission had gone far enough and headed south toward the ocean. They tried to walk to Texas, then turned back to the Mississippi. There, they built boats and sailed down to the Gulf of Mexico. Four years and 4,000 miles after the expedition started, 311 men ended up in Mexico. There had been no gold, no colonies established for the glory of the European God and the Spanish Empire. But they had accomplished a momentous feat, exploring the continent as far north as the Smokies and as far west as Texas. Two Florida counties — Hernando and DeSoto — would later be named for the fallen explorer.

Of course, it looks good in the tourist brochures to say "De Soto landed here," so there's been competition for the honor. Cynics would argue that the right answer is important only to historians. Historians counter that the expedition's descriptions of sixteenth-century North America are less valuable unless you can establish the starting point in order to identify each place described after that.

Cooking demonstration at the De Soto National Memorial. *De Soto National Memorial*

In 1939, on the landing's 400th anniversary, a congressional commission of the Smithsonian Institution concluded it was on the south side of Tampa Bay; the park was established there a decade later, on this 25-acre site west of Bradenton. But in 1947, a series of articles argued De Soto had landed at Charlotte Harbor, about 100 miles to the south. A 1966 book repeated that proposition. Those reports cite a 1590 account that says the distance to a village now identified as being in the Tallahassee area better fits Charlotte Harbor. One scholar places landfall around Sanibel Island, off the coast of Fort Myers. But accounts by three other participants in De Soto's march give distances that would support Tampa Bay. Some historians argue Charlotte Harbor wouldn't have been deep enough for De Soto's ships.

Many scholars have thrown up their hands and said the debate will never be settled because the geographic references are, one wrote, "hopelessly vague." Others say a 1612 account clearly identifies Tampa Bay and says it is where De Soto landed. The state has thrown its lot with the Tampa Bay landfall. Archaeologists across the South scrambled to identify De Soto's passage in time for the 450th anniversary, in 1989, and gather hundreds of artifacts collected along the route and believed to have come from the expedition. Florida then began a major campaign to promote the De Soto Trail, which starts at the national monument and goes to the Georgia state line. A national commission has been established to extend the commemorative trail throughout the Southeast.

The De Soto National Memorial is about five miles west of downtown Bradenton. Write Box 15390, Bradenton 34280-5390. Call (941) 792-0458. Website: www.nps.gov/deso

Take State Road 64 (Manatee Avenue) to 75th Street North, which becomes 75th Street North West, then north about two and one half miles.

Admission to the memorial is free. It is open every day during daylight hours except New Year's, Thanksgiving, and Christmas. The visitors center is open 9 A.M. to 5 P.M. A 21-minute De Soto film is shown on the hour.

Camp Uzita, a living history exhibit with reenactors in Spanish costume, recreates the Indian village De Soto commandeered for his base camp; it operates from December 1 to Easter.

Anna Maria Island Chamber of Commerce: 5313 Gulf Drive N., Holmes Beach, 34217. Call (941) 778-1541. Website: www. annamariaislandchamber.org

Bradenton Area Convention and Visitors Bureau: Call (941) 729-9177. Website: www.flagulfbeaches.com

Read More About It
Bourne, Edward G. *Narratives of the Career of Hernando de Soto.* 1905, London, David Nutt.
Milanich, Jerald. *Hernando de Soto and the Indians of Florida.* 1993, Gainesville, University Press of Florida.
Swanton, John R., chairman. *Final Report of the De Soto Expedition Commission.* 1939, Washington, Smithsonian Institution.

Gamble Mansion

Ellenton

Where the Confederacy met its ignoble end

The Confederate States of America began in glory and ended in ignominy. Its great cities lay in ruins, its farms denuded, its men dead and bleeding, its president, Jefferson Davis, captured in flight disguised as a woman. And the Gamble Mansion, where the Confederacy's Secretary of State, Judah Benjamin, hid en route to exile in Europe, was later used to store cow manure.

People don't usually think of Florida when they recall the South's antebellum plantation era, but there were many places like the Gamble spread. Few, however, were in the sparsely settled peninsula.

The Gamble Plantation State Historic Site now stands off the main road in Bradenton, between convenience stores and shops, its glory a little dulled by the years, but not gone. Only 16 of its 3,500 acres remain, and the two-story, ten-room building is the only surviving antebellum plantation mansion in southern Florida.

The house, designed to stay cool in hot Florida summers, is made of red brick and "tabby," a mixture of water, shells, and limestone. The outer walls of the two-story mansion are nearly two feet thick. Eighteen columns support the roof and upper verandahs, which extend around three sides of the house. The north section of the house was built first and is separated from the main building by the breezeway or "dogtrot," as it was called. Like many homes built before air conditioning, the mansion was designed for cross breezes, with strategically placed windows and a breezeway between wings.

Today, the second-floor balcony offers a view south to a

neighborhood. Once, clear land stood between the mansion and the north bank of the Manatee River, about a half-mile away.

Grocer in St. Marks

Major Robert Gamble built the plantation up from the river to protect it from flooding. He had moved with his family in 1827 from Virginia to Tallahassee, where his brother John established a large plantation. After serving in the Second Seminole War (1835–1842), Robert Gamble was lured to the fertile soil of Manatee County in 1844.

Southwest Florida was a wilderness far from the nearest civilization in Tallahassee. Major Gamble chose this unlikely spot to build a sugar plantation that would eventually cover 3,500 fertile acres along the Manatee River, northeast of what is now Bradenton. Gamble brought the latest technology for his sugar refinery. Soon, the plantation was successfully producing sugar cane, molasses, citrus, grapes, and olives, which were shipped to New Orleans.

The nearest grocer was in St. Marks, south of Tallahassee on the Panhandle coast and a very long boat ride away. Gamble employed a "factor," a sort of broker and buyer, just to pick up basics.

Too much sulfur and salt in the groundwater supply prohibited Gamble from sinking wells, so he set up an elaborate water catchment and filtration system that still stands. Gutters collected rain water and funneled it to a trough that led to a building that could hold 40,000 gallons. Water then filtered from one side of the cistern, seeping through a wall of tabby.

In 1850, his best year, Gamble shipped 115 tons of sugar and 10,000 gallons of molasses. But he'd had bad years too, the result of hurricanes and fires. In 1856, Gamble's delicate credit structure collapsed amid falling sugar prices and bad crops. He sold the entire estate for $190,000 to Archibald McNeil, the Confederacy's Deputy Commissary for the Manatee district.

Civil War to the Present

During the war, Union soldiers broke up the giant Gamble sugar mill, several miles away — perhaps for the $50,000 bounty, perhaps just for the scrap metal. The mill's ruins are on private property and may not be toured.

As the Confederacy foundered, its Secretary of State, Judah Philip Benjamin — pursuers on his heels and a $40,000 dead-or-alive

The Gamble Mansion is southern Florida's last antebellum mansion. *Eliot Kleinberg*

price on his head — came through in May 1865. He was disguised as M. Bonfal, a French journalist, and later as Mr. Howard, a farmer and potential buyer of the property. He stayed at the mansion for three days, once fleeing the house and hiding elsewhere on the property as Union soldiers searched the building for him. Supporters found a boat in nearby Sarasota, and Benjamin fled to Bimini, then to a new life as a leading barrister in England.

The house was sold in 1872 to the Patten family for $3,000. In 1895, Major George Patten built a second, smaller home on the property for his son that may also be toured. But the cost of maintenance forced the Pattens to sell, and the house stood empty and rotting for years.

From 1920 to 1925, a fertilizer company that had bought the house for back taxes stored manure in it. The 1926 hurricane, which leveled Miami, crossed the peninsula and slammed the mansion, knocking down some of the 18 pillars that support the roof and balcony on three sides; a photograph from the mid-1920s shows other columns rotting.

The United Daughters of the Confederacy bought the estate in 1925, fixed it up, furnished it with period furniture, and deeded it to the state of Florida. The guest bedroom is the only one still displaying the original wooden flooring; it was rotted throughout most of the house by age and the manure, and only enough for one room could be salvaged piecemeal from the others. The original furniture was stored in a barn; it was destroyed years later in a fire.

Visitors to the impressive two-story Greek Revival mansion can hear the story of Gamble Plantation from tour guides who explain the difficulties early settlers faced trying to run a business in the Florida wilderness.

The grounds around the mansion were cleared of vegetation for security — from Seminole Indians and more mundane dangers such as snakes, vermin, and fire. But two-century-old oak trees remain.

The plantation complex also includes the Patten House, an excellent example of a pioneer Florida farmhouse, a rapidly vanishing style of architecture. The furnishings and memorabilia in the house show the way of life in pioneer days.

Gamble Plantation Historic State Park: 3708 Patten Ave., Ellenton 34222. Call (941) 723-4536. Park open every day from 8 A.M. until sunset, admission is free. The Visitor Center is open Thursday through Monday from 8 A.M. to 4:30 P.M. Tours of the mansion are at 9:30 A.M. and 10:30 A.M. and 1:00 P.M., 2:00 P.M., 3:00 P.M. and 4 P.M. The tour costs $5 for adults and kids 6 to 12 are $3. Website: www.floridastateparks.org.

Manatee Chamber of Commerce: Box 321, Bradenton 34206. Call (941) 748-3411. Website: www.manateechamber.com

Bradenton Area Convention and Visitors Bureau: Call (941) 729-9177. Website: www.flagulfbeaches.com

Read More About It

Evans, Eli N. *Judah Benjamin: The Jewish Confederate*. 1988, New York, Free Press.

Hannah, A.J. *Flight Into Oblivion*. 1959, Bloomington, Ind., Indiana University Press.

Schofield, Arthur C. *Yesterday's Bradenton*. 1975, Miami, E.A. Seeman Co.

Ringling Museum and Home

Sarasota

The John and Mable Ringling Museum of Art, Cà d'Zan Mansion, Circus Museum, and Hisotric Asolo Theater

John Ringling stares down at you, bigger than life, in a room of the mansion he named for himself. Out in front of the art museum, bright yellow school buses pull up, and kids pour into one of the state's most prominent cultural centers.

The 66-acre, state-run Ringling estate, between U.S. 41 and Sarasota Bay, comprises four showcases: the Cà d'Zan Mansion, the Museum of Art, the Circus Museum, and the Historic Asolo Theater — along with many acres of landscaped grounds featuring huge banyan trees and Mable Ringling's rose garden. The Florida State University Asolo Center for the Performing Arts, part of Florida State University's Cultural Campus, stands on the other side of a parking lot. Right next door are the campuses of New College, which is the honors college for the state of Florida, and the Sarasota-Manatee branch of the University of South Florida. Not bad for a guy who made his fortune with clowns, elephants, and peanuts.

In 1882, Ringling, still a teenager, and four brothers started Yankee Robinson and Ringling Bros. Great Double Shows, Circus and Caravan. Two years later their first traveling circus began. In 1890, they abandoned wagons and began moving the circus by train. In 1907, after Phineas T. Barnum and James A. Bailey both died, the Ringlings bought their show. They ran their circus, the Barnum and Bailey operation, and a third, smaller circus separately before merging them in 1919 to a conglomeration with a name nearly as long as its performances: Ringling Bros. and Barnum & Bailey Combined Shows. John and Mable Ringling first visited Sarasota in 1909 and bought the property along the bay where their mansion and art museum would later stand. In 1913, Mable Ringling completed work on her rose garden. Through his circus, real estate, and railroads, Ringling was a wealthy man by the mid-1920s.

"Florida is a nice place," he'd tell an interviewer in the rapid-fire staccato voice of a showman, waving his ever-present cigar for emphasis. "You ever been there? You ought to see it. Blue water, and green and lavender in the bay. Lovely at sundown. Beautiful light and air."

Cà d'Zan Mansion

John and Mable Ringling built their mansion for $1.5 million between 1924 and 1926 and furnished it for another $400,000. He called it "Cà d'Zan" — Venetian dialect for "House of John." It stands in the company of many other showcases built by Florida's barons, who might have been engaged in an outrageous contest to see whose digs were fanciest: Ringling's Cà d'Zan, Flagler's Whitehall, Deering's Vizcaya.

Fronting an 8,000-square-foot terrace with a magnificent panorama of Sarasota Bay, it is 200 feet long, with an interior 2 1/3-story living room, 30 other rooms, 15 bathrooms, kitchens and pantries, as well as servants' quarters in a wing to the south. A tower in the mansion was lighted when the Ringlings were in residence. Mable Ringling, John's wife since 1905, was the driving force for the mansion and directed its construction and furnishing. Period furniture was bought used from great estates, but these are not garage sale purchases; many were also gathered during a grand European buying spree.

"It is my house," the enigmatic Mable Burton Ringling would tell her architect. "I know what I want, and that is that."

Ringling's tastes sometimes bordered on the gaudy or even bizarre. Besides the giant portrait of himself, he also had himself and Mable painted in costume on the ceiling of his gaming room by the famous muralist Willy Pogany. Mable died in 1929 of diabetes. She was 54 and had been in Cà d'Zan only three years. Ringling remarried 18 months later.

In 1996, Cà d'Zan was the setting for a modern film version of

TOP: John Ringling's mansion, the Cà d'Zan. *John and Mable Ringling Museum of Art*

LEFT: Rubens Gallery, Ringling Museum. *John and Mable Ringling Museum of Art*

Dickens' *Great Expectations*. The great house was coated with removable dark paint and plastic cobwebs.

After a six-year, $15 million restoration, Cà d'Zan reopened in April 2002 to record crowds in all of its Roaring Twenties splendor.

The John and Mable Ringling Museum of Art

Ringling built the museum in the 1920s and opened it in 1932. Building upon the Ringling collection, the Museum has since acquired more than 16,000 objects, both classic and contemporary. It includes 1,000 original paintings, 1,000 prints and drawings, 500 pieces of sculpture, and an abundance of decorative art. Only a portion can be shown at a time in the 47,000-square-foot building's 21 galleries, in two wings connected by a lobby. Some of the giant paintings are the size of garage doors. The "old master" European paintings are the core of the collection, many of which Ringling procured himself. Every visitor must see the room filled with Peter Paul Rubens' giant "cartoons," which are paintings made as studies for tapestries.

Ringling, always a showman, loved to be daring and controversial. When the city of Philadelphia, which had commissioned a statue of a girl bound to a bull, was shocked to see she was naked and banned the sculpture, Ringling bought it.

His fortune all but wiped out by the Depression, Ringling lost control of the circus but held on to his art trove until he died at age 70 from pneumonia in 1936.

The last chapter of the Ringling saga is a sad one. For decades after their deaths, the remains of John, Mable, and John's sister Ida, lay in temporary vaults in New Jersey while relatives squabbled over their final repose. The three were moved in 1987 to unmarked crypts in a Port Charlotte cemetery, and finally buried in 1991 at the Museum grounds.

Although Ringling had donated his museum on his death to the state, lawsuits by creditors, the IRS, and relatives tied it up in court until 1946 when it transferred to the people and the State of Florida. In 2000, the State of Florida transferred stewardship to Florida State University, making it the largest university museum complex in the nation. Beginning in 2006, a series of new buildings has opened, including the Circus Museum's Tibbals Learning Center, a Visitors Pavilion featuring the reinstalled Asolo Theater, new art galleries, and an education center.

The Historic Asolo Theater

The Asolo Theater (not to be confused with the Asolo Center for the Performing Arts), is a 270-seat theater built in the 1798 in Asolo, Italy. It was removed from the castle of Caterina Cornaro to make way for a movie theater. After it sat in storage in Italy for two decades, A. Everett Austin, Jr. the legendary first director of the Ringling Museum bought it and had it shipped over and reassembled in the Museum of Art. For years, the tiny jewel box of a theater was alive with actors and cheering audiences on the Ringling grounds, then closed for years. It has been recently restored and opened in a beautiful new

Visitors Pavilion just inside the historic Cà d'Zan Gatehouse on the Ringling Museum estate.

The Circus Museum

The newest of the Ringling showcases is the Ringling Circus Museum's Tibbals Learning Center. The original Circus Museum was established in 1948 and the Tibbals Learning Center was completed in January 2006.

The Circus Museum collected artifacts from around the world to tell John Ringling's story, from his talent as a circus logistics master to his love for art.

Displays honor Emmett Kelly and Lou Jacobs, perhaps the world's most famous clowns, and the Flying Wallendas high-wire team. You can even see the cannon used to send the Flying Zacchinis flying.

There are clown masks and heads, trapeze and ringmaster outfits, some of the baggage wagons, rolling cages for animals, and a calliope that drew people like a pied piper during the circus parades through town. A recorded voice calls, "Ladies and gentlemen, children of all ages . . . "

The big top entrance to the Ringling Circus Museum's new Tibbals Learning Center leads to a world of wonder for children of all ages. With two floors of exciting new exhibitions, visitors discover a new delight around every turn.

Colorful circus posters — some so large that the horses are life-size — are featured on the lower floor.

The main attraction is an enormous miniature: the Howard Bros. Circus. Philanthropist and circus enthusiast, Howard Tibbals captures the Big Show's arrival in small-town America ca. 1919 to 1938 in this time capsule of the great American tented circus. It is the largest miniature circus in the world and shows in precise detail America's most anticipated and beloved form of entertainment.

The miniature covers 3,800 square feet and unfolds just as the circus came to town. Visitors are greeted by a steam engine emitting real steam and the sounds of a busy arrival on 996 feet of miniature custom-designed steel rail and a 57-car circus train. The circus lot is packed with eight main tents, 152 wagons, 211 exotic animals in the menagerie, and 1,300 individual circus artists, workers, and staff. That doesn't even account for the many spectators and John Ringling himself.

The excitement continues on the second floor of the Tibbals Learning Center, where visitors experience the story of the circus. Displayed artifacts include P.T. Barnum's bizarre furniture, Buffalo Bill's Wild West on parade, and Tom Thumb's tiny saber. There is also a collection of vibrant costumes from the contemporary circus, including Ringling Bros. and Barnum & Bailey, The Big Apple Circus, and Cirque du Soleil. They are displayed against the pulsating footage of thrilling circus acts projected from floor to ceiling.

The Ringling Museum of Art is at 5401 Bay Shore Road, Sarasota 34243. (941) 359-5700. Take University Parkway seven miles west of I-75, cross U.S. 41 and into museum. Grounds are open seven days a week, 10 A.M. to 5:30 P.M. Admission: $15 for adults, $13 for seniors and military; $5 for students 6 and older, with ID. Museum members are free and Florida teachers $5 with ID. Price includes admission to mansion and circus museum and grounds. Free admission on Mondays to the art galleries only. Website: www.ringling.org

Sarasota County Chamber of Commerce: 1945 Fruitville Road, Sarasota 33236. Call (941) 955-8187. Website: www.sarasotachamber. com

Sarasota Convention and Visitors Bureau: (800) 522-9799. Website: www.sarasotafl.org

Read More About It

Matthews, Janet Snyder. *Sarasota: History to Centennial.* 1985, Tulsa, Okla., Continental Heritage Press.

Weeks, David Chapin. *Ringling: The Florida Years, 1911–1936.* 1993, Gainesville, University Press of Florida.

Historic
Spanish Point

Osprey

Centuries of history

Historic Spanish Point is a little finger of land in Little Sarasota Bay, but it's packed with five centuries of history.

Open to the public since 1982, the Historic Spanish Point Museum, on 30 acres eight miles south of downtown Sarasota in Osprey, features prehistoric sites, a nineteenth-century pioneer homestead, and lush gardens.

The site holds one of the largest intact prehistoric villages in Florida. Surviving are a burial ground and two middens, basically garbage dumps. One of the two middens was despoiled by construction in the 1920s, but archaeologists have saved the shell walls. A cutaway view lets visitors see the different layers left by centuries of dumping bone, shell, and other items.

Modern settlement began in 1867 when John and Eliza Webb and their five children fled cold New York. They named the place Spanish Point because a Spanish trader they met in Key West had recommended it and for the high point of land that extended into Little Sarasota Bay.

For more than four decades, the Webbs farmed on ten acres. With no railroad, they built a packing house at the waterfront to sort fruit and other crops, which were then loaded onto their schooners for shipment to Key West. They also ran Webbs Winter Resort, the first tourist attraction in Sarasota County.

A pioneer house has been furnished as it was during their lifetimes, and the museum has recreated the citrus packing house and Mary's chapel, next to the cemetery where Webbs and other settlers are buried.

At the turn of the twentieth century, wealthy Chicago widow

Guptill House. *Courtesy of Gulf Coast Heritage Association, Inc.*

Bertha Matilde Honore Palmer bought a giant chunk of what's now Sarasota County and built a winter manse and estate at Spanish Point, naming her digs Osprey Point. While she protected the ancient structures on her property, her mansion didn't survive her; it fell into disrepair after her death in 1918 and was eventually razed. But many of her lawns and gardens, including a sunken garden and a jungle walk, have been restored.

Palmer's heirs donated the 30 acres to the nonprofit Gulf Coast Heritage Association. Volunteers continue the area's legacy of boat building, restoring and constructing wooden boats using traditional tools.

Historic Spanish Point is at 337 North Tamiami Trail (U.S. 41) in Osprey; about halfway between Sarasota and Venice. Write Box 846, Osprey 34229. Call (941) 966-5214. org. Open 9 A.M. to 5 P.M. Monday through Saturday, noon to 5 P.M. Sundays. Admission: adults $9, kids 6–12 $3. Florida residents and seniors $8. Price includes guided tours; call for times. Plan to spend about two hours. No tickets sold after 4 P.M. Website: www.historicspanishpoint

Read More About It
Almy, Marion M. *Spanish Point: Guide to Prehistory* 1987. Osprey, Spanish Point at the Oaks.

South Central Florida/ Lower Gulf Coast

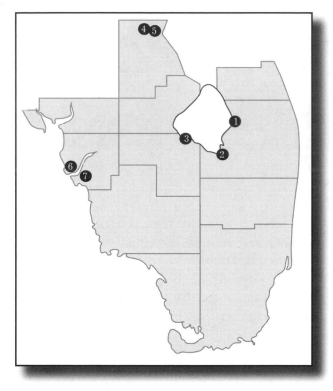

1. Port Mayaca Cemetery, *Palm Beach County*
2. Clewiston Inn, *Clewiston*
3. The "Lone Cypress," *Moore Haven*
4. Kenilworth Lodge, *Sebring*
5. Sebring International Raceway, *Sebring*
6. Koreshan, *Estero*
7. Edison and Ford Homes, *Fort Myers*

Port Mayaca Cemetery

Palm Beach County

A monument to the night 2,000 died

At the Port Mayaca cemetery, a tall, narrow granite tombstone points down into the ground. It's high ground, a few hundred yards from the tall dike that surrounds Lake Okeechobee. The dike wasn't here in 1928. But the cemetery was. So when the bodies kept popping out of the ground in the saturated Glades, they were brought here, perhaps as many as 1,600. The high ground would hold them. So they piled them up and they dumped them in. Many more were buried in West Palm Beach.

Some say 1,800 died that long night. Some say more than 3,000. But September 16, 1928, will always be known simply as "The Night 2,000 Died." In 2003, forecasters announced they would officially change the death toll to 2,500. That would make the storm the second deadliest natural disaster in U.S. history, behind the Galveston hurricane of 1900, which killed 5,000 to 6,000, and ahead of the Johnstown flood in 1889, which killed 2,200. But this 1928 storm had already killed 2,000 to 4,000 before striking Florida.

In 1928, hurricanes didn't get names. For this region, it is not a hurricane, but *the* hurricane.

Down U.S. Highway 98 in Belle Glade, a sculpture in front of the county library bears motionless and silent testimony to the power and terror of the storm. A man, woman, and boy are running. The woman carries an infant in her arms. As they look over their shoulders, they raise their arms in a feeble attempt to ward off an unseen wall of water.

Below the statue, a concrete relief shows houses, people,

The 1928 Hurricane leveled West Palm Beach before moving on to devastate the Glades. *Palm Beach Post*

vegetation, and animals swirling helplessly in the water that enveloped the lake area. Its legacy is the death it brought in previously unimagined proportions to the hardy pioneers. Decades later, farmers plowing fields would find more bodies. Some have never been accounted for.

The storm leveled homes and buildings from Palm Beach to Fort Pierce to Okeechobee. Damage estimates were $50 million in 1928 dollars — more than $350 million by 1990s standards. Many cities were without power for a week. About 15,000 families were left homeless.

"It leaves you with the feeling that anything can happen at once," survivor Helen McCormick said in a 1988 interview for the storm's 60th anniversary. She still teared up as she recalled the night she lost 18 of 20 relatives when a wall of water rushed over Belle Glade.

"I live with it every day," she said.

Suffering Beyond Words

The day of the storm, a Sunday, started clear and sunny in West Palm Beach and cloudy around the big lake, where just a few thousand people lived. The technology of weather forecasters was far inferior to what it is now, and radio reports had indicated the storm would pass to the north.

But it did not.

About 5 P.M., it came ashore, bringing a huge tidal surge and furious winds, estimated at 145 mph. Jupiter's historic 105-foot brick lighthouse swayed 17 inches. A foot-deep layer of sand was deposited on Palm Beach's Ocean Boulevard.

Before moving inland, the storm caused — in 1928 dollars — $13.8 million in damage in West Palm Beach, $10 million in Palm Beach, $4 million in Lake Worth, and about $1 million each in Jupiter, Kelsey City — now Lake Park — Delray Beach, Boynton Beach, and Riviera Beach. Fort Pierce suffered $150,000 in damage.

About 5 A.M. Monday, Tommy Rickards Jr., 14, and his family ventured out from the county courthouse in West Palm Beach, where they had weathered the storm.

"It was horrendous," Rickards, then 74, recalled in 1988 on the 60th anniversary of the storm. "It looked like a war scene."

Rickards later continued to live near downtown West Palm Beach and kept the letters written by him and his father, then a county coroner and justice of the peace.

"The town looked flat, and it was, practically," young Tommy wrote then to his Aunt Kate in North Carolina. "The street was shoulder-deep in debris."

And his father wrote, "The suffering throughout is beyond words. Individual tales of horror, suffering, and loss are numberless."

"The monster began to roll"

At the lake, residents heard radio reports from West Palm Beach that the storm was headed inland.

With no National Hurricane Center, no TV weather reports, there was little warning for those who had settled in the farmland that only a few decades earlier had risen from the swamps of south Florida's outback. Their greatest fear was the 760-square-mile body of water that helped make the surrounding countryside among the most productive agricultural areas in the nation.

Lake Okeechobee is a shallow frying-pan-shaped lake no more than 12 feet deep anywhere. It sloshes easily in storms. In 1928, the only thing keeping the lake from overflowing along its southeast shore was a 47-mile-long, five-foot-tall earthen dike. Built between 1923 and 1925, it had been erected strictly to protect crops from flooding after heavier than normal rainfall raised the lake level to unusual heights for two consecutive years.

Ironically, had there been no dike, fatalities might have been minimal. Most of the deaths occurred because water built up behind the dike and then rushed out suddenly when parts of it gave.

After dark, the storm arrived from the southeast. "It woke up old Okechobee [sic] and the monster began to roll in his bed," author Zora Neale Hurston wrote in 1937 in *Their Eyes Were Watching God*, which climaxes with the storm's assault. Because of the storm's spiral, winds hitting the towns along the southeast shore came from the lake, throwing waves of water that reached ten feet at South Bay.

As the storm neared, with no roads yet built to the west or south, residents had only two escape routes: north into the teeth of the winds or east right into the storm. So many stayed put.

The storm crossed Lake Okeechobee, pushing water into the low-lying surrounding countryside along the northwest shore. When the eye passed and the winds shifted, all that water came roaring back into the lake, then over the five-foot-high earthen dike at the southeastern corner.

The dike broke.

"The house was moving"

When the winds began to pick up, 63 people had climbed into the attic of a large farmhouse near Lake Harbor, about 100 feet from the canal that rims the lake. One of them was a 14-year-old boy named Vernie Boots.

As they waited and prayed and screamed, the house suddenly lurched from its foundation. "You could tell the house was moving," Boots, a farm equipment designer living in Belle Glade, recalled in 1988. He said the house moved 75 to 100 yards before ramming into the high ground where U.S. 27 was being built.

"It made two bounces," Boots said. "The house went down. Walls and everything came apart. Everybody went under water. The lake was everywhere."

Boots clung to a piece of ceiling and floated for hours in ten feet of water, fighting waves that crested at three to four feet. By daybreak, he had floated two and a half miles. He lost his parents and was one of only six of the 63 to survive. He doesn't know why.

"You have to accept things," he said. "It's just not good to question the Lord."

Carmen Salvatore sat at the dining room table of his Pahokee home in 1988 with his great-grandson Adam, then 17, and remembered the hurricane that had nearly killed him in the same spot 60 years earlier.

"We never had been in a hurricane," said Carmen Salvatore, who had come from New Jersey to farm early in the century. "Nobody knew from experience what it was going to be like."

At the storm's height, winds began to shake his home, and he feared it would come down.

"(Wife) Mary would holler, 'Oh Lord, don't let the house blow away,'" Salvatore recalled. "One of my kids said, 'The Lord's asleep.'"

The family eventually abandoned the house and headed to a neighbor's home for safety. In winds that drowned out shouts and sheets of rain that reduced visibility to inches, it took 80 minutes for Salvatore, his wife, and three children to walk 900 feet. Along the way, he fell into a canal with a child in each arm; his wife pulled him out.

"The rain and water was so thick, you couldn't see your hand in front of your face," he said. "You couldn't stand up."

When the storm had passed, Salvatore had lost his home, his crops, and his seed. But his family had survived.

Helen McCormick's family wasn't so lucky. Sixty years later, the horror of her most horrible night was still fresh and painful. She was only 13 when 18 of her relatives gathered at the family home to have dinner and hunker down for the storm's duration. As it got worse, everyone climbed through the roof. Suddenly, she recalled, she was in the water. She thought she had slipped off. She learned later the house had flipped over. She floated all night, and in the morning found her stepfather. He told her only the two had survived the night.

"It wasn't me that saved me," she recalled in 1988. "A 13-year-old kid couldn't have saved herself. It just wasn't my time, I guess."

Burning bodies
Between 8 A.M. September 15 and 4 P.M. September 17, almost ten inches of rain fell. By the end of the week another nine inches would come down.

The countryside stank with death. The area was quarantined. Volunteers performed the grim work of pulling bodies from the muck.

As many as could be were moved out for burial. Others, including those of animals, were simply gathered into piles, covered with lime and burned. Officials loaded 69 bodies onto a barge and sent it down the canal to West Palm Beach. A drag line dug a mass grave, and the bodies were laid into the ground at Woodlawn Cemetery, along U.S. 1 in downtown West Palm Beach.

Life in south Florida changed forever.

Work began in 1930 on a giant levee around the lake. The Herbert Hoover Dike was finished in 1961.

Eventually a government entity was born and a network of canals carved for flood control. The agency's mission later grew to include water supply and quality, and it became the powerful South Florida Water Management District.

The Port Mayaca Cemetery is on the south side of State Road 76, about two miles east of U. S. 441/98 at Lake Okeechobee.

Stuart/Martin County Chamber of Commerce: 1650 S Kanner Hwy, Stuart 34994. Call (772) 287-1088. Website: www.goodnature. org

Read More About It

Hurston, Zora Neale. *Their Eyes Were Watching God.* 1978, Champaign, Ill., University of Illinois Press.

Will, Lawrence. *Okeechobee Hurricane and the Hoover Dike.* 1978, St. Petersburg, Outdoors Publishing.

Clewiston Inn

Clewiston

A sweet night's stay

If the cypress-paneled walls could talk.

Many a sweet deal has been closed in the Clewiston Inn, a quaint lodge along Sugarland Highway, the main street of "America's Sweetest Town." The inn stands out on the busy highway, with its Southern architecture, highlighted by pillars, lanterns, and tall arched windows.

Built in January 1938 by U.S. Sugar — the "company" in this company town — to host visiting executives, it is the oldest hotel in "The Glades," the sugar growing area between Lake Okeechobee and the Everglades. It is a state historic site and is on the National Register of Historic Places.

The inn, still owned by U.S. Sugar, has hosted scores of business leaders and elected officials. Herbert Hoover stayed there in 1961 when the former president dedicated the giant dike around Lake Okeechobee, named for him.

A predecessor to the inn was built in 1926 along a ridge where the lake's banks stood, before the Herbert Hoover dike was built. It was on the town's highest point, one of the few places that wasn't swampland. It was even built with sugar. The wood frame building's interiors and exteriors were made of Celotex, the fiber material left over when sugar, molasses, and water are extracted from cane.

After the original inn burned in 1936, the current building went up. It was made of steel frame with brick and was even air-conditioned. A 1953 anniversary edition of *The Clewiston News*

Clewiston Inn: a sweet place to stay. *Clewiston Inn*

praised "the modern efficiency and comforts of a metropolitan hotel with the quiet and dignity of a country estate."

During World War II, this Southern inn took on a British flavor as many of the 1,325 Royal Air Force cadets who trained at nearby Riddle Field between 1941 and 1945 would gather around the piano to sing. When two hurricanes struck the area in the same summer, 1947, the Inn served as a storm shelter. Two babies were born there in one storm.

The Inn, with 48 rooms, features a wide staircase with brass and wrought iron handrails; the spartan dining room still sports the original pine tables and chairs. The lobby has sofas and beamed ceilings and wood-burning fireplaces. In one corner stands a period switchboard, complete with pull cords, used from the hotel's inception until 1986.

One of the highlights of the hotel is a giant Everglades wildlife mural covering the four walls of the lounge. It was painted in 1945 by Palm Beach artist J. Clinton Shepherd, who lived at the inn for several months, making trips into the Everglades to sketch animals. He then returned to Palm Beach to create the four-panel painting. A legend available at the inn identifies the birds, alligators, and other animals on the work. Shepherd died at age 86 in 1975; the mural's worth has been estimated at more than $40,000.

The Clewiston Inn is at 108 Royal Palm Avenue in downtown Clewiston. Call (863) 983-8151 or (800) 749-4466. Website: www. clewistoninn.com

Read More About It

Gregware, Bill and Carol. *Guide to the Lake Okeechobee Area*. 1997, Sarasota, Pineapple Press.

Will, Lawrence. *Cracker History of Lake Okeechobee*. 1964, St. Petersburg, Outdoors Publishing Co.

The "Lone Cypress"

Moore Haven

A piece of Lake Okeechobee's past

The "Lone Cypress" leans at an awkward angle toward the Caloosahatchee Canal. Its trunk juts out of a wooden deck next to the canal's concrete wall across the street from the city library in the downtown of tiny Moore Haven.

From this spot, you can gaze north, under the U.S. 27 overpass, only as far as where the canal curves away into the brush. About a half-mile beyond it, on the other side of a towering earthen dike, is the unseen Lake Okeechobee. Try to imagine that this tree once was an important landmark for fishermen and mariners. That's because this spot once was on the edge of the big lake. The tree hasn't moved. But the lake has.

The fall from grace of the "Lone Cypress" dates back to early efforts to drain swamplands and build farming empires.

In 1881, Hamilton Disston of Philadelphia, whose family had made its fortune selling Disston saws, bought four million acres of Central Florida — about 11 percent of the state's total land area. He paid $1 million — 25 cents an acre. Some of that property now is inhabited by Walt Disney World, and real estate values have increased just a bit.

One of Disston's first projects was to carve a canal bridging the three-mile gap from where the Caloosahatchee dead-ended into Lake Hicpochee only three miles from Lake Okeechobee.

That stretch eventually would become a key link in the Okeechobee Waterway, a 125-mile marine route across the peninsula from the St. Lucie Canal through Lake Okeechobee and down the Caloosahatchee to Fort Myers.

Boaters on Lake Okeechobee then began using the "Lone

The "Lone Cypress" once stood along Lake Okeechobee. *Fort Lauderdale Historical Society*

Cypress," standing on the shore, to guide them into Disston's "Three-Mile Canal."

The 30-foot-tall tree, believed to be more than two centuries old, served as a natural marker for three decades. Settler James Moore built the town of Moore Haven around it.

But hurricanes indirectly stole the tree's glory. After the 1926 and 1928 storms killed more than 2,000 people around the lake, the government built the giant dike to prevent future catastrophic floods. In the process, the lake's size was shrunk. Now the great tree that once helped sailors find their way home stands quietly across from a playground.

The "Lone Cypress" is at the eastern end of Avenue J, on Riverside Drive along the Caloosahatchee Canal in downtown Moore Haven.

City of Moore Haven, 99 Riverside Dr. SW, Moore Haven 33471. Call (863) 946-0711.

Read More About It

Gregware, Bill and Carol. *Guide to the Lake Okeechobee Area.* 1997, Sarasota, Pineapple Press.

Johnson, Lamar. *Beyond the Fourth Generation.* 1977, Gainesville, University Press of Florida.

Will, Lawrence. *Lawrence Will's Cracker History of Lake Okeechobee.* 1977, Belle Glade, Belle Glade Historical Society.

Kenilworth Lodge

Sebring

A good book, and maybe a ghost

As you check in at Sebring's Kenilworth Lodge hotel, you might be surprised to see Mr. Parker at the front desk. That's because he's dead.

Mr. Parker, a former manager, died in the 1950s at the historic hotel. It is said his ghost still haunts the third floor of the north wing. Some employees swear furniture, doors, and air conditioning knobs move, and taps are heard on doors from the inside of empty rooms.

George Sebring, of Sebring, Ohio, laid out the town on the east shore of Lake Jackson, designing it in the pattern of the ancient Egyptian city of Heliopolis (city of the sun), with streets radiating from a central park site.

He built the Spanish-style Kenilworth, the oldest continuously operating hotel in Highlands County, on 320 acres in 1916. It competed for northern tourists with the grand resorts of the two Henrys, Flagler on the east coast and Plant in the Tampa Bay area.

Initially open only during the "season," the Kenilworth catered to snowbirds from mid-Atlantic and Midwestern states. Guests rode the Orange Blossom Special train from the Northeast to central Florida.

At the Kenilworth, they played golf, strolled through an orange grove, crossed Lake Jackson in sailboats and motor launches, and fished and hunted in the surrounding wilderness.

Both tourists and land speculators were attracted by the hills, lakes, and pristine rural countryside and, perhaps most important, real estate prices far lower than those for the more famous coastal cities.

The historic Kenilworth Lodge might include a ghost.   *Kenilworth Lodge*

During the boom-and-bust 1920s, the hotel had four different owners, the last obtaining it at auction in 1927 and operating it during the Depression. It went through at least three more owners, the second losing it to foreclosure, and the current owners performed major renovations in the 1980s.

The three-story wood and stucco lodge building hosts 117 rooms, with wooden doors, glass doorknobs, and porcelain bathtubs. Fifteen cottages and duplexes, containing a total of 20 poolside units, were built in the 1970s.

The lobby features a brick fireplace. You can also curl up with a good book from the hotel's honor-system library. Guests and friends have slowly built up its inventory over the years by donating books; you're welcome to grab one and take it upstairs into your room.

Sebring's downtown is listed on the National Register of Historic Places. It features tree-lined streets, canopied storefronts, and antique lamp posts.

The Kenilworth Lodge is at 1610 Lakeview Drive, at Lakeview and Kenilworth in downtown Sebring, 33870. Call (800) 423-5939 or (863) 385-0111. Website: www.kenlodge.com

   Greater Sebring Chamber of Commerce: 309 Circle Park Dr., Sebring 33870. Call (863) 385-8448. Website: www.sebringflchamber.com

   Sebring Downtown Merchants and Professional Association, Box 1322, Sebring 33871. Website: www.sebring-florida.com

Read More About It

Chamber of Commerce History Committee. *History of Sebring, Highlands County, Florida.* 1965, Sebring.

Sebring Semi-Centennial Committee. *The First 50 Years of Sebring, 1912–1962.* 1962, Sebring.

Sebring
International
Raceway

Sebring

Where speed reigned

When the cars aren't running, they leave a roaring silence. Then, Sebring International Raceway is a vision of empty bleachers, bright advertisements shouting to no one, a dark press box, an unused pedestrian bridge across the dormant 3.6-mile-long track.

In a row of metal sheds, workers load a modern racing car into the back of an 18-wheeler. And nearby, a small plane or two might land or take off from the small municipal airport that serves this otherwise sleepy central Florida town. It's different in March, when the gentlemen start their engines for the 12 Hours of Sebring, the track's centerpiece event. It's America's oldest sports car race and largest sports car endurance event. Thousands of fans pack one of the south's premier racing venues.

Sebring's racing year is highlighted by the March race, first called "the Sam Collier Memorial Grand Prix of Endurance" and renamed in 1963. Drawing 28 entries for its first running, it now limits to 75 to 80 cars, luring the race world's stars and drawing more than 90,000 fans per four-day weekend.

When the Hendricks Field military air base, built in Sebring in 1941, was deactivated five years later, it remained active as a municipal airport — and still does — but local race organizers saw potential in its snaking access roads. They spent a year assembling rules, planning for safety and preparing for crowd control.

The effort was led by track founder Alec Ulmann, an automobile and aviation parts engineer who watched his first sports car race at age six in his native Russia before the Bolsheviks chased out his

Sebring International Raceway. *Josh Martin*

family. He was taught to drive by the family chauffeur.

The first race was held on New Year's Eve, 1950. It was the nation's first endurance race. Sebring firemen set up a three-and-a-half mile course for a six-hour event witnessed by about 3,000 fans. It started at 3 P.M. with the traditional Le Mans open — the 28 drivers standing in a line on the track, then sprinting to their cars. A portion of the active airport runways was commandeered for the race, a practice that would continue into the mid-1980s. The average speed of the winner was about 67 mph.

The second race, a 12-hour event in March 1952, was backed by American and international racing groups and was the first on the 5.2-mile course. The next year's running was recognized as the world sports car championship race. In 1956, it instituted its first winner's purse: $10,000.

In December 1959, the track hosted the United States Grand Prix at Sebring, the nation's Grand Prix race for Formula One cars, the highest level of racing in the world. In 1960, when a dispute kept many racers home, the track established "support races" for the weekends leading up to the big event. That practice continues, with three races in the days before the big 12-hour race.

The track has had its share of tragedy. Driver Bob Goldich

was killed in 1957. In 1960, George Thompson, a *Tampa Tribune* photographer standing where drivers who failed to negotiate hairpin turns could pull off, was struck and killed by driver Jimmy Hughes, who also died. In 1966, driver Bob McLean was killed in the race; later Mario Andretti collided with another driver and four spectators were killed. Several other drivers were killed in practice accidents.

In 1974 the world's energy crisis prompted organizers to cancel the races. But 2,000 fans showed up and partied anyway. In 1999, the track underwent a $20 million renovation, adding a luxury hotel overlooking the famed hairpin turn, as well as new pits and bridges, corporate skyboxes, and a year-round racing school.

Sebring International Raceway is about six miles southeast of Sebring at 113 Midway Drive, Sebring 33870. Call (800) 626-RACE (7223). Website: www.sebringraceway.com

The track is not open for tours between races, but is active with testing, driving schools, club racing, and other activities.

Greater Sebring Chamber of Commerce: 309 Circle Park Dr., Sebring 33870. Call (863) 385-8448. Website: www.sebringflchamber.com

Read More About It
Breslauer, Ken. *Sebring: the Official History of America's Greatest Sports Car Race.* 1996, David Bull Publishing.

Koreshan

Estero

One man's vision of New Jerusalem

Welcome to New Jerusalem. Dr. Cyrus Reed Teed, an upstate New York surgeon spurred by a vision in 1869, led about 200 of his faithful to this spot 15 miles south of Fort Myers. He saw a sprawling city, home to ten million people. Ironically, his followers' gift of the 305-acre settlement to the state has kept it from joining the sprawl that has changed southwest Florida.

Visitors can stand on the promenade, feel the gravel crunch underfoot, tune out the traffic on U.S. 41 just a few yards away, and listen carefully for the strains of the long-gone marching band, its music bouncing off the trees that line the Estero River.

They may squint upward at the crumbling wood and concrete Founder's Home and try to imagine it in its splendor. The curious who tour the Koreshan (pronounced koh-RESH-en) State Historic Site tend to snicker at Teed's theory — that we don't live on the Earth's surface but rather line the underside of the hollow, 8,000-mile-diameter shell, with the planets and stars revolving around the sun at the globe's core. But they might be impressed with the visionary philosophies of the group — racial and religious tolerance, equality of gender, and ecology.

The Koreshan Unity also disdained profanity, tobacco, and liquor, and embraced celibacy and communal property ownership. A giant piece of concrete reading "Cyrus Shepherd, Stone of Israel" is all that remains of Teed's tomb.

The charismatic leader was a pied piper spurred by a "divine revelation" in 1869. The self-proclaimed prophet of his time recruited 200 devotees to the property, donated by a converted landowner.

Soon the settlement boasted 60 buildings, including schools and

TOP: The Koreshans believed we live inside the earth.
Koreshan State Historic Site

CENTER: The former Koreshan village is now a state historic site.
Palm Beach Post

BOTTOM: Cyrus Teed envisioned a "New Jerusalem" on Florida's Gulf Coast. *Koreshan State Historic Site*

businesses, and a publishing house. You can still see the eight remaining buildings, which include the bakery and meeting hall and the partially restored home of Cyrus Reed Teed. The grounds have been restored to approximate how the site looked at the turn of the century.

When Teed died at age 69 in 1908, his flock, clinging to its belief in resurrection, stood vigil at his body for six days in a hot sun, until the local health inspector stepped in. When a hurricane 17 years later swept his tomb away, but left the tombstone, their faith was stirred by what they saw as an act of God.

Over the next three decades, celibacy and infighting reduced the colony to a few dozen and, in 1961, when the last of the original Koreshans died, their last four surviving believers deeded the property to the state.

In a glass Nautilus-shaped building across U.S. 41, Koreshan Unity Inc., a corporation supported by donations, maintains historic archives. Inside, shelves hold hundreds of books and piles of brochures, photographs, and other materials from the original community.

The foundation at one time presented an annual fall solar festival and spring lunar observance. And it continues to press for intelligent use of resources — a popular idea now, but in many ways as bizarre a concept 100 years ago as the others put forth by the Koreshans.

The Koreshan State Historic Site is south of Fort Myers. Take Interstate 75 to Corkscrew Road, then west. Cross over U.S. 41 and the entrance is about 1000 feet down on the right. Tours at 10 A.M. weekends. Admission: $4 per vehicles, $3 single-passenger vehicles, $1 for pedestrians or cyclists. Tours: Adults $2, under 12 $1. Call (239) 992-0311. Website: www.floridastateparks.org

Koreshan Unity Alliance: Box 2061, Ft. Myers 33902.

Lee County Visitor and Convention Bureau: 12800 University Drive, Suite 550, Ft. Myers 33907. Call (800) 237-6444. Website: www. fortmyers-sanibel.com

Read More About It

Herbert, Glendon M. *Koreshan Unity Settlement, 1894–1977.* 1977, Winter Park, Architects Design Group of Florida.

Mackle, Elliott James. *The Koreshan Unity in Florida, 1894–1910.* 1971, Coral Gables.

Teed, Cyrus Reed. *The Cellular Cosmogony, or: The earth, a concave sphere.* 1975, Philadelphia, Porcupine Press.

Edison and Ford Homes

Fort Myers

Where the wizard set up shop

Street lights? No thanks, Thomas. They'd just keep the cows awake.

That's how this town reportedly declined an offer by its most famous winter resident to build a power plant to light the city. The story is now dismissed, but chances are Edison would have shrugged and gone on with his tireless work.

From 1885 to 1887 and 1901 to 1931, the man considered one of the modern world's greatest geniuses, the man who had conquered darkness and changed forever the way we live, tinkered away and entertained at "Seminole Lodge," his sprawling estate on the banks of the Caloosahatchee. The spread, bequeathed to the city by Edison's widow in 1947, is now a historic site. So is the home of the next-door neighbor, a fellow named Henry Ford.

Some 300,000 people a year visit the Edison complex of two houses, a laboratory, museum, and gardens, to walk on his wooden porch, gaze out to the wide Caloosahatchee beyond the foliage, and peek inside his rooms from the wide verandah vantage point.

The estate sprawls on both sides of McGregor Boulevard, the busy thoroughfare that leads south from downtown. The royal palm trees that line the road are just one of Edison's abundant gifts to Fort Myers and helped earn it the nickname "City of Palms."

The Wizard Heads South

Thomas Alva Edison was already in his late 30s and an established

TOP: Edison was already an established inventor when he bought "Seminole Lodge."

BOTTOM: The view from Edison's porch. *Eliot Kleinberg*

inventor when he first visited the tiny town. His doctor in New Jersey had told him that working 15 to 20 hours a day was bad enough, but doing it in the cold north was wearing down the Wizard of Menlo Park. He already suffered a spate of ills, including ulcers and diabetes.

Having already perfected what would become perhaps his greatest invention, the light bulb, Edison was drawn to Fort Myers, then a settlement of 350, for the warm winter weather, but also because the bamboo he sought as a filament source could be grown in the subtropical climate. Edison, then widowed with three children, settled on a 14-acre site on an old cattle trail on the banks of the wide river, about 14 miles east of the Gulf of Mexico. He paid $2,750 for the property.

He had the two spruce houses prefabricated in Maine and sent by schooner to the town, which had no paved roads. Furnishings were comfortable and expensive.

The main home has wide French doors, with windows on the first floor and a 14-foot veranda. One story says Edison put the dining area and kitchen in the guest cottage — almost a twin of the main house and connected by a walkway — because he didn't like the smell of cooking food. He also banned any smoking, although he did enjoy chewing on stogies. His swimming pool, built in 1910, is fed by an artesian well.

In March 1887, Edison turned on lights at his home for the first time. They were powered by a plant in his laboratory. Curious neighbors gathered to see the miracle. Edison returned north two years later; he would not come back to live in Fort Myers for 14 years. But his presence was still powerful in 1898 when the city threw the switch and became connected to its new power plant.

The banyan tree in front of the visitors center began as a four-foot shoot, a 1925 gift from tire king Harvey Firestone. Now, a circumference of roots covering an acre snakes along the ground or drops down vertically from branches like table legs.

The estate's gardens contain some 300 trees, many of them exotic plants comprising one of Florida's richest collections.

Spurred by separate $25,000 offers from Firestone and next-door neighbor Henry Ford, Edison experimented with many of his plants in search of a new source of rubber, then exclusively imported. Late in life, Edison did create a type of rubber from the common goldenrod. Exhibits explaining this work and many of his other experiments are in the laboratory near the visitors center.

"Discovery is . . . an accident"

With nearly 1,100 patents, the list of common household items invented or dramatically improved by Edison is staggering: the light bulb, movies, phonograph, microphone, toaster, electric coffee pot, fan, waffle and curling irons, hot plate, water softener, Christmas lights, spark plugs.

There's more: wax paper, transparent tape, plate glass, distillation, fruit preservation techniques, talking dolls, electric meters, and workable typewriters — early models had been slower than longhand.

"Discovery is not invention," Edison would say. "A discovery is more or less in the nature of an accident. A man walks along the road intending to catch the train. On the way his foot kicks against something and . . . he sees a gold bracelet embedded in the dust. He has discovered that — certainly not invented it."

Edison's home is almost exactly as it was in his lifetime; rooms contain personal items, drawers hold clothes, and laboratory cabinets are still lined with vials and devices.

In the dank lab, now a museum, is a very early phonograph, marred on the frame by teeth marks. Edison found that if he placed his ear close to the speaker and his teeth on the frame he could better hear the sounds. The wizard was almost completely deaf. In fact, Edison had proposed to his second wife, Mina, by tapping into her palm in Morse code during a horse ride in New Hampshire. Edison died at age 84 in October 1931. Mina Miller Edison died 16 years later, willing the property to the city.

Henry Ford partially credited his success to his friend, whom he had met in 1896. Ford's adjacent estate was bought by the city in 1988 as a historic site.

The estates have just finished a $9.2 million restoration of the Edison buildings.

The Edison and Ford Homes are at 2350 McGregor Blvd., south of downtown Fort Myers 33901. Call (239) 334-7419. Open 9 A.M. to 5:30 P.M. Monday through Saturday, noon to 5:30 P.M. on Sundays. The last guided tour leaves at 4 P.M. Admission: both homes, adults $20, kids 6-12 $11. Florida residents: adults $14, kids 6-12 $7.50. Website: www.edison-ford-estate.com.

Lee County Visitor and Convention Bureau: 12800 University Drive, Suite 550, Ft. Myers 33907. Call (800) 237-6444. Website: www. fortmyers-sanibel.com

Read More About It

Baldwin, Neil. *Edison: Inventing the Century.* 1995, New York, Hyperion.

Fritz, Florence. *Bamboo and Sailing Ships: The Story of Thomas Alva Edison and Fort Myers, Florida.* 1949, Fort Myers.

Godown, Marian, and Alberta Rawchuck. *Yesterday's Fort Myers.* 1975, Miami, E.A. Seeman Co.

Newton, James D. *Uncommon Friends.* 1987, San Diego, Harcourt Brace Jovanovich.

Smoot, Tom. *The Edisons of Fort Myers: Discoveries of the Heart.* 2004, Sarasota, Pineapple Press.

South Florida

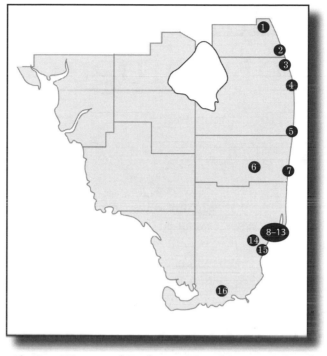

1. Gilbert's Bar House of Refuge, *Hutchinson Island*
2. Jonathan Dickinson State Park, *Hobe Sound*
3. Jupiter Lighthouse, *Jupiter*
4. Whitehall, *Palm Beach*
5. Boca Raton Resort and Club, *Boca Raton*
6. Alligator Alley
7. Stranahan House, *Fort Lauderdale*
8. Hialeah Race Track, *Hialeah*
9. Orange Bowl, *Miami*
10. Freedom Tower, *Miami*
11. Vizcaya, *Miami*
12. Miami City Hall, *Miami*
13. The Barnacle, *Coconut Grove*
14. The Biltmore, *Coral Gables*
15. Cape Florida Lighthouse, *Key Biscayne*
16. Everglades National Park

Gilbert's Bar House of Refuge

Hutchinson Island

Shelter from the storm

Imagine you're on a ship lurching through a nineteenth-century hurricane. The vessel is dashed onto the rocks. You somehow make your way to the deserted beach. In the darkness and blinding rain, a light is shining in the distance, beckoning you to shelter.

Ten buildings built in a string along Florida's east coast in the late 1800s could not have been more appropriately named. They were called Houses of Refuge. Only one remains: Gilbert's Bar House of Refuge, east of Stuart on Hutchinson Island. The 1876 building, the second of the ten to be built, is listed on the National Register of Historic Places. The house was built on the site of a midden, a habitation site used by the local Ais peoples. Exhibits on the Ais have been added to the home's displays. The building's endurance is credited to the wall of reef that has kept the ground under the house from eroding.

Over the centuries many a ship, lacking the current luxuries of a National Hurricane Center and mass media, was surprised by a hurricane and sank to the bottom with its precious cargo. That history has earned the area the nickname "the Treasure Coast." Eleven ships sank in the 1715 hurricane alone. Finally, the U.S. Life Saving Service established a string of Houses of Refuge, budgeting $2,900 for each. Keepers were first paid the then-hefty sum of $40 a month. In the nineteenth century, a pirate named Gilbert worked the waters around what is now called Hutchinson Island. The offshore reef, or bar, was named for him.

Keepers of the Gilbert's Bar refuge lived on the first floor of the

Gilbert's Bar House of Refuge
still stands on Hutchinson Island.
Florida News Bureau

house; a dormitory upstairs could sleep up to 24. That area is closed
to the public. On the first floor, a kitchen displays original cooking
utensils, a rum keg, and a "food safe." A parlor and bedroom have
been transformed into exhibits featuring period furniture, clothing,
and artifacts.

Next to the building is "the boathouse," built in 1914. It's a
small gift shop, and it displays marine artifacts, early life saving
equipment, and model ships. You'll find a two-headed turtle, bones
of sea creatures, and the propeller from a freighter sunk in 1942 by a
German U-boat.

Outside is a hand-built reproduction of a 150-year-old surf boat.
And about 300 yards offshore, in 15 feet of water, accessible to divers
and snorkelers, is the wreck of the *Georges Valentine*, a barkentine en
route to South America that went down on Oct. 16, 1904. It has been
designated the tenth Florida Underwater Archaeological Preserve.
Inside the house, a log gives testimony to all the ships that were
dashed to pieces or disappeared beneath the unforgiving waves.

The home is also said to be haunted; keepers have reported
inexplicably smelling beef stew and finding slivers of a nonexistent
mirror on an upstairs bed. Visitors entering the room have stopped
short, saying they sense something foreboding, and refused to enter.

The home was deactivated in 1945 and abandoned until Martin
County stepped in and bought it in 1953. The local Soroptimists Club
restored it. It's leased to and operated by the Historical Society of
Martin County.

Gilbert's Bar House of Refuge Museum is on Hutchinson Island, at 301 S.E. MacArthur Blvd., Stuart 34996. Call (772) 225-1875. From downtown Stuart, take East Ocean Boulevard east across the Intracoastal Waterway to the ocean. Turn right at the first light, MacArthur Boulevard, and travel 1 1/2 miles. The house is on the left. Open 10 A.M. to 4 P.M. Monday through Saturday, 1 P.M. TO 4 P.M. Sunday. Admission: adults, $4; children 6 to 13, $2. Educational groups free by arrangement. The house is operated by the Historical Society of Martin County, 825 N.E. Ocean Blvd., Stuart 34996. Call (772) 225-1961.

Stuart/Martin County Chamber of Commerce: 1650 South Kanner Highway, Stuart 34994-7199. Call (772) 287-1088. Website: www.goodnature.org

Read More About It

Hutchinson, Janet. *History of Martin County.* 1975, Hutchinson Island, Martin County Historical Society,

Stewart, Laura, and Susanne Hupp. *Historic Homes of Florida.* 1995, Sarasota, Pineapple Press.

Jonathan Dickinson State Park

Hobe Sound

Secrets in the sand

The white sands of Jonathan Dickinson State Park hold a history both ethereal and tangible. The 16-square-mile park's name honors the ordeal three centuries ago of the shipwrecked Jonathan Dickinson and his family, who walked adjacent beaches en route to St. Augustine and rescue. Its more current history can be found in the sand itself; spent bullet shells dating back to the park's incarnation as Camp Murphy, a strategic World War II training site. And tours travel deep into the wilderness to visit the domain of the wild man of the Loxahatchee River, Trapper Nelson.

Jonathan Dickinson, a Quaker merchant traveling from Jamaica to Philadelphia with his wife and six-month-old son, was stranded with two dozen other passengers when the ship on which they were riding, the *Reformation*, was beached on nearby Jupiter Island in 1696. Natives threatened to kill the party, then relented. For the next two months, Dickinson and his family trudged on a trek of more than 200 miles through the Florida wilderness. They eventually made their way to Philadelphia. Dickinson later published *Jonathan Dickinson's Journal*, a story of faith and determination that is also considered one of the most important eyewitness accounts of the original Indians, long ago exterminated by European aggression and disease.

Two and a half centuries later, when World War II broke out, the military came to Florida, looking for land to place installations. From 1942 to 1945, more than 10,000 men moved through the camp; as many as 6,000 were there at one time, giving the site a larger population than the nearby town of Jupiter. Camp Murphy was deactivated in

187

Jonathan Dickinson State Park recalls a historic shipwreck and the sounds of war. *Palm Beach Post*

October 1944 and most of the property was turned over to the state to become the park.

The park also stretches into the wilds along the Loxahatchee River, the only waterway in Florida listed by the federal government as a Wild and Scenic River.

The most colorful character in the park's past may well be Victor Nostokovich, better known as Trapper Nelson, "the wild man of the Loxahatchee." He came into the area in the 1930s and lived the frontier life, eating wildlife he'd trapped. He moved inland into the wilderness and bought up land as he went.

People from locals to Palm Beachers began visiting his camp, which became a tourist attraction of sorts. He added picnic tables and grills and built cages into which he put some of the wild animals he caught.

He began charging for dock space and cabin rentals and used the money to buy more land, eventually owning 858 acres. But Trapper fell on hard times. His zoo closed. His health declined. He began felling trees across the river to block boats and placed them across a road into his camp. He turned away uninvited visitors, chasing off some with a shotgun.

Trapper Nelson was one of the region's most colorful characters. *Palm Beach Post*

In 1968, Trapper was found dead of a shotgun blast. His death was ruled a suicide, but some still believe he was murdered. For years, rumors insisted he'd hidden a treasure somewhere on his property. In 1984, rangers pulled away some mortar near a fireplace and found more than 5,000 coins totaling $1,800.

Jonathan Dickinson State Park is near Hobe Sound in southeastern Martin County. Write 16450 S. E. Federal Highway, Hobe Sound 33455. Call (772) 546-2771. Web page: www.floridastateparks.org.

From Interstate 95 take exit 96, then east on Bridge Road to U.S. 1 and south three miles to park entrance. From Florida's Turnpike, take exit 116, east on Indiantown Road to U.S. 1, then north five miles to entrance. Hours: 8 A.M. to sunset. Park admission: $4 per car, $3 single occupancy car, $1 pedestrians. Camp sites and cabins available. Loxahatchee River tours and canoe rental available.

Hobe Sound National Wildlife Refuge is on the east side of U.S. 1, across from the state park. $5 parking in island parking lot. Call (772) 546-6141. Website: www.fws.gov/hobesound

Hobe Sound Chamber of Commerce: 8779 S.E. Bridge Road, Hobe Sound 33475. (772) 546-4724. Website: www.hobesound.org

Read More About It

Dickinson, Jonathan. *Jonathan Dickinson's Journal*. 1988, Port Salerno, Florida Classics Library.

Jupiter Lighthouse

Jupiter

Sweeping the seas

The Jupiter Lighthouse first lit up the shallow waters off the Jupiter Inlet on July 10, 1860. General George Meade, who would later win the battle of Gettysburg, designed the lighthouse to guide mariners over the treacherous shallows. Except for brief outages, it has sent its beam sweeping 18 miles across the dark seas ever since.

Distracted by fear of Indian attacks, the troops took six years to build the 105-foot structure. During the Civil War, Confederate blockade-runners familiar with the waters didn't need the light and didn't want it revealing them to Union patrols. Assistant keeper August Oswald Lang, a German immigrant who had become a proud citizen of the Confederate States of America, ordered his boss to surrender the lighting mechanism. J. F. Papy, loyal to his federal paycheck, first said no, but was convinced otherwise. The rebels hid the light, and it was recovered after the war. It was relighted June 28, 1866.

The 1928 hurricane first came ashore at the Jupiter Lighthouse. "It seemed as if things were approaching a crisis," Jupiter Inlet pioneer Bessie DuBois would later write. "About all that held our house together was the chimney and the cement back porch. . . . Finally the unbearable strain was broken in a dramatic manner. The wind began to ring the ship's bell on the back porch which we used to summon the family to meals. The wind had changed, the center of the hurricane had passed."

The storm buffeted the lighthouse; it swayed a remarkable 17 inches as mortar squeezed from between bricks like toothpaste. The storm then moved inland. It emptied Lake Okeechobee and sent a wall of water into the Glades, drowning perhaps up to 3,000 people. But the lighthouse had held. A lens had blown out, and the electricity for the newly converted light died. The keeper brought out the oil lamps

The Jupiter Lighthouse dates back to the 1860s.
Florida News Bureau

and kept the lighthouse shining. The light was quickly reactivated.

In the 1980s, retired Army Colonel David Meredith III uncovered secret documents showing that during World War II, the lighthouse was a secret listening post called U.S. Naval Supplementary Radio Station, Jupiter, Florida, with the code name of Station "J."

In 1929, the Navy had acquired 8.4 acres of the lighthouse reservation and broadcast weather information and monitored ship-to-shore and aircraft distress calls. They were ordered to stop in 1939, and by 1940 the lighthouse entered the coming war as a listening post.

At its busiest, 95 men at Station "J" monitored diplomatic messages with a priority on locating German submarines in the Atlantic. The U-boats would surface every night to charge batteries and transmit their location and current weather. Thirty enemy submarines were destroyed in the Atlantic in May 1943 and 37 in

June, some possibly spotted by Station "J."

After World War II, allegations arose that President Franklin Roosevelt, realizing the awesome consequences of Nazi conquest and needing an excuse to pull a reluctant America into the war, learned of the imminent attack on Pearl Harbor but withheld the information from the military. A major investigation was launched, but officials denied Station "J" intercepted a Japanese "Winds" signal to start the raid on Hawaii.

The lighthouse, placed on the National Register of Historic Places in 1975, was staffed by the Coast Guard until 1987, when it became fully automated. Some electrical problems briefly darkened the light in the late 1980s.

In 1994, the U.S. Coast Guard turned the lighthouse over to the Florida History Center and Museum, now the Loxahatchee River Historical Society, signing a 30-year lease. The society spent $858,000 from 1999 to 2000 to restore and repaint the lighthouse. Donations and proceeds from tours will pay to maintain the lighthouse and keep its beam shining across the waters.

The Jupiter Lighthouse is on the Intracoastal Waterway at Jupiter Inlet. From Interstate 95, take Indiantown Road to U. S. 1, then north across Loxahatchee River; the lighthouse is on right. Write c/o Loxahatchee River Historical Society, 805 N. U.S. 1, Jupiter 33458. Call (561) 747-6639. Admission: $6 per person. Tours 10 A.M. to 4 P.M. Saturday through Wednesday. Last tour leaves at 3:15 P.M. Sunset tours the last Wednesday of the month. Height minimum for children: 4 feet. Website: www.lrhs.org

Jupiter-Tequesta-Juno Beach Chamber of Commerce: 800 N. U.S. 1, Jupiter 33477. Call (561) 746-7111. Website: www.jupiterfl. org

Read More About It

De Wire, Elinor. *Guide to Florida Lighthouses*. 2001, Sarasota, Pineapple Press.

DuBois, Bessie Wilson. *The History of Jupiter Lighthouse*. 1981; *The History of the Loxahatchee River*. 1981; *Shipwrecks in the Vicinity of Jupiter Inlet*. 1975, Jupiter, Bessie Wilson Dubois.

Meredith, David III. *Spy Station Jupiter, A History of the U. S. Naval Supplementary Radio Station, Jupiter, Florida*. 1988, David Meredith.

Whitehall

Palm Beach

*The home of the man who
built Florida*

It was a wedding gift from Florida's seminal figure to his new wife. It was the largest home on Florida's jewel resort island when finished in 1902. It was built for the then-remarkable cost of $2.5 million — plus another $1.5 million for furnishings. The owners would throw lavish parties there, and it became a center of the social set. Henry Flagler called the place Whitehall.

In February 1894, the opening of Henry Flagler's landmark Royal Poinciana Hotel had marked the unofficial birth of a narrow island that only eight years earlier had been given the simple name of Palm Beach. Flagler's newest possession would become "The Queen of Winter Resorts," the brightest gem in his gaudy necklace of Gay '90s society getaways. Over the next century, a sprawl of about a million people would rise from the swamp and scrub. And his mansion would become the king's castle.

Palm Beach and the other towns Flagler founded outright or converted from fishing village to tourist mecca changed Florida from a wilderness of less than a half million people — the last frontier east of the Mississippi River to be settled — to America's fourth largest state. Not everyone is happy with the Florida of today. Many mourn the old Florida that disappeared under the shovels of people like Henry Flagler. But no one disputes the extraordinary changes he wrought.

Inside the six towering white pillars of Whitehall that Flagler had built was a 110-by-40-foot entrance hall, dripping with artwork, and a very private second floor. It had 22 servants' rooms and 14 guest

Whitehall is a monument to Henry Flagler. *Flagler Museum*

rooms — each with a distinctive look, private bath, and walk-in closet. The master bedroom had a dressing room and sunken bathtub.

After Flagler's death in 1913, Whitehall was sold in 1924; the new owners built a ten-story, 300-room tower and converted it into a hotel. Flagler's granddaughter repurchased it in 1959 for a reported $2 million, tore down the tower, and turned it into a national historic site and museum. Jean Flagler Matthews saved Whitehall from becoming a health spa by establishing the Whitehall Foundation and buying the property.

"One day . . . I heard that a spa was going to open at Whitehall, and that the Marble Hall would be used for dressing room cubicles — that did it," she said. Though she never knew her grandfather, Whitehall's patron saint had the mansion immaculately restored. In 1960, a gala ball celebrated the opening of Whitehall as a museum and historic site — and, with The Breakers, the last vestige of Flagler's incredible Palm Beach dream.

Henry Morrison Flagler

Henry Morrison Flagler's fortune started with a five-cent piece, four pennies, and a five-franc coin he carried the rest of his life, a reminder of the lesson in the biblical parable of the talents: no risk, no gain. He was a conservative financier who sometimes risked everything. He built a fortune, saw it collapse, and within a half-decade was the second-in-command at Standard Oil and on his way to becoming one of America's wealthiest men.

His success was tempered by great personal loss. A daughter

died in childbirth, and he was estranged from his son. He lost one wife to disease and another to insanity. He was a private, aloof man who always made sure to be dressed formally and always stood tall and stiff, even in his later years. He was an honorable man who nevertheless bought his way out of serving in the military in the Civil War. His advertisements crowed of the natural beauty of Florida, but, like so many of his era, he bulldozed native trees and Indian burial sites to make room for his railroads and buildings. He made more money than he would ever need but still sought immortality. So at an age when most people retire, he began a second career that made him the pivotal character in Florida's modern history.

The Man Who Built Florida

Flagler was a descendant of political refugees. His family fled Germany in 1710 during attempts by the French king Louis XIV to conquer their homeland. Flagler's father was running a small church in upstate New York when he was born January 2, 1830. By foot and boat, the 14-year-old came to Republic, Ohio, near Cleveland, for a five-dollar-a-month job in a general store. Eight years later, he became a broker in his family's grain business. There, he met a young grain merchant named John D. Rockefeller.

After losing a fortune when his salt works failed at the end of the Civil War, Flagler vowed to minimize risk in future ventures by getting co-investors. In 1870, he joined forces with his old friend Rockefeller, now in the burgeoning oil industry. Within five years, he was the number two man in the company, which was quickly becoming one of the mightiest in history.

In the ensuing decades, government would battle Standard — accused of freezing out rivals and squeezing railroads for desirable transportation deals. That battle would come to symbolize the anti-monopoly movement. But it would be 1911 before the U.S. Supreme Court finally dismantled the empire. By then, Flagler was two years away from his death and had already played out a triumphant second career as the man who built Florida.

In the late 1870s, Flagler and his wife, Mary, suffering from tuberculosis, made their first visit to Florida. They hoped the climate would improve her health. But Mary died in 1881. In June 1893, the 55-year-old Flagler married Ida Alice Shourds, Mary's companion. For their honeymoon, they came to St. Augustine. Flagler was struck by a vision of making the town "The Newport of the South" — an affluent resort to rival Rhode Island's playground of the rich.

Inspired by a festival honoring Juan Ponce de León, who in 1513 had claimed Florida for Spain, Flagler decided to build a hotel. At the time, Flagler, still involved with Standard, saw Florida as almost a hobby. But soon his relationship with the booming state had become far more compelling.

Even as the $2.5 million, four-story, 450-room Hotel Ponce de Leon, then the largest concrete structure in the world, was opening its doors, Henry Flagler was buying up more land in St. Augustine. But the fates were unkind to America's first city. On January 1, 1886, the high of 22 was only eight degrees warmer than the high in Manhattan. A yellow fever epidemic in 1888 led to a poor 1889 season.

Flagler had already begun moving his railroad south. His impetus came from the state; to encourage settlement, it had already been promising 3,800 acres for every mile of track laid. Now, it was upping the ante to 8,000 acres for every mile built south of Daytona Beach. Considering what now lies on either side of Flagler's tracks, which run along U.S. 1, the deal was an advantageous one — probably for both sides.

As Henry Flagler was setting up shop in St. Augustine, Palm Beach was an isolated settlement of 30 to 40 cottages. Less than 1,000 residents were reported living between the St. Lucie River and Key West.

Flagler had been irritated from the start by the lack of railroad service in Florida. The tracks then ended at the St. Johns River in Jacksonville, and St. Augustine could be reached only by ocean passage or by floating down the St. Johns to a landing, then by a small railroad east 15 miles to the coast.

Flagler built a bridge across the St. Johns, linking the peninsula with the rest of the country for the first time. His first rail move to the south was to Ormond Beach. He bought the Hotel Ormond, tore down the natural pines, and replaced them with palmettos. Then, between June 1892 and February 1893, he extended the railroad through Daytona Beach to New Smyrna Beach, Titusville, Cocoa, and finally, Rockledge.

From those stops, his steamship line would take people to his next potential resort, the place to which his tracks were inching. He had first visited Palm Beach — clandestinely — in 1892 and returned to say he had found "a veritable paradise."

An 1894 publication described the area as "the Orient and the Occident rivaled. The climax of the great American Riviera. Far excelling that of the Old World. Perpetual spring, tempered by the breezes of old ocean on the east and the health-giving pampas on the west...a union of all that is lovely in nature, art, and luxury, and yet not the half is told!"

He would eventually buy about 100 acres for $300,000. There, he decided to build a hotel. As he broke ground on May 1, 1893, his railroad and construction workers began a race. The hotel won.

The Royal Poinciana

The Royal Poinciana cost Flagler more than a million dollars. It was advertised as the world's largest wooden resort hotel. A thousand workers and artisans had labored on it, completing it in only nine months. As many as 20 died rushing to build it. Materials made an arduous journey through the wilderness via train and boat.

Environmental concerns were unheard of at the time. Workers dumped thousands of carloads of dirt to fill in swamps and marshlands. They planted rows and rows of Australian pines, now recognized as one of Florida's greatest pest trees.

"Like a myth from the Arabian nights, rising at the touch of a modern Aladdin, the Royal Poinciana has grown upon the shore of beautiful Lake Worth in the marvelous short space of nine months," reads a program published for the hotel's opening season. On the day the Poinciana opened, in February 1894, it had 17 guests and one big no-show: a railroad.

At the time, the 35-hour train trek from the northeast came to a stop at Fort Pierce. The next leg was a 50-mile, 14-hour ride to Jupiter in a 22-passenger stern wheeler, followed by a ride on the narrow-gauge Celestial Railroad, which linked Juno to Lake Worth, then by small motorboat to West Palm Beach and by flat-bottom steamer across to the island. It would be two months before the line was completed to West Palm Beach and more than two years before a wooden railroad spur — now the Flagler Memorial Bridge — crossed the lake to the front door of the Royal Poinciana.

Once Henry Flagler had pointed across the lake to the west and said, "In a few years, there will be a town there as big as Jacksonville." He had bought a 45,000-acre site and laid out an entire town on 200 acres, set in a grid with streets named alphabetically for plants: Banyan, Clematis, Datura. He said he was building a city "for my help." West Palm Beach began as a giant servant's quarters, freeing up the island for the beautiful people.

Flushed with the success of the Poinciana, Flagler had almost immediately begun his next project, the Palm Beach Inn. It opened for the 1896 winter season. In 1901, he doubled its size and gave it a name, for a well-known Rhode Island resort: The Breakers.

Just two years later, The Breakers burned. Insured for only $100,000, its loss was estimated at $400,000. Only two weeks later, Flagler insisted he would rebuild, and he did. Misfortune would strike again when the hotel, nearly restored, burned again. But he somehow got it open for the 1904 season. And the clientele came. They were among "The 400," the cream of the Gilded Age's Northern society. They included Vanderbilts, Belmonts, and Astors. They paid as little as $6 and as much as $100 a night to stay at Flagler's hotels. They basked in luxury, attending extravagant banquets and balls late into the evening, with copious 12-course menus to overwhelm the heartiest gourmand.

From 11 A.M. to 1 P.M. — and only at those times — guests far too dressed for bathing lounged at the beach. At 4 P.M., they gathered for afternoon tea at the Coconut Grove, a wooded area on the hotel's southwest side. In the evening, they dressed full-tilt to watch black employees dance the cakewalk. For several years, not a single one of those newfangled automobiles was permitted on the island. Guests traveled via bicycle, horseback, donkey-pulled trolley, or the Afromobiles.

Guests enjoyed the paradox of lounging at a society resort just a few yards from a rapidly vanishing jungle. An alligator farm operated on the present site of the Everglades Golf Course. Mules carried people for walks through lush forests. And wildcats were killed within earshot of the hotel.

While the season would later be extended, at that time it began around New Year's Day and came to a climax on Washington's birthday, February 22. Within a few days the hotels would be deserted. Meanwhile, Flagler had opened a new world, and speculators and investors poured into Florida. Raw land rocketed in value; an 1896 hotel program says land was selling for $1,000 to $15,000 an acre, while 40 miles to the south, in what is now the Fort Lauderdale area, it went for as little as $1.25 an acre.

Back in St. Augustine, hard freezes in 1894 and 1895 had weakened the tourist trade and demolished North Florida's citrus industry. Flagler had sent an assistant from Palm Beach down to the pioneer settlement at Biscayne Bay. One of its leaders, Julia Tuttle, showed the man how the frost hadn't reached Miami, which was in full triumphant bloom. The two collected a bouquet of flowers, which Flagler's assistant brought back to St. Augustine.

Flagler was impressed, but he believed Miami would never be more than a fishing village. He built a hotel there anyway. It is probably a leap to say Julia Tuttle's symbolic act alone convinced him to come to Miami. There was a far more substantive enticement. Tuttle gave Flagler more than half her land — property now covering most of downtown Miami and of incalculable value.

Whitehall

Even as Flagler was reveling in his public success, his private life was heading in the other direction. The mental health of his wife, Ida, appeared to be deteriorating, and there were several embarrassing public displays. She showed a doctor pebbles she said would cure paralysis and make sterile women pregnant, and she said she was in love with the czar of Russia, whom she'd never met. Flagler finally had her placed in an upstate New York mental institution and declared insane.

In the meantime, he had become involved with Mary Lily Kenan, daughter of a prominent North Carolina family. But New York and Florida laws allowed for divorce only on grounds of adultery. Flagler opted to file in Florida, then lobbied the Legislature to soften its divorce laws. There was an uproar when charges were leveled that Flagler had bribed legislators, but the bill became law, and Flagler married Mary Kenan in 1901. The next year, he built Whitehall for her.

Whitehall opened January 26, 1902, signaling the start of Mary Lily's first season as Mrs. Flagler. Her husband, meanwhile, had one last accomplishment in mind before his long life came to an end: the monumental task of building a 128-mile-long railroad through the sea to link the mainland with the isolated island of Key West.

The railroad, at the time one of America's largest privately financed engineering projects, cost Flagler $20 million, two-fifths of Flagler's total Florida investment. Detractors called it "Flagler's Folly." But in 1912, after seven years of work by 3,000 to 4,000 men, the railroad had come to Key West. While *The Miami Herald* would call it the eighth wonder of the world, critics who said the railroad would never pay for itself were eventually proven right, and the wonder would last less than a quarter century before it was demolished by the 1935 Labor Day hurricane and replaced by the Overseas Highway.

But on that glorious day in January 1912, a stooped and weak Flagler made a triumphant entrance to a frenzied Key West, where he was overcome by the welcome and the import of the moment.

The Godfather of Florida

While his friend John Rockefeller was trying to make it to age 100 in Ormond Beach — he failed by three years in 1937 — Flagler was also falling victim to age. His hearing and eyesight were failing. He had became introspective and lonely, and would be seen sitting silent and alone in a rocking chair or in one of his infamous Afromobiles.

A year later, in January 1913, while entering a first-floor bathroom around the side from Whitehall's dramatic lobby stairway, he failed to negotiate the high step down and fell, breaking his hip. He would later slip into a coma. His son, Harry, who had not seen his father since he married Mary Kenan 12 years earlier, rushed to his side, but he never regained consciousness. Flagler died May 20, 1913, at 83 in the cottage adjoining Whitehall.

Flagler had bought the current site of Woodlawn Cemetery in West Palm Beach, then a pineapple grove, and deeded it to the city. But Flagler was reportedly furious when West Palm Beach tried to annex Palm Beach in 1911, forcing the island settlement to itself quickly incorporate. So the man who put Miami and Palm Beach on the map was buried instead in St. Augustine, next to the Flagler Memorial Presbyterian Church. He lay in state at his Ponce de Leon Hotel in St. Augustine; strangely, none of his Standard Oil colleagues attended. Then he was buried in the cemetery. His first wife, Mary Flagler, and his daughter, Jennie, with her stillborn baby in her arms, had all been buried there earlier.

The reading of Flagler's will would reveal an estate valued at $100 million.

"I have spoken of the godfather of this state. May the state of

Florida recognize his benefits," Rev. George Morgan Ward said at services a year later in Palm Beach's Royal Poinciana Chapel. "I have spoken of one of the great men of history. The coming years will make clear how wise was his judgment. . . ."

Henry Flagler's Legacy

After his death, Flagler's Long Island estate was sold to film director D. W. Griffith. In 1924, Whitehall was sold by Mary Lily's heir, her niece, Louise Clisby Wise. In 1926, ten stories were added, and the mansion became a luxury hotel. In the 1940s, the hotel tower behind the mansion was torn down.

The Breakers caught fire again in March 1925, and burned to the ground; flames spread to another Flagler property, the Palm Beach hotel, and burned it as well. It was again rebuilt, with 1,200 workers and $6 million. It still stands as the grand dame of a former era.

The great 1928 hurricane hit the Royal Poinciana hard, especially in the north wing; an engine room was reduced to rubble, and the building was twisted from its foundation. The garishly leaning structure was razed and rebuilt in time for the 1929 season, but the hotel was still forced to undergo its first season without a Washington's Birthday ball. The hotel, however, could not overcome a man-made catastrophe: the Depression. Hampered by the declining economy and the emergence of a new breed of wealthy Americans not steeped in society, the Poinciana held its last ball in 1931.

" . . . while we regret the necessity of having to reach the decision regarding the Hotel Royal Poinciana, it would not be good judgment to open that house unless there would be a sudden change in conditions throughout the country," a hotel official wrote to the Palm Beach Chamber of Commerce in October 1932.

Just before Labor Day of 1935 — tragically, days before Henry Flagler's railroad to Key West would itself lay in shambles — his demolished Royal Poinciana Hotel was a pile of splinters enveloped in haze and smoke. It would live on when its wood was used to build 500 houses. On its site, a residence tower now stands.

In 1960, a historical marker was erected at the old Poinciana site to identify the spot where Palm Beach was born. Just a few feet away, the tall, white pillars of Whitehall stand in tribute to the town's patriarch.

The Henry Morrison Flagler Museum (Whitehall) is at One Whitehall Way in Palm Beach. Write Box 969, Palm Beach 33480. Call (561) 665-2833. Website: www.flaglermuseum.us

From downtown West Palm Beach, take Flagler Memorial (middle) Bridge to Palm Beach, then south on Cocoanut Row to the first traffic light; the museum is on the right. Museum open 10 A.M. to 5 P.M. Tuesday through Saturday, noon to 5 P.M. Sunday. Adults, $15; 13 to 18, $8; 6 to 12, $3; under 6 free. Group rates available.

Palm Beach Chamber of Commerce: 400 Royal Palm Way, #106, Palm Beach 33480. Call (561) 655-3282. Website: www. palmbeachchamber.com

Read More About It

Amory, Cleveland. *Florida, the Last Resorts*. 1952, New York, Harper.

Akin, Edward N. *Flagler: Rockefeller Partner and Florida Baron*. 1988, Kent, Ohio, Kent State University Press.

Curl, Donald W. *Palm Beach County, An Illustrated History*. 1986, Northridge, Cal., Windsor Publications.

Martin, Sidney Walter. *Florida's Flagler*. 1949, Athens, Ga., University of Georgia Press.

McIver, Stuart. *Yesterday's Palm Beach*. 1976, Miami, Seeman Publishing.

Boca Raton Resort and Club

Boca Raton

Pretty in pink

Boca Raton and Palm Beach are two different places; you need only eyeball their prevalent colors. Henry Flagler painted Palm Beach canary yellow. When Addison Cairns Mizner went south to create Boca Raton, he wanted his own tint. So he did everything in pink. That included his hotel, now the Boca Raton Resort & Club.

Mizner, who grew up in California, had developed an interest in Spanish architecture while in Guatemala with his missionary father. Later, while building country homes on Long Island, he met Paris Singer, part of the sewing machine family empire. Singer invited him down to Palm Beach in 1918. Soon Mizner was one of the wealthy island enclave's most sought architects. In all, Mizner would design or build 67 structures in Palm Beach, another 11 in other parts of the county, and 27 in Boca Raton.

When Mizner decided to branch from designing to developing, he looked to Boca, then a tiny settlement 20 miles south of Palm Beach. Mizner was the brains of the operation; his brother Wilson, the salesman. The two bought 17,000 acres with the idea of creating the "greatest resort in the world." Today, the value of that acreage — the equivalent of 27 square miles — is too dizzying to contemplate. But even then, the brothers, riding the boom, were at one point doing $2 million in sales — in 1920s dollars — per *week*.

To draw potential buyers, Mizner spent $1.25 million to build the Cloister Inn, then the costliest 100-room hotel ever built. It opened in February 1926. Part of the entertainment was Mizner himself. He thought nothing of walking the resort in silk pajamas, parading on his shoulder his pet monkey Johnnie Brown or a pet macaw and leading

203

his two chows. The Cloister's glory days lasted less than a year before the boom busted and so did the Mizner brothers. Mizner Development was taken over in July 1926 and eventually fell into bankruptcy. Addison would die in February 1933, Wilson two months later.

Utilities magnate Clarence Geist, an early Mizner investor, bought the Cloister in 1928 and spent $8 million on renovations, reopening it two years later as the Boca Raton Club. Geist pumped money into the resort to keep it going during the Depression; by the time he died in 1938, the property was four times its original size.

The place got a special batch of guests during World War II, as it housed officers from the nearby Boca Raton Army Air Field, now the Boca Raton municipal airport and Florida Atlantic University campus.

Hotelier and theater magnate J. Myer Schine then bought the resort at a fire-sale price of $3 million, refurbished it, and opened it in 1945 as the Boca Raton Hotel and Club. Eleven years later, it became part of the Arvida empire. Arthur Vining Davis, a founder of the ALCOA aluminum company, bought it from Schine for $22.5 million; at the time, it was the biggest real estate deal in Florida history.

Meanwhile, Davis was buying up large pieces of Boca Raton. They now include some of the area's most luxurious neighborhoods. Myrtle Butts, whose family bean fields were bought by Arvida and eventually became some of those neighborhoods, remarked in 1993, "We sold it by the acre. It's sold by the inch now."

The resort's ownership passed to separate investment firms in 1983 and 1993, and in 1997 it became, of all things, a subsidiary of a hockey franchise. H. Wayne Huizenga, the Blockbuster video rental giant and owner of the Miami Dolphins football team, Florida Marlins baseball team, and Florida Panthers hockey team, bought the resort for $325 million. In 2004, an affiliate of the Blackstone Group private investment banking firm bought the resort and its four Florida sister properties for $1.2 billion. The following year, it launched a $140 billion refurbishment.

The resort still sports Mizner's trademark Spanish Mediterranean, Moorish, and Gothic influences with hidden gardens, barrel tile roofs, archways, ornate columns, fountains, and beamed cypress. But it's now part of a sprawling complex that sports more than a thousand rooms and an abundance of amenities on 356 prime coastal acres southeast of downtown Boca Raton. There's the original hotel, along with a yacht club, a hotel tower, and condos. There are also a beach

Gates to the Boca Raton Resort and Club, circa 1940. *Florida State Archives*

club, yacht club, and country club. There are two conference halls, two golf courses, 30 tennis courts, a spa, six pools, an indoor basketball court, a 32 slip marina, and a half mile wide private beach.

One of the hotel's unique features is a room with a pool under the floorboards. After Geist bought the Cloister, he brought in the famous architect team of Schultze and Weaver to expand the resort. Geist had an indoor salt water pool installed. But in south Florida, no one needed to swim indoors when they could do it outdoors even in the winter. In 1938, Geist had the pool covered with a wooden floor and created a room that was an auditorium and theater. It later became a conference room called the Valencia Room. At 2,900 square feet, it holds 140 people.

The Boca Raton Resort & Club is on Camino Real between U.S. 1 and State Road A1A. Exit Interstate 95 east to U.S. 1, south about a half mile to Camino Real, then east to the traffic circle. Write 501 East Camino Real, Boca Raton 33431. Call (888) 478-2822. Website: www. bocaresort.com.

Read More About It
Curl, Donald, and John P. Johnson. *Boca Raton: A Pictorial History*.
    1990, Virginia Beach, Donning Co.

Alligator Alley

An adventurous trek acorss the Everglades

The 79-mile-long Alligator Alley is no longer Alligator Alley. Not officially, anyway. In March 1993, contractors wrapped up a seven-year project to change it from a deadly two-lane configuration to a safer, divided four-lane highway. Although mapmakers say they'll still include the name, the road south Florida loved and hated for nearly a quarter century is now just another stretch of Interstate 75, a 1,787-mile superhighway from Michigan to Miami. But to those who have crossed it, it will always be The Alley.

The road has been a romantic route through old Florida since it opened in 1969. Motorists can gaze at the Everglades stretching to the horizon on either side, undisturbed by towns, buildings, or billboards.

They might see thick black clouds of mosquitoes or mating love bugs, black crows perched atop fences, or white egrets and blue herons soaring lazily over algae-covered pools. They might see one of the road's namesake alligators sunning on a bank or submerged in a waterway with only its eyes and nostrils showing. And, until fencing across The Alley's length was completed, they might have had to dodge gators casually waddling over the road or a rare Florida panther dashing across or the remains of animals that didn't make it.

They might see buzzards swoop for a road kill, pick at it, and wait until cars are almost upon them before sharply winging away in a dangerous game of buzzard's "chicken." They might find their way blocked by blinding brush fires so fierce the pavement crawls with snakes flushed from the bush by the heat and smoke.

But the old two-lane, a pitch-black, unlit highway, was also a killing ground where a careless or dozing or drunken driver would drift across the yellow stripe of paint and slam into a vehicle hurtling the other way. The deep canals on either side, formed by workers gouging out earth to elevate the highway out of the swamp, gave motorists no escape. Hundreds have died, many in head-on crashes. Agencies don't have fatality totals for The Alley, but the Florida Department of Transportation and the Florida Highway Patrol report 94 deaths just between 1986 and 1993.

For more than 20 years, John Herl watched from his perch at South Florida Water Management District pump station S-140, atop a dike, about a third of the way from Fort Lauderdale to Naples.

"I've seen more head-ons and people killed on the road," Herl says. He dreads the fog and the smoke from the Everglades fires, which can leave motorists blinded. "We had a camper crash once," Herl says. "It went over the bridge. Dropped 20 feet. Somebody had crossed the line. It had no place to go."

"They Ruined It"

In the 1960s, with environmentalism not yet a force in Florida, opposition to carving a highway through the Everglades focused mostly on practicality. It made no sense to spend $17 million extending State Road 84 across the southern peninsula, opponents argued, when motorists already had two routes to the west coast — Tamiami Trail from Miami and State Road 80 from West Palm Beach. The state first called its project the Everglades Parkway. Detractors snidely suggested Swamp Pike, Alligator Lane, and, finally, Alligator Alley. That stuck and became the official name during five painstaking years of construction.

Even as it opened in 1969, The Alley's extinction was already in the works. For decades, I-75 snaked through the Midwest and South before coming to a dead end in Tampa. Even in the 1960s, planners saw The Alley becoming part of it. In the 1980s, a series of projects extended I-75 from Tampa to Naples and a section was built in Dade and Broward Counties that connected to existing expressways. Starting in 1986, the two lanes of the old Alley were made eastbound, and two new lanes were built to the north, with a grassy median between. The work was completed in November

1992. The last project was the installation of fences on both sides of The Alley — a requirement of all interstate highways. The fences also protect wildlife from vehicles. Thirty-six underpasses in Collier County guide panthers and other wildlife beneath the road.

About halfway across the monotonous Alley, the air-conditioned Miccosukee Service Plaza's giant sign rises out of nowhere, beckoning weary motorists. It is the oasis of the entire stretch. Cars line up at pumps outside the facility, which is privately operated on Miccosukee land under a contract with the tribe. Inside, travelers browse the combination convenience store, delicatessen, and diner. It offers the usual tourist wares: belts, postcards, license plates, beef jerky, and little wooden alligators and pelicans. Atop the deli counter, a sign inside the jaws of a real stuffed alligator head says: "Try our delicious sandwiches. Nobody likes a coward." A giant stuffed shark hangs from the ceiling. On the wall are paintings of Indians — not Seminoles or Miccosukees, but western Indians.

Once a hunter came in who had shot himself in the foot. Once a resident of the reservation who was in labor got as far as the parking lot. Sometimes motorists stranded by disabled cars stay overnight in the 24-hour diner; sometimes they stay two or three days, waiting to be rescued by friends.

"Sometimes they don't have enough (toll) money to get across. Sometimes they have to borrow money," says Cecilia Tigertail, a Seminole from the nearby Big Cypress Reservation. Grateful motorists may leave pagers or driver licenses as collateral and always promise to mail the money back, Tigertail says. She says most do.

Just behind the service plaza, where dust leads to mud and then to standing water, a rusting contest is under way. The contestants: pipes, oxygen tanks, and several vehicles — a blue sedan, trailers, a pickup on concrete blocks — abandoned by motorists and stripped by vehicular cannibals.

At the west end of the road, the expressway is a mostly vertical line on the map all the way to Michigan. On the east-west Alley, Interstate 75 signs saying "north" or "south" have been bureaucratically correct but geographically inaccurate.

While it cost more than $189 million just to four-lane The Alley — 11 times the original $17 million to build it — $151.2 million of that money came from Washington, D.C. The original state bond issue was paid off in 1984, years ahead of its planned date of 1991. But the tolls

Alligator Alley tollbooth
Florida Department of Transportation

This well-known sign once lined Alligator
Alley. *Florida Department of Transportation*

— the only ones on the 1,787-mile length of I-75 — will stay in place into the twenty-first century, to pay for maintenance and to cover the $21 million the state spent on the wildlife underpasses. Everyone paid 75 cents at one end and another 75 cents at the other when The Alley opened in 1969. Starting in 1999, the toll was collected once, $1.50 as motorists entered. In 2006, for the first time since the Alley opened, the Florida Department of Transportation upped the toll, raising it to $2.50.

One untarnished "Alligator Alley" sign hangs in the Fort Lauderdale office of Barbara Kelleher, public information director for the Florida Department of Transportation's District Four. Knowing it would have sentimental value, she grabbed it from the warehouse several years ago before it was posted on the highway. As they finished up, contractors took the last of the signs — rusted, worn, and full of bullet holes — from the road.

"But," Kelleher says, "everybody still refers to it as The Alley. And I think they always will."

The Night Andytown Died

More than a quarter century after Andytown fell under the bulldozer, maps still identify the spot at the corner of Alligator Alley and U.S. 27. The town never had more than 11 official residents, but it became an oasis for truckers, hunters, and fishermen.

The sounds, sights, and smells of Greece always seemed out of place in south Florida's western frontier, where people are more likely to hear country music blaring from a pickup. The bar that was the town's centerpiece was never fancy; it had the usual Formica tables, pinball machines, and illuminated beer signs. A sign over the bar said: "This is the town that Andy built. God Bless Andy."

Andy Poulos had come to the deserted crossroads at the edge of the Everglades in 1947. Twenty miles east lay the growing town of Fort Lauderdale. Andy bought ten acres, including an existing coffee shop and gas station, for $50,000.

The place became a running joke in south Florida. Television weathermen would give its forecast. Newspaper editors would victimize new reporters by assigning them to take a ride out there and find out what was on the city council agenda.

Andy took on nephew Konstantinos "Gus" Tsanos and John Theodore as partners in 1963. They took over Andytown when Andy died in 1972. In 1967, the Florida Department of Transportation bought Andytown for $180,000. Its buildings would eventually be knocked down to make way for an expressway interchange.

Closing night came on Halloween 1979. Tsanos and Theodore, their wives, their barmaid, and a crush of friends packed the place. The liquor flowed for free. Tsanos wept. The next morning — November 1, 1979 — Tsanos handed the state the keys to Andytown. The owners vowed it would rise from the ashes somewhere else on State Road 84. They opened a restaurant and a bar about a mile from each other and several miles east of the old site. They eventually sold the restaurant; now the only legacy is Andy's Lounge, a small establishment in the shadow of I-595 in western Fort Lauderdale. The original Andytown highway sign still hangs on the bar's wall. And the town, long gone, is still on the map.

Alligator Alley runs 79 miles from western Broward County to just east of Naples.

Florida Department of Transportation: 3400 W. Commercial Blvd., Fort Lauderdale 33309. Call (954) 486-1400 or (866) 336-8435. Website: www.dot.state.fl.us

Greater Fort Lauderdale Convention and Visitors Bureau: 100 E Broward Blvd, Suite 200, Fort Lauderdale 33301. Call (800) 22-SUNNY (227 8669). Website: www.sunny.org

Greater Naples Marco Island Everglades Convention and Visitors Bureau: 3050 N Horseshoe Dr, Suite 218, Naples 34104. Call (800) 688-3600. Website: www.paradisecoast.com

Read More About It

Burghard, August. *Alligator Alley, Florida's most controversial highway.* 1969, Washington, Lanman Co.

Stranahan House

Fort Lauderdale

The little house in the big city

As the city grew around it, Stranahan House has stood, since the beginning, on the New River. Fort Lauderdale's oldest structure stands as a monument to Frank Stranahan, considered the city's founder, and to Ivy Stranahan, who survived her husband's economic ruin and suicide and saw the city emerge as a metropolis.

Frank had come from Ohio in 1893 to establish a ferry crossing across the New River for the Bay Biscayne Stage Line, along the road from Lantana to North Miami. He'd been invited by his cousin, Guy Metcalf, publisher of one of the region's early newspapers and the first superintendent of Palm Beach County schools.

Ivy Julia Cromartie came from north Florida to Miami's Lemon City, then came to Fort Lauderdale in 1899 to work as the city's first schoolteacher. She was 18.

It was in 1901, a decade before Fort Lauderdale incorporated, that Frank picked the spot on the river for his trading post. Frank served settlers and Seminoles alike. Soon the place was a post office, a community center, and a town hall. Frank became a renaissance man, simultaneously wearing the hat of postmaster, banker, and businessman. He met and wed Ivy a year after she arrived. Soon the building's upper floor hosted dances, festivals, and community events. In 1906, it became the couple's personal home.

Ivy was an abstainer and convinced Frank not to sell alcohol. When the plume trade almost wiped out area birds, she convinced Frank not to sell the accessories. She was an ardent suffragette. And

212

Stranahan House.

she spent much of her life befriending, teaching, and fighting for area Seminoles.

Like many of his contemporaries in the real estate boom, Frank Stranahan roller-coastered from prosperity to collapse. He went from millionaire to a broken man. And he was devastated that friends who'd invested with him had also been wiped out. In 1929, deep in debt and stricken with cancer, he tied a piece of metal to himself and, just behind his pioneer home, leaped into his beloved New River.

Ivy, left an impoverished widow and all alone — the couple had no children — wore mourning clothes for a decade. For years, she stayed in the home's upstairs and leased the first floor for use as a restaurant. For decades, she used her influence as a city icon to keep the truth of her husband's death out of the local papers. Ivy died in 1971; two years later, the home was placed on the National Register of Historic Places. In 1979, the restaurant closed down. The property eventually was turned over to the Fort Lauderdale Historical Society.

The society and the Fort Lauderdale Board of Realtors undertook a major restoration. Stranahan House now looks much as it did in the 1910s. Even then, it had electric wiring, indoor plumbing, and running water, as well as interior stairways, bay windows, and wide porches. Its hardy Dade County pine has seen it through many a storm, but over the years most of its original furniture was sold or given away. It's now stocked with period furniture.

The historic home, with its white exterior and green trim, is now the eastern bookend of River Walk, a waterfront park connecting Fort Lauderdale's historic district with a cultural district that includes the Broward Center for the Performing Arts and the Museum of Discovery and Science.

And ghost hunters claim Frank and Ivy both haunt the place.

Stranahan House is at Las Olas Boulevard in downtown Fort Lauderdale. Follow Interstate 95 to Broward Boulevard, then east to U.S. 1. Bear right before tunnel and follow signs to Las Olas. The house is directly ahead. Write 335 S.E. 6th Ave., Ft. Lauderdale 33301. Call (954) 524-4736. Website: www.stranahanhouse.org

Hours: 10:00 A.M. to 3:00 P.M. Wednesday through Saturday; 1:00 P.M. to 3:00 P.M. Sunday. Tours given on the hour, last tour starts at 3:00 P.M. Admission: $10 for adults, $9 senior citizens, children $5. Call ahead about group tours.

Read More About It
Kersey, Harry A. *The Stranahans of Fort Lauderdale: A pioneer family of New River*. 2003, Gainesville, University Press of Florida.

Hialeah Race Track

Hialeah

The pink lady of racing

Where will the flamingos go?

Hialeah Race Track, Florida's grand old dame of horse racing, is a far cry from its halcyon days when it was virtually a synonym for the sport of kings. Back then it was a blur of pink: striped awnings, clubhouse, tablecloths, napkins, carnations. Tuxedo-clad waiters served giant stone crab claws and strawberries. Admirers called it "the lady." The lady continues to hang on.

The track's design, which won an award at the 1936 Paris exposition, was so magnificent some bettors found it distracting. Longtime sports writer John Crittenden, who wrote a history of the track, says that, compared to Hialeah, playing other tracks was "like shooting craps in the back of a filling station."

Drawing the top horses, jockeys, and trainers, it also attracted the glitterati of society, entertainment, sports, and politics. A special train, the Biltmore Special, took Palm Beach socialites down to Miami and, via a spur, to the front of the race track. Its 40-day racing season marked the peak of the social season.

The facility, built on a 200-acre site by the Miami Jockey Club, opened January 25, 1925, at the height of Miami's real estate heyday. A crowd of 7,000 attended. By May, the state legislature had declared gambling a felony and called for a five-year prison term and the then-hefty fine of $5,000. But the track operated with no scrutiny save some winks.

The 1926 hurricane that killed Miami's boom — killing 242

215

Hialeah Race Track's beloved flamingos. *Hialeah Race Track*

people and destroying 5,000 homes — wiped out a third of the town of Hialeah, and while the track suffered little damage, its local and tourist clientele plummeted. Another blow came a year later, when the Florida Supreme Court strengthened its ban on betting, closing the track for the season. The track returned in 1929, finding a way to keep operating. It sold postcards of horses. If the horse on your card won, it bought the card back at a premium price that just happened to match the winning odds.

By 1930, with a new owner and with gambling again legal, the track began its climb toward fame. Hialeah was the first to use a photo-finish camera with a mirror, the first to use the totalizator system in which the money bet set the odds, the first to use a horse identification system, and the first to use a saliva test for doping. The facility was sidetracked only when the White House shut it down during World War II.

Changes in the surrounding neighborhood contributed to the track's decline. The state briefly considered buying the track as a historical and tourism landmark, but abandoned the idea as too costly. By the mid-1970s, it entered a series of bidding wars and spitting matches over racing dates, the lifeblood of south Florida's competing tracks. Shut out of favorable dates for the 1989-90 season, it shut down for 23 months.

In the fall of 1991, the track reached an agreement with Calder, next to Joe Robbie Stadium in northern Dade County, and Gulfstream, a little farther north in Hallandale. Hialeah, with the early spring dates, was still in business, but only as a remnant of its colorful past.

The track shut down altogether in 2001 when it lost its permit after it failed to get the Legislature to continue regulating racing dates so it could race competition-free. In the summer of 2005, track owners were unable to get courts to restore the permit and said they were pursuing rezoning the property for commercial or residential use. But lovers of Hialeah said they were trying to get the track declared a National Historic Landmark in hopes of saving it.

Hialeah Race Track is at N.W. 79 Street, about two miles west of Interstate 95 and one mile east of the Palmetto Expressway. Write 2200 E. 4 Ave., Hialeah 33013. Call (305) 885-8000.

Greater Miami Convention and Visitors Bureau: 701 Brickell Ave, Suite 2700, Miami 33131. Call (800) 933-8448. Website: www. gmcvb.com

Read More About It
Crittenden, John. *Hialeah Park: A Racing Legend.* 1989, Miami, Pickering Press.

Orange Bowl

Miami

More than football

Leftover American Legion bleachers started it. Presidents spoke in it. Rockers rocked in it. Millions have become Americans in it. Broadway Joe guaranteed and delivered in it. The Dolphins moved out of it. And a multitude of Cuban exiles is expected to swarm it for the greatest fiesta of the century if and when their favorite villain falls from power. He's not invited.

It was born Roddey Burdine stadium in 1937, and it has stood in the same spot, in many forms, since Miami's boom years. It has seen better days, to be sure. But the Orange Bowl is still the grand dame of Florida stadiums.

And when the annual New Year's Day gala that showcases south Florida to the freezing north played its 62nd game on January 1, 1996, it was the last time The Orange Bowl would be played in the Orange Bowl. Traditionalists cried foul in 1994 when the Orange Bowl executive committee voted to move the New Year's classic out of the arena for which it is named and up the road to Joe Robbie Stadium. Supporters of the move said the place was just too old, the neighborhood too run down, the access and parking too cramped.

But the stadium will be filled with plenty of other events. Miami High School has played there since the beginning, and the Bowl is the home of many other big Miami-Dade County high school games.

The Miami Dolphins called it home from their birth in 1966 until 1986, when they left for the new stadium named for their owner. In 1972, it was the home field for the National Football League's only perfect season. The University of Miami has played there since the college opened in 1926.

The first New Year's Day games were played in 1927. But they were not in the same league as California's Rose Bowl game. The first Palm Festival, forerunner to the Orange Bowl, was played in 1933 at Moore Park, a city park near Biscayne Boulevard with a makeshift 3,000-seat grandstand. The first game to bear the name "Orange Bowl Classic" and to be played at the stadium's current site — then called simply Miami Field — took place January 1, 1935. The University of Miami lost 26-0 to Bucknell in front of only 5,134 fans, many of whom walked in off the streets for free. They sat on 5,000 wooden parade-viewing bleachers bought by the city from an American

The Orange Bowl has hosted everything from football to political rallies. *Orange Bowl*

Legion national convention in 1934. A local promoter convinced the city he'd have enough motorcycle races and other events to justify the expense.

The father of the Orange Bowl was city recreation director Earnie Seiler, who pushed the Depression-era Works Progress Administration to pay for the stadium. He made the game the nationally renowned classic it is now and earned fame for his spectacular half-time shows. Because the WPA required that money be used only to upgrade existing facilities, the city had to build at the same spot. It took less than a year to build the $340,000, 23,330-seat steel and concrete stadium. It was dedicated December 10, 1937.

By 1948, the city had rejected a plan to build a new stadium at another site for $1.2 million. Instead, it added a second deck, expanding seating to 60,000. The following year, it got its current name: the Orange Bowl. The stadium, and the New Year's Day classic for which it was a showcase, had gone big-time.

The stadium got a lot of use. In 1956, legendary baseball showman Bill Veeck, owner of the minor-league Miami Marlins of the International League, brought a game into the Bowl. The round peg didn't fit easily into the rectangular hole; right field was only 216 feet and left field 250. Still, the event drew 51,713. In 1962, President Kennedy addressed 35,000 in the aftermath of the failed Bay of Pigs invasion of Cuba. He promised to return the Brigade 2506 flag to "a free Havana." And three years later, people filled the stadium to watch a giant television screen showing man walking in space.

The stadium got a million-dollar facelift the following year, and soon got something else: the Miami Dolphins, who began playing in 1966. A tank was built in the open east end zone; a dolphin from the *Flipper* television series was brought in for games from the nearby Seaquarium. He was trained to leap into the air after touchdowns and bat footballs from the tank with his nose after field-goals and point-after-touchdown kicks. The tank lasted two years.

In 1969, after a Doors concert at Coconut Grove's Dinner Key auditorium got out of hand, with lead singer Jim Morrison allegedly exposing himself, the stadium hosted about 30,000, most of them young people, for a "rally for decency" featuring entertainers Jackie Gleason and Anita Bryant.

The stadium even got into the movies. Portions of *Black Sunday*, in which terrorists attempt mass murder of fans at a Super Bowl game, were shot at the 1976 game. Other projects continued to increase seating; capacity for football actually dropped in 1977 from 80,010 to 75,153 when end zone bleacher seats were removed. It holds up to 82,000 for other events.

In 1992, the city of Miami, the stadium's owner, spent $21 million to upgrade the stadium. By then the Dolphins were already gone, lured in 1986 to northern Dade County by a sparkling new stadium. Dolphins owner Joe Robbie had built it when city voters balked at major upgrades or building a new stadium downtown.

City fathers say tearing the Orange Bowl down is not an option. Cuban-Americans have reportedly booked it for a giant rally the day Fidel Castro falls from power. Orange Bowl officials promise that whenever that is, the stadium will be waiting.

The Orange Bowl is at 1501 N.W. 3rd St. Miami 33125. Call (305) 643-7100. Website: www.orangebowlstadium.com

The stadium is just west of downtown Miami. From points east or west or the airport, take State Road 836 west to Northwest 12th Ave., then turn left (south) to N.W. 7 Street and turn right. Stadium is on the left.

Tri-Rail/MetroRail service available for University of Miami games and selected events. Guided tours available.

Read More About It

Smith, Loran. *Fifty Years on the Fifty: The Orange Bowl Story.* 1983, Charlotte, N.C., East Woods Press.

Freedom Tower

Miami

Florida's Ellis Island

Florida's version of the Statue of Liberty stands empty and rotting, a dead shell that once thrived with the teeming masses of south Florida's immigrant experience. From 1962 to 1974, the Freedom Tower was a processing center for the wave of Cubans fleeing Fidel Castro. Now Miami's first skyscraper, three-fourths of a century old and all alone, awaits its own rescue from a wave of lethargy and lawsuits.

The building started as a newspaper office. Ohio Governor James Cox, who ran for president as a Democrat in 1920 — his running mate was then-New York Governor Franklin Roosevelt — and lost to Warren G. Harding, then bought the *Miami Metropolis*, the city's first newspaper. He renamed it *The Miami Daily News*.

For his paper's headquarters, he hired architects Schultze and Weaver of New York, who also designed Biltmore hotels in Coral Gables, Los Angeles, and Atlanta. The 65,000-square-foot structure was completed in 1925. To commemorate its new building and the city's 29th anniversary, *The Miami News* published a commemorative 22-section, 504-page edition on July 26, 1925. It weighed seven and a half pounds; at the time it was the fattest newspaper in world history.

The 17-story tower, inspired by the fifteenth-century Giralda Tower in Seville, Spain, stood out on the skyline of fledgling Miami, visible to ships six miles out at sea. In its opulent lobby, a chandelier encircled a globe, representing the newspaper's ties to the world through the remarkable telegraph. Illustrations on elevator doors showed symbols of newspapers and the pioneer days of printing.

The News moved out in 1957. The building was dormant for five years. Then, in July 1962, the federal government, facing

Freedom Tower was Miami's Ellis Island. *Miami News*

overwhelming numbers of Cuban refugees, leased the four main floors of the empty building for what it called the Cuban Refugee Center. It got a new name: Freedom Tower. Over the next 12 years, 650,000 refugees passed through its doors. Castro stopped the Cuban Airlift in April 1973, and the center shut down again the following year.

It was then empty for another 14 years, even as other parts of downtown were rejuvenated in the booming 1980s. Critics dubbed the lonely edifice "The Dowager of the Boulevard." Rescue schemes came and went. In 1976, grateful Cuban refugees started a campaign to raise $2 million to buy the building for a cultural and trade center. Nothing came of it. Another group wanted to turn the building into a trade mart. The government worried about its structure as street people occupied it, building fires and stripping much of the interior.

The tower had a chance at a new life in late 1987; with great fanfare, a Saudi sheik who had paid $8.7 million for the building kicked off a renovation that would cost another $12 million. The sheik planned a private club, banquet hall, and private offices as part of a rejuvenation of that part of Biscayne Boulevard, for years a dead spot across from what is now Bayfront Marketplace. But the project stalled after only a few months of work. The sheik and a partner became embroiled in a lawsuit. In the meantime, marauders broke its windows and doors, and trashed the inside. The sheik later lost the building to bankruptcy.

A mysterious group based in the European duchy of Liechtenstein later bought the building and hired a Miami real estate agent and management firm to restore the tower to good condition and put it on the market. Miami-Dade Community College, which has a downtown campus just a few blocks away, expressed interest in making it a school of the arts. But the college couldn't meet the asking price.

Later, exile leader Jorge Mas Canosa bought the tower for $4 million, with plans to house the Cuban American National Foundation in it and make it a museum of the Cuban immigration experience. The Mas family eventually sank $14 million into renovations.

The Terra Group development firm bought the Freedom Tower in February 2005 for $38 million. According to published reports, Terra planned a $500 million project to wrap a 62-story condominium around the historic tower. The group said it would tear down the "back house," the part of the complex that once housed *The Miami News* presses and storage.

Terra also announced plans for a museum, to open in 2007, that would show the history of the building and its importance to local and American history.

The Freedom Tower is at 600 Biscayne Boulevard in downtown Miami. It is not currently open for visitors.

Freedom Square Foundation: Call (305) 372-9640. Website: www. freedomsquare.org

Greater Miami Chamber of Commerce: 1601 Biscayne Blvd., Miami 33132. Call (305) 350-7700. Website: www.greatermiami.com

Read More About It
Kleinberg, Howard. *Miami, The Way We Were*. 1989, Tampa, Surfside Publishing.

Vizcaya

Miami

Miami's exalted place

When Pope John Paul II made his historic visit to south Florida — first ever by a pontiff — in September 1987, one of the most lasting images was that of the pope and then-President Reagan walking among the magnificent foliage, architecture, and adornments of Vizcaya. The word, from Spain's mysterious Basque language, translates to "high place," a fitting description of the stunning 34-room Italian renaissance villa sitting on 28 acres along Biscayne Bay — itself named for Spain's Bay of Biscay. The house, tucked into a neighborhood adjacent to downtown Miami, is now a museum displaying 2,000 years of European art history. It hosts about 185,000 visitors a year.

As with Whitehall, the former Palm Beach residence of Henry Flagler, one walks through Vizcaya both marveling at the magnificence and wondering how anyone might have used it as a normal home. It's impossible to imagine kids racing down its marbled halls.

About 1,000 workers — one in ten Miamians at the time — toiled from 1914 to 1916 to build a winter home for James Deering of Chicago, founder of the International Harvester farm machine empire. The use of local limestone gave the place a Florida look and feel. Deering roamed across Europe, studying architecture and collecting art; he was especially influenced by country homes in northern Italy's Veneto region, which surrounds Venice. His idea was for Vizcaya to appear as a sixteenth-century Italian estate that had been occupied by several generations for 400 years.

Miami's dramatic Vizcaya estate. *Vizcaya*

Ten acres of formal gardens surround the building. World War I delayed completion of the gardens until 1921. The estate's famed European fountains are surrounded by sculptures and urns. The attraction also features a small café and gift shop.

Deering died in 1925, and the great hurricane the following year caused extensive damage. His heirs tried to operate the estate as an attraction but later sold off much of the land. Dade County bought it in 1952 for $1 million in revenue bonds; the family donated its contents.

While the cool breezes from adjacent Biscayne Bay allowed for Vizcaya's high ceilings and open courtyard to perform natural air conditioning, they also carried salt spray and humidity for decades, forcing several renovation projects. The open-air building was enclosed and air-conditioned in 1987. In 1992, Hurricane Andrew destroyed two small gardens, blew some statues off the Great Stone Barge situated ten feet offshore, and caused a reported $1 million in flood damage, little of it visible. The home and gardens and barge have now been repaired. Vizcaya reopened two months after the storm.

Vizcaya is sometimes confused with the Deering Estate, about 20 miles to the south in the Cutler Ridge neighborhood. The estate, built by Deering's half-brother Charles Deering in 1922 and 1923, covers about 400 acres and is one of the largest natural areas maintained by Miami-Dade County. A wooden building constructed in the 1890s in the original Cutler settlement later became the Richmond Inn and was expanded twice in the ensuing decade. Deering built his three-story stone house, facing the bay, and connected it to the wooden structure. He died in 1927, but his family held on to the property until 1985, when they sold it to the state. The estate, close to Andrew's landfall, suffered extensive damage in the storm — especially the wooden buildings — and closed as an attraction indefinitely.

Vizcaya Museum and Gardens is at 3251 S. Miami Ave., just south of downtown Miami (33129). Call (305) 250-9133. Take Interstate 95 to Exit 1A and follow signs. Open 9:30 A.M. to 4:30 P.M. Adults, $12; Miami-Dade County residents: $9. Children 6 to 12, $5, under 6 free. Web page: www.vizcayamuseum.org

Greater Miami Convention and Visitors Bureau: 701 Brickell Ave., Suite 2700, Miami 33131. Call (800) 933-8448 or (305) 539-3000. Website: www.gmcvb.com

Read More About It
Harwood, Kathryn Chapman. *The Lives of Vizcaya: Annals of a Great House*. 1985, Miami, Banyan.
Littlefield, Doris Bayley. *Vizcaya*. 1983, Miami, Martori Enterprises II, Inc.

Miami City Hall

Miami

Monument to airlines' romantic past

It may be the only city hall in America that was once an airport. It hearkens to a romantic time when lumbering seaplanes opened up the world of travel. When city government set up in the former Pan American Seaplane Base and Terminal Building in 1954, it was to be a temporary move. Since then, there have been many efforts to move City Hall to a more convenient location in downtown Miami, about five miles north. Critics complain many city offices are already downtown and a run over to City Hall takes about 15 minutes on a good day, a lot more during rush hour. But the city commission still meets at the old terminal at Dinner Key.

Pan Am was the first U.S. airline to operate a permanent international air service, use radio communications and emergency life-saving equipment, provide regular service across the Atlantic, employ cabin attendants, and serve an in-flight meal. The fledgling airline, founded in 1927 with mail service between Key West and Havana, later moved to Miami and became an important international carrier. Its first base opened in 1929 in what was then the boondocks, on Northwest 36th Street, northwest of downtown. The site later became Miami International Airport, now America's fifteenth-busiest airport in passenger volume.

Later, it moved to a ragged patch of Biscayne Bay waterfront in Coconut Grove, an enclave of pioneers, writers, and adventurers that is still one of south Florida's most colorful communities. During World War I, the U.S. Navy had built a base at Dinner Key — so named because early settlers picnicked on it — and filled in the tidal

Miami City Hall was once a seaplane base. *Historical Association of Southern Florida*

flats between the key and the mainland. Pan Am built its first hangar in 1931. Workers began building the main terminal and did more dredging. A houseboat shuttled passengers to offshore docks where they boarded the seaplanes. When the building, which cost $900,000, opened in May 1934, it was the first built exclusively for commercial seaplanes and was considered the largest marine air terminal in the world.

A *Miami News* report on the terminal's opening said the three-story concrete and steel building, on 12 acres, fronted a seven-foot deep, 700-foot-wide, mile-long channel into the bay to serve the "flying boats." The terminal could handle four planes at once and 1500 passengers a day but never saw more than 600 a day. Its planes served 32 countries in the Caribbean and Central and South America. One of the early pilots was Charles Lindbergh. The famed aviator planned and tested Pan Am routes from the terminal.

Standing at the end of the palm-lined Pan American Drive, the terminal featured ticket counters, immigrations and customs offices, a dining room for 100, and a wrap-around second-floor balcony with a view of the bay. Its centerpiece was the ten-foot, multicolored relief globe — at that time one of the largest in America — built for Pan Am by Rand McNally. It showed all the air routes of the period and rotated by electric motor on a metal ring every two minutes. The entire structure weighed more than three tons.

In the 1930s and early 1940s, about 50,000 passengers a year moved through the Pan Am terminal. During World War II, Dinner Key again hosted a Navy base. When President Franklin Roosevelt boarded a seaplane there for a summit in Casablanca, he was the first president to travel by air while in office. But the war changed air travel, and land-based airports began springing up. Pan Am returned to its original base at Miami International Airport. The last Pan Am flight left Dinner Key on August 9, 1945. The next year, Pan Am sold the terminal and hangars to the city for $1.1 million.

Two of the four old Pan Am hangars are now used by a local boatyard; the future of the other two is uncertain. The city is hoping a developer will preserve them as a boatyard or public market. The city first leased out the terminal building to a private restaurant, the Marina. In 1948, police raided the place and seized 16 slot machines. In August 1951, the globe was moved to Miami International to tout Pan Am's new terminal there. But it sat in a warehouse. It eventually was moved to the Science Museum, where it is today.

Finally, in 1954, the city decided to use the old Pan American building as its city hall. After renovations, it opened the next year as a "temporary" city hall that is still used.

Miami City Hall is at 3500 Pan American Drive, Miami 33133. Call (888) 311-DADE.

Take U. S. 1 to S.W. 17 Avenue, left to Bayshore Drive, and right on Bayshore about a mile. City Hall is on left, just before S.W. 27 Ave.

No guided tours; most administrative offices closed to public. Commission chambers and lobby are open.

Greater Miami Chamber of Commerce: 1601 Biscayne Blvd., Miami 33132. Call (305) 350-7700. Website: www.greatermiami.com

Greater Miami Convention and Visitors Bureau: (800) 933-8448. Website: www.gmcvb.com

Read More About It

Kauffman, Sanford B. *Pan Am Pioneer: A Manager's Memoir, from Seaplane Clippers to Jumbo Jets.* 1995, Lubbock, Texas, Texas Tech University Press.

Parks, Arva Moore. *Miami, Magic City.* 1981, Tulsa, OK, Continental Heritage Press.

The Barnacle

Coconut Grove

A peek at early Miami

When Commodore Ralph Middleton Munroe remarried, he decided to add a second floor to his home along Biscayne Bay. But "The Barnacle" had been built in a way that made it impractical to build up. Munroe, unfazed, just jacked up the entire home and built a new floor under it. Munroe reflected the pioneer spirit of the few hundred hardy souls who, a little more than a century ago, were the only inhabitants of what is now one of the world's most important cities.

In the 1880s, "Cocoanut Grove" (the spelling was changed to "Coconut" in 1923) was a paradise of hammocks and sandy beaches along unspoiled Biscayne Bay, about five miles south of what is now downtown Miami.

Munroe's estate along Biscayno Bay in Coconut Grove, which sprawled across 40 acres, has shrunk to five acres. It is now a state historic site and a snapshot of the "Era of the Bay." The home, damaged by Hurricane Andrew in 1992, reopened less than a year later, but access is now limited to guided tours.

When Munroe was 26, a relative invited him to sail a schooner to Key West, where they met Miami pioneer William Brickell. He took them up to Biscayne Bay, where they saw a wild and magnificent wilderness. In 1877, Munroe liquidated his business and moved to Coconut Grove with his infant daughter and tuberculosis-racked wife, Eva, and several relatives. He would later lose both wife and daughter.

Munroe took up permanent residence in Coconut Grove in 1886, obtaining 40 acres for $400 and a boat. He built The Barnacle in 1891. He also persuaded Charles and Isabelle Peacock to build the

The Barnacle was the home of Miami pioneer Ralph Middleton Munroe.
Barnacle State Historic Site

first hotel on south Florida's mainland. Munroe set up shop designing boats with minimal drafts that could navigate the shallow bay and its dangerous shoals, bars, and reefs. He taught newcomers how to live with the land among mosquitoes, hurricanes, and isolation. He helped found the Biscayne Bay Yacht Club, believed to be the oldest continuous club in south Florida, and was its commodore for 22 years.

Soon, "the Grove" became home to an eclectic stew of black Bahamians, Key West "Conchs," and New England intellectuals. Its reputation as a haven for the offbeat, the adventurer, the free spirit, and the maverick continues today, although it is slowly being taken over by office high-rises and young professionals in expensive condominiums and homes.

Munroe, originally from New York's Staten Island, had been influenced early in life from contacts with Henry David Thoreau and Ralph Waldo Emerson; he became an ardent conservationist at a time when nature was a limitless expanse. When he bought The Barnacle property, he left the hammock untouched. He argued against filling the shoreline, instead advising laying rough stones with cement grouting to prevent erosion. In the 1920s, he fought efforts to build artificial islands south of nearby Dinner Key. And he convinced Coconut Grove to go with septic tanks when its larger cousin, Miami, opted to pipe raw sewage into Biscayne Bay.

The Barnacle features tropical architecture and a dramatic view of the bay from its sprawling porch. The upstairs — the former downstairs — contains four bedrooms, a sitting room, a landing, and a bathroom, although the site is "interpreted" for its pre-indoor plumbing era. Downstairs is a living room, dining room, kitchen, a display room showing period artifacts, and two special rooms containing Munroe's mementos, including nautical charts, curios, and a model of the *Micco*, an eight-foot boat with shallow draft that he built in 1881.

The boat went through several owners, then through a stroke of luck, was reunited with The Barnacle. But it was reduced to kindling by Hurricane Andrew, which damaged the cupola and knocked off roof tiles. Andrew also blew out the walls of the boathouse, which Munroe had rebuilt after it was destroyed by the 1926 storm. He had employed blow-out walls that preserved the structure; his concept worked in Andrew, but the 11-foot surge took out the front and back walls, and the floor was washed away as the waters receded.

Also on display are photographs by Munroe, described in an 1896 *Miami Metropolis* article as "an amateur photographer of considerable ability." They are some of south Florida's earliest visual records.

The Barnacle Historic State Park, in the Coconut Grove section of Miami, is at 3485 Main Highway, Miami 33133. Call (305) 442-6866. From U.S. 1, take McDonald Street (S.W. 32 Ave.) east. Turn left to the end, left on Grand Avenue, then a quick right onto Commodore Plaza. Go one block to Main Highway, then right to entrance. Park on the Main Highway. Open 9 A.M. to 4 P.M. Friday through Monday. Guided tours at 10 A.M., 11:30 A.M., 1 P.M., and 2:30 P.M. Ages 6 and over, $1. Open Tuesday through Thursday for group tours and advanced reservations. Website: www.floridastateparks.org.

Coconut Grove Chamber of Commerce: 2820 McFarlane Rd, Coconut Grove 33133. Call (305) 444-7270. Website: www.coconutgrove.com

Greater Miami Convention and Visitors Bureau: 701 Brickell Ave., Suite 2700, Miami 33131. Call (800) 933-8448 or (305) 539-3000. Website: www.gmcvb.com

Read More About It

Coulombe, Deborah A., and Herbert L. Hiller. *Season of Innocence.* 1998, Miami, Pickering Press.

Munroe, Ralph Middleton. *The Commodore's Story.* 1967, Miami, Historical Association of Southern Florida.

The Biltmore

Coral Gables

The jewel of Coral Gables

The Biltmore has had more lives than a cat. It has outlived guests ranging from the Roosevelts and Vanderbilts to injured World War II GIs and gangster Al Capone. And it has suffered many painful deaths and as many resurrections.

Symbolic of young Miami's boom and bust, the 275-room orange-and-brown hotel opened in 1926, just months before a hurricane flattened the city. It was designed by famed architects Schultze and Weaver, who also fashioned Biltmores in Los Angeles and Atlanta and the *Miami News*/Freedom Tower. Shultze also helped create New York's Grand Central Terminal.

Like the Freedom Tower, the Biltmore boasts a replica of the 500-year-old Giralda tower in Seville, Spain. The Biltmore's copper-clad roof rises 300 feet above quiet, Moorish-designed neighborhoods. It's one of eight Florida hotels on the National Trust for Historic Preservation's Historic Hotels of America program. And it hosted opening ceremonies and a banquet for the Summit of the Americas, December 9–11, 1994. It was also one of six south Florida hotels selected to house the 33 world leaders participating in the event. And it's even said to be haunted by the ghost of gang hit man Thomas "Fats" Walsh, cut down March 7, 1929, in the thirteenth floor gambling suite; like the hotel, he refuses to die.

City of Dreams

The hotel, a lasting symbol of Coral Gables, was built by the same man who gave birth to "The City Beautiful." But it shone long after

The Biltmore is a symbol
of Coral Gables' beauty.
The Biltmore

fate had cruelly beaten down George Edward Merrick. Merrick
named his city for his family home, its roof gables made with native
coral. Merrick wasn't out just to make tons of money, but to establish
the city of his dreams, with schools, a library, and plenty of lush
green space, at a time when planned cities were unheard of in south
Florida.

By 1925 he had spent $100 million to build Coral Gables and
another $5 million to promote it. Merrick splashed the name "Coral
Gables" in the middle of Times Square and had real estate offices
across the North shouting the melodious words. He was the first of the
big-time Florida developers to advertise in national magazines. And
he hired no less eminent a pitchman than William Jennings Bryan,
the three-time presidential candidate and defender of the Bible in the
famed "Monkey Trial." Merrick paid Bryan a remarkable $100,000 a
year   half in cash and half in land.

On Friday, March 13, 1925, Merrick broke ground for the "Miami
Biltmore." He wanted to cash in on the instant recognition of booming
Miami. Built for an astounding ten million dollars and completed in
a dizzying ten months, it opened January 15, 1926, on a spot where
eight years earlier Merrick's family had grown tomatoes. The hotel
featured 400 rooms and suites, each with a private bath, and a staff
of 1,000. There were three ballrooms. The giant swimming pool was
then touted as the largest in the world and now proclaimed as the
largest in the continental United States. A gala dinner dance was
limited to 1,500 of the cream of society; another 3,500 were turned
away. To appease them, Merrick scheduled a week of fashion shows
featuring $250,000 worth of attire. Despite Prohibition, there was
plenty of alcohol to go around at the various bashes. A gondola was
brought in from Italy to meander the vast pool; a guest tipped it.

As with the rest of south Florida, Coral Gables' crash was helped along by a hurricane. For the Keys, it would be the Labor Day storm in 1935. In the Lake Okeechobee region, it was the 1928 catastrophe. For the Gables, it was the 1926 blow. On the morning of September 18, 1926, Merrick dropped into the mail 2,000 letters announcing his winter season. Twenty-four hours later, Miami was in shambles. At least 113 died. Newspapers across America declared the city dead and buried. The Biltmore had lived up to its builders' boasts, standing tall in the winds — the gauge at the hotel broke at the 128-mph point — and serving as a shelter for about 2,000 people. But windows had been blown out and draperies, carpets, and furnishings damaged by wind and rain. It was the beginning of the end for George Merrick.

An aquatic show, featuring alligator wrestling and exhibitions by future Tarzan Johnny Weissmuller and other swimming greats, continued to make money for the hotel. But Merrick had built 2,000 homes, and many stood unsold. The operator of his fish camp in the Keys fled with the profits. In April 1929, Merrick's Coral Gables Corporation filed for bankruptcy protection. A year later, the Biltmore went into default. An ungrateful city commission asked Merrick to resign.

A six-week, cross-country motor tour with his brother ended with the two opening a new real estate office on Miami Beach and setting up another fishing lodge in the Keys. The 1935 Labor Day hurricane blew the fish camp away. Meanwhile, Merrick's old partner in the Biltmore, Jack Bowman, tried to line up new partners for the hotel. But a year later he was dead.

"A Terrible Turkey"

In 1931, a new Biltmore owner, Henry L. Doherty, began pushing south Florida as a year-round — not just winter — resort. He began pumping money into both the hotel and the area. He gave out-of-town reporters dollar-a-night rooms and free libations; they turned the lobby into a press center and began putting "The Miami Biltmore" in datelines. He bankrolled the first Orange Bowl Classic football game, then called the Palm Festival. Celebrities once again came to the Biltmore to see and be seen, including Dorothy Lamour and Glenn Ford. Entertainment was provided by, among others, a young Cuban performer named Desi Arnaz. The nation's top song was "Moon over Miami." But by 1938, Doherty, like Merrick before him, gave up the

Biltmore. In ill health, he sold it to a friend who privately called it a "white elephant." One columnist was even less kind, calling it "a terrible turkey."

World War II came too close to the Biltmore. With U-boats sinking freighters just offshore, the hotel had to turn out its lights. War washed out the season. Salvation came in the form of Uncle Sam. The War Department bought the Biltmore for $895,000 — less than a tenth of its original value. The military dumped valuable furnishings and dinnerware onto the streets outside the hotel. It unceremoniously renamed the once-splendid Biltmore "Army Air Forces Regional Hospital, 28th AAF Base Unit."

In 1942, Merrick himself died of a heart attack at age 56, still paying off his debts. His last post had been a $7,000-a-year job as Miami postmaster.

"A Thing of Lasting Beauty"

After the war, the Army kept the hotel, renaming it Pratt General Hospital. It was later taken over by the Veterans Administration, which moved to Jackson Memorial Hospital in 1968, leaving the hotel again empty but still federal property. At one point, it was a kennel for dogs used in medical experiments; mutts lay where the cream of society once relaxed.

This time, local residents began a "Save the Biltmore" campaign. The federal government tried to sell the Biltmore to a developer; the public fought it amid fears the businessman would level the hotel for high-rise condominiums. In 1973, the federal government gave the hotel to the city. Residents cleaned it up for a 1920s-era prom; people nationwide sent in old Biltmore trinkets. Other groups scheduled galas there.

In 1983, the city approved a four-year, $47 million refurbishment. In January 1987, 61 years and one day after it opened, the reborn Biltmore opened its doors. A souvenir menu carried the words of the hotel's original publicity pitches: "Many people may come and go but this structure will remain a thing of lasting beauty."

But the development company to which the city had leased the hotel fell on hard times, and the hotel had to shut its doors in 1990. A year later, Seaway Hotels, a Florida hotel management company, leased the hotel from the city and put another $3 million into it. It reopened yet again in August 1992 — ironically, two months early, to house out-of-town emergency workers and their families brought in to help rebuild after Hurricane Andrew. By January 1996, it was doing such a rush of business it didn't have space to throw a 70th birthday bash.

The Biltmore is at 1200 Anastasia Ave., Coral Gables 33134. Call (800) 727-1926 or (305) 445-1926. Take U.S. 1 two streets south of LeJeune Road to Granada, then right, then about a mile. Website: www.biltmorehotel.com

　　Coral Gables Chamber of Commerce: 224 Catalonia Ave., Coral Gables 33134. Call (305) 446-1657. Website: www.coralgableschamber. org

　　Greater Miami Convention and Visitors Bureau: 701 Brickell Ave., Suite 2700, Miami 33131. Call (800) 933-8448. Website: www. gmcvb.com

Read More About It

Coral Gables Historical Preservation Board of Review. *Coral Gables: Yesterday, Today and Tomorrow*. 1982, Miami, Coral Gables Historical Preservation Board of Review.

Muir, Helen. *The Biltmore: Beacon for Miami*. 1987, Pickering Press, Miami.

Cape Florida Lighthouse

Key Biscayne

A brave sentinel

When Hurricane Andrew slammed Dade County in August 1992, the magnificent woods of Key Biscayne, the picturesque community across Biscayne Bay from downtown Miami, were laid horizontal. Sticking up alone from the kindling, in defiance of Andrew and other hurricanes that have failed to budge it in nearly a century, was the 95-foot Cape Florida Lighthouse. It is the oldest standing structure in Dade County, now Miami-Dade County. The 400-acre state recreation area surrounding it was severely damaged by Andrew, but the park opened again a year later, almost to the day.

When the lighthouse was first built in 1825 to aid boats around the end of the peninsula, Florida had been American territory for four years. It would not be a state for two decades. And only about 500 non–Native Americans lived in south Florida.

For nearly two centuries, the solid brick structure — tapering in thickness from five feet at the base to two feet at the top — has withstood storms, the onslaught of the elements, invaders, and the encroachment of development. Perhaps its greatest stand came against an attack by Seminole Indians and the botched suicide attempt of a panicking assistant keeper named John Thompson.

On July 23, 1836, the lighthouse was stormed by Seminoles who set its base afire. Trapped on the catwalk at the top, Thompson decided there was only one way out: to throw a keg of gunpowder down the flaming interior of the lighthouse, blowing up himself and the Indians. His plan was to be quick-fried instead of slow-roasted

Cape Florida Lighthouse is Miami-Dade County's oldest structure.
Miami-Metro Department of Publicity and Tourism

and become a martyr of the Second Seminole War. Instead, the tower turned into a giant Roman candle, scaring off the Indians; the fire was smothered when the interior stairway collapsed. When the smoke had cleared, the lighthouse was saved. Thompson was alive — dazed and slightly shot up.

It was later learned that the builder, to cut his brick costs in half, had secretly built hollow walls much of the way up. In 1842, a contractor bolstered the tower; he may have completely leveled it and built a new structure. In 1855, the military extended the lighthouse's height to 95 feet and then headed north to build the lighthouse at the Seminole War outpost of Fort Jupiter. The leader of that endeavor, George Gordon Meade, would later win the historic Civil War clash at Gettysburg.

The Cape Florida Lighthouse was abandoned in 1878 when a new one was built at Fowey Rock, several miles to the southeast in southern Biscayne Bay. That lighthouse is now the official one used for navigation. But a century later, in 1978, the U.S. Coast Guard reestablished the light at Cape Florida Lighthouse.

The structure is finally feeling the effects of the elements, and a private effort is under way to raise money to maintain it.

Cape Florida Lighthouse is in Bill Baggs Cape Florida State Park, at the end of Key Biscayne. Write 1200 S. Crandon Blvd., Key Biscayne

33149. Call (305) 361-5811. Hours: 8 A.M. to sunset. Tours of lighthouse arc Thursday through Monday, 10 A.M. and 1:00 P.M. Admission: $5 per car, $3 per single-occupant car, $1 for pedestrians and cyclists. Web page: www.floridastateparks.org.

Key Biscayne Chamber of Commerce: 88 W. McIntyre St., Suite 100, Key Biscayne 33149. Call (305) 361-5207. Website: www.keybiscaynechamber.org

Greater Miami Convention and Visitors Bureau: 701 Brickell Ave., Suite 2700, Miami 33131. Call (800) 933-8448 or (305) 539-3000. Website: www.gmcvb.com

Read More About It

Blank, Joan Gill. *Key Biscayne: A History of Miami's Tropical Island and the Cape Florida Lighthouse.* 1996, Sarasota, Pineapple Press.

McIver, Stuart. *100 Years on Biscayne Bay.* 1980, Miami, Seeman Publishing.

Everglades National Park

A global treasure

On December 6, 1947, Harry S. Truman took time out during one of his Key West vacations and rode up U.S. 1 to the mainland. There, on a wooden platform, and with 57-year-old Marjory Stoneman Douglas at his side, he dedicated America's newest national park.

"Here are no lofty peaks seeking the sky, no mighty glaciers or rushing streams," Truman said at the park opening. "Here is land, tranquil in its quiet beauty, serving not as the source of water but as the last receiver of it."

More than a half-century later, Truman is long gone. Douglas, even then one of America's leading environmental activists, lived to 108; she died in 1998. Everglades National Park is still around. But the future of the Everglades is in doubt.

The park was dedicated the same year Douglas published her landmark book, *The Everglades: River of Grass.* "There are no other Everglades in the world," she wrote. "They are, they have always been, one of the unique regions of the earth, remote, never wholly known." Douglas asserted the Everglades was a giant, shallow river, moving and filtering water across the peninsula and driving south Florida's rain machine. But now a giant dike rings Lake Okeechobee. Tamiami Trail bisects the peninsula, forming a giant boom to block the flow. Demands by urban south Florida have drawn down the cushion of water. And farm runoff has compromised its quantity and quality. Once, the Everglades covered some 7,000 square miles from Lake Okeechobee to Florida Bay. The state later drained the northern regions to form sugar and vegetable growing areas.

Parts of the Everglades still exist as far north as Palm Beach County in the Arthur R. Marshall Loxahatchee National Wildlife Refuge and in state-operated water conservation areas and Everglades National Park. Spanning 1.5 million acres, or more than 2,300 square

TOP: Everglades National Park is a natural treasure. *Florida News Bureau*

BOTTOM: Marjory Stoneman Douglas fought for decades to save the Everglades. *New York Times*

miles, the park is third in size among national parks only to Death Valley and Yellowstone. The East Everglades expansion in 1991 added more than 100,000 acres.

It is home to dozens of species, from the ever-tormenting mosquito to the rare Florida panther, as well as wood storks and spoonbills, bald eagles and osprey, snails and kites, crocodiles and alligators, sea turtles and manatees, black bears, snook and sea trout, redfish and tarpon.

"The First Martyr"

The crusade that led to Everglades National Park may have well begun with the martyrdom of Guy Bradley, raised on Hypoluxo Island, near Palm Beach, and son of one of that region's pioneer families. By the turn of the century, egrets and other birds of the Everglades were being hunted almost to extinction; their feathers were in demand as hat decorations. The fledgling Audubon Society was able to push through state laws to protect the birds, but Florida couldn't afford wardens, so the society raised money to hire four. One was Bradley.

"That man Bradley is going to be killed sometime," a famed bird expert who had toured the area with Bradley said. "He has been shot at more than once, and someday they are going to get him."

On July 8, 1905, 35-year-old Bradley was found dead, floating in his skiff. Suspected were Walter Smith and his two sons, habitual game violators. The killing was a national sensation. Witnesses claimed Bradley shot first. But furious local residents torched Smith's house. Five months later, a grand jury in Key West ruled there wasn't enough evidence to try Smith. Bradley left a wife and two sons. A marker in the park says he "gave his life for the cause to which he was pledged."

The murder, and that of another Audubon warden three years later in Charlotte Harbor, helped boost public support for bird protection. Conservationists targeted the consumer end of the slaughter, New York's garment district, and pushed through a state law there that banned use of feathers in hats, despite the efforts of lobbyists and cries of industry officials that thousands would be left jobless. After the industry began sneaking the feathers in through Europe, the federal government passed similar laws. But back in south Florida, conservationists argued more was needed than a handful of rangers paid with private money. Soon the movement wasn't just about protecting birds. As south Florida's real estate boom began gearing up, and completion of a road from Florida City in 1915 spurred interest in farming the area, the fight became one of preserving a unique ecosystem.

In 1916, Royal Palm State Park was established 15 miles southwest of Homestead. In 1930, Congress heard the first call to establish a national park. It would take another 17 years of lobbying, stalled by a depression and a world war, and revived when the state gave $2 million to buy private lands and donated another $800,000 of state lands.

In its first year, Everglades National Park had only 7,482 visitors. With improvements to the facilities and approach routes, and the increasing significance of the park, that figure is now approaching 1.5 million a year.

There are three entrances — at Everglades City, Homestead, and Shark River. Visitor centers at all three locations are staffed by naturalists who offer guided boardwalk strolls, hikes, boat tours, and tram rides through different regions. The United Nations designated the park as an International Biosphere Reserve in 1976 and as a World Heritage Site in 1979 and a Wetland of International Importance in 1984.

Hurricane Andrew caused about $54 million in damage to park facilities and carved a 25-mile-wide scar, downing thousands of trees. But the Everglades has been in the path of hurricanes for eons. Much of its wildlife survived the storm and new vegetation rapidly overtook downed trees. The park reopened less than four months after the storm.

Everglades National Park main entrance is about ten miles southwest of Homestead. Write 40001 S.R. 9336, Homestead 33034. Call (305) 242-7700. Take Florida's Turnpike south until it ends; turn west on State Road 9336 to the park entrance. Open 24 hours, daily. Admission: $10 per vehicle; $5 for pedestrians and cyclists. Website: www.nps.gov/ever/

Shark Valley entrance (open 8:30 A.M. to 6 P.M.): 17 miles west of Florida's Turnpike on U.S. 41 west of Miami. Tram tours (305) 221-8455. Everglades National Park Boat Tours: (239) 695-2591. Park campgrounds at Long Pine Key and Flamingo. Flamingo Lodge, Marina and Outpost Resort, Flamingo 33030, (305) 253-2241. The Flamingo area is currently closed due to hurricane damage, please call ahead.

Greater Homestead/Florida City Chamber of Commerce: 43 N. Krome Ave., Homestead 33030. Call (888) 352-4891 or (305) 247-2332. Website: www.chamberinaction.com

Greater Miami Convention and Visitors Bureau: 701 Brickell Ave., Suite 2700, Miami 33131. Call (800) 933-8448. Website: www. gmcvb.com

Read More About It

Carr, Archie Fairly. *The Everglades*. 1973, New York, Time-Life Books.

Douglas, Marjory Stoneman. *The Everglades: River of Grass* (updated edition). 1987, Sarasota, Pineapple Press.

Tebeau, Charlton W. *Man in the Everglades: 2,000 Years of Human History in Everglades National Park*. 1968, Miami, University of Miami Press.

The Keys

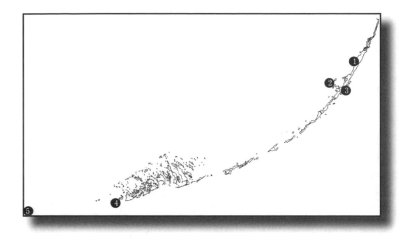

1. Monument to the Labor Day Storm, *Islamorada*
2. Indian Key
3. The Wreck of the San Pedro, *Indian Key*
4. The Hemingway Home, *Key West*
5. Fort Jefferson, *Dry Tortugas*

Monument to the "Labor Day Storm"

Islamorada

The end of a dream

Forget Andrew. Forget Katrina. Forget the great Galveston hurricane or the 1928 Lake Okeechobee storm.

The most powerful hurricane ever to strike North America is still the monster that ripped through the Florida Keys on Sept. 2, 1935. Top sustained winds were at least 160 mph and may have reached 185 mph. Its barometric pressure, the standard by which meteorologists determine a storm's might, bottomed out at 26.35, the lowest ever recorded in a U.S. landfall. Like many other profound hurricanes, the Labor Day Storm changed the course of Florida history; it took Henry Flagler's railroad to the sea and washed it into the sea.

A monument off U.S. 1 in Islamorada, installed in November 1937, honors the storm's victims

The memorial stands on a 65-by-20-foot plot. A crypt holds the remains of dozens of victims. It is covered by a ceramic tile map showing the stretch from Key Largo to Marathon. An obelisk stands 18 feet high, marked with a sculpture of a tidal wave and palms bending in powerful winds A marker reads: "Dedicated To The Memory Of The Civilians And The War Veterans Whose Lives Were Lost In The Hurricane Of September Second 1935."

In 1905, having already put Florida on the map, Flagler, then nearing the autumn of his life, had one more mission: building a 128-mile-long railroad across the ocean to Key West. From there, steamers would be only 90 miles from Havana. The project cost Flagler $20 million, in early twentieth-century dollars, of his own money. Critics called it "Flagler's Folly," but Flagler lived — barely — to see the first

1935 Hurricane
Monument.
Bruce Hunt

DEDICATED
TO THE MEMORY OF THE
CIVILIANS AND WAR VETERANS
WHOSE LIVES WERE LOST
IN THE HURRICANE OF
SEPTEMBER SECOND, 1935

train arrive in Key West in January 1912. He died only 16 months later.

But the wonder would last less than a quarter century. By the 1930s, a new dynamic was challenging the iron horse: the car. A series of roads and causeways through the Keys was planned to accommodate motor traffic. It needed a labor force. Many World War I veterans had come back from Europe to find no jobs available at home. Frustrated and embittered, they challenged the federal government to take care of them. Franklin Roosevelt's New Deal set up camps in the Keys to house some 700 veterans working on the highway.

When the storm approached, officials planned to send a rescue train, but it was Labor Day weekend, and they had trouble rounding up crews. Problems with drawbridges and mechanical trouble further delayed the train. Storm surge came ashore moments after the train arrived in Islamorada, but everyone aboard survived, according to

Willie Drye, author of *Storm of the Century: The Labor Day Hurricane of 1935.*

The official death toll is 408; some estimates are as high as 600. About 260 of the victims were the veterans working on the road. The storm leveled a ten-mile stretch of the Keys. And it washed away the railroad. With trains losing their prominence, and cars on the rise, the motorways were rebuilt, but the railroad was not.

The Monument to the "Labor Day Storm" is in Islamorada, just east of U.S. 1., off old State Road 4-A at milemarker 81.5, across from the library.

Historical Preservation Society of the Upper Keys: Box 2200, Key Largo 33070. Website: www.keyshistory.org.

National Hurricane Center: 11691 SW 17th Street, Miami 33165. Website: www.nhc.noaa.gov

Read More About It

Drye, Willie. *Storm of the Century: The Labor Day Hurricane of 1935.* 2003, Washington D.C., National Geographic Society.

Reilly, Benjamin. *Tropical Surge: A History of Ambition and Disaster on the Florida Shore.* 2005, Sarasota, Pineapple Press.

Indian Key

From county seat to massacre site

From the Overseas Highway, this looks like just another mangrove-covered dot along the Florida Keys. Tiny Indian Key's solitude belies a legacy as one of nineteenth-century south Florida's most important locales. The island, still accessible only by boat, is now a state historic site with an observation tower, boat dock, shelter, and trails. There is no restroom or picnic area, no power or water, no telephones.

Here a pioneer family was killed by Seminoles. And here was the first seat of Dade County, now one of the most populous, cosmopolitan, and prominent counties in the world. If the historic 27-story county courthouse, built in downtown Miami in 1927, was cut into square-foot chunks, it would cover nearly two thirds of the tiny key. But Dade County — now Miami-Dade County — now occupied by nearly 2.4 million residents, was a different animal in 1836. After eons as home to indigenous peoples and two and a half centuries under the Spanish crown, Florida had been an American possession for only 15 years and would not achieve statehood for another nine. The region's first U.S. census, in 1830, placed 517 people in the peninsula's entire southern half. A handful of them lived around a little settlement that would become Miami.

South Florida's most important city — in fact, the only one of significance — was Key West, seat of Monroe County, which spanned north to Lake Okeechobee. Isolated in the string of unconnected islands that was the Keys, it nevertheless enjoyed a strategic location at the mouth of the Gulf of Mexico. It was a key port and, more importantly, wreck salvaging center. Like the pirates, and the drug smugglers that would follow them into the 1990s, the opportunistic residents of Key West profited handsomely from mariners' misfortunes.

Jacob Housman, formerly of Staten Island, was a mover in Key

Indian Key was Dade County's first county seat. *Florida Park Service*

West's wrecking trade. When other wreckers alleged he was fast and loose with the law, he left in the 1820s for Indian Key, drawn by its proximity to both fresh water and treacherous reefs that chewed on ships. Housman built a store, hotel, homes with cisterns, warehouses, and wharves, and set up a busy port with about 50 residents. Suddenly, Indian Key was one of south Florida's metropolises.

Tired of dealing with officials in Key West, Housman pushed the legislature to create Dade County on February 4, 1836, and make Indian Key its seat. Two years later, Dr. Henry Perrine, a physician intrigued with tropical plants, set up a nursery. Business then soured for Housman. He lost several court battles over wrecking claims. The Second Seminole War broke out in 1835, and he lost his trade with the Indians. The feds later yanked his salvager's license for improprieties.

Jacob Housman's stockpile of merchandise and ammunition was a dangerous enticement, and he sought government protection. Forces came to nearby Tea Table Key. But in the early hours of August 7, 1840, more than 100 Indians raided Indian Key. Housman and his wife escaped; Indians sacked the settlement as residents swam offshore or hid. Dr. Perrine secreted his wife, two daughters, and a son in a cellar beneath a trap door and convinced the invaders he would treat wounded and provide medicine later on if they would just leave now. They did, but juiced by Housman's rum, soon returned. Shrieking and whooping, they chased Perrine, shot him, trashed his library, and burned his home.

His family, roasting beneath the floorboards, was able to sneak to a nearby boat through a turtle kraal, or holding pen, and escape. Another man, his wife, and two small children weren't as lucky; they were beaten and shot dead. A 12-year-old boy died as he hid beneath a burning building; another boiled in a cistern under a flaming warehouse. Four blacks were abducted as slaves. The Indians repelled a weak federal counterattack and continued their plunder. When the smoke had dissipated, between six and 13 residents were dead. The key had been leveled, except for one building and the stone foundations of the others, which remain today.

Vengeful troops chased the Seminoles into the Everglades, wiping them out and slaying their leader, Chekika, whom they strung up in a tree as a grim warning. Only a few settlers returned after the attack. Housman, financially ruined by the destruction of Indian Key, went to Key West, where he signed on a wrecking ship. A year later, on a rough sea, he was crushed between two boats.

Meanwhile, his utopia fell into disrepair. It was sparsely settled after that and has been uninhabited since the turn of the twentieth century, even as the Keys have exploded with development. The county seat moved to Miami in 1844, then to Juno in 1888, and back to Miami for good 11 years later.

The state acquired the property in the early 1970s and made it a park. Now visitors walk among its ruins and look at the descendants of Henry Perrine's plants, which have overgrown the deserted colony.

Indian Key State Park is about a half mile off U.S. 1 on the Atlantic Ocean side, about three miles south of Islamorada. Due to hurricane damage the island was only accessible via canoe or kayak at the time of this printing. Write: Box 1052, Islamorada 33036. Call (305) 664-2540. Website: www.floridastateparks.org

Islamorada Chamber of Commerce: Mile Marker 83.2 on the bayside, Islamorada 33036. Call (305) 664-4503 or (800) FAB-KEYS.

Florida Keys and Key West Visitors Bureau: 1201 White Street, Key West 33040. Call (800) FLA-KEYS (352-5397). Website: www.fla-keys.com

Read More About It

Schene, Michael G. *History of Indian Key*. 1973, Tallahassee, Florida Division of Archives, History and Records Management.

Viele, John. *The Florida Keys: A History of the Pioneers*. 1996, Sarasota, Pineapple Press.

The Wreck of the *San Pedro*

Indian Key

Lost treasure on the ocean floor

Barely visible beneath about 20 feet of silty ocean, a limestone marker brought all the way from Indiana marks the grave of the *San Pedro*. For more than 250 years, the 100-foot Spanish merchant ship, scuttled by a hurricane, has sat on the ocean floor a little more than a mile off tiny Indian Key, the first county seat of Dade County and now a state park.

Over the centuries, salvagers, scavengers, and vandals have picked it clean so all that remains are the ballast stones and, buried in the sand beneath them, the ship's wooden hull. In that time, the ship's skeleton has attracted coral and sea life that always gravitates to it, making the *San Pedro* one of Florida's oldest artificial reefs. Now it is the nucleus of San Pedro State Underwater Archaeological Preserve, dubbed by state underwater archaeologists "a living museum in the sea."

The *San Pedro* was one of a dozen Spanish ships in the New Spain fleet, heading in June 1733 from Havana to the Spanish port city of Cadiz. Four armed galleons escorted 18 merchant ships laden with treasures from Asia and Spain's colonies in the Philippines and Mexico. The 287-ton Dutch-built *San Pedro* had been carrying 16,000 silver Mexican pesos and several crates of porcelain from China, as well as leather goods, ceramics, and art from Spain's colonies. The fleet was caught off-guard by a hurricane; the ships tried to turn back to Havana, but the storm sank all but one of them, scattering them over 80 miles.

Because the water where the ships sank is no deeper than

The wreck of the *San Pedro* is an underwater state park. *Indiana University*

about 20 feet, Spanish crews were able to salvage most of the cargo, including some smuggled goods not on the original manifests. Ships were returned to Havana or abandoned.

In 1977 and again in 1988, archaeologists mapped out the sites and did a biological survey of the myriad sea life living in and around them. The *San Pedro* project involved Florida's Bureau of Archaeological Research as well as the state's Department of Natural Resources. In 1988, they were assisted by students at Florida State University and Indiana University, which operate field schools in underwater archaeology in conjunction with the state. The *San Pedro* was selected for the preserve because of its proximity to the Indian Key park and another state park at Lignumvitae Key, an island on the Florida Bay side of the Overseas Highway. In addition, the ship is still in relatively good shape. It is in shallow water, and the reef that has grown on and around it is busy and picturesque. The Islamorada Chamber of Commerce mobilized local businesses to donate money, services, and press for the park's creation.

A sand and gravel company from Islamorada, a few miles up the road, volunteered to craft seven 400-pound concrete replicas of the Spanish cannon that had once peered out from the proud galleon. They used a mold from a cannon off another fleet ship that wrecked in the same storm and whose remains are about ten miles away. That cannon is now on display at the Florida Museum of History in Tallahassee.

The firm also constructed six one-ton concrete mooring blocks to mark the site and allow boaters to tie up for diving. On the 700-pound plaque, made of Indiana limestone and carved by Indiana craftsmen, an inscription, identifying the site and recognizing supporters, is painted in bright colors and sealed in thick glass. Organizers hope it will last for years and draw people to the new park.

The San Pedro State Underwater Archaeological Preserve is in about 18 feet of water about 1.25 nautical miles (1.43 statute miles) south of Indian Key. Boats must tie to mooring posts; no anchoring. It is open 8 A.M. to sunset, 365 days a year. Write to: P.O. Box 1052, Islamorada, 33036. Call (305) 664-2540. Website: www.floridastateparks.org

Islamorada Chamber of Commerce: Mile Marker 83.2 on the bayside, Islamorada 33036. Call (305) 664-4503 or (800) FAB-KEYS.

Florida Keys and Key West Visitors Bureau: 1201 White Street, Key West 33040. Call (800) FLA-KEYS (352-5397). Website: www.fla-keys.com

The Hemingway Home

Key West

Where Papa wrote and played

Many literary giants at one point called Key West home: John J. Audubon, Tennessee Williams, Robert Frost, and Wallace Stevens. None is more famous, or infamous, than "Papa." Local residents — Conchs — honor the author every summer during a week of Hemingway Days. They cheer as one look-alike contestant after another mounts the stage at Sloppy Joe's. And they drink to the likeness, frozen forever in a portrait with beard and turtleneck; perhaps as much a symbol of the outlandish city as the conch shell.

About nine blocks from the legendary bar is Hemingway's home at 907 Whitehead Street. The two-story, green-shuttered, green-and-ivory coral rock home, built in 1851, is a national historic landmark and tourist attraction. Perhaps its most well-known feature is the colony of about 50 six-toed cats, believed to be descendants of his pets, who roam the one-acre tropical grounds.

Ernest and Pauline Hemingway moved in on December 19, 1931, three years after Papa first visited the island city. For the next decade, he wrote, drank, fished, and lived the tropical life, taking time to referee Friday night open-arena boxing matches.

It was at this home that he wrote *Death in the Afternoon, Green Hills of Africa,* and *To Have and Have Not,* and began *For Whom the Bell Tolls*.

One night at a party, poet Wallace Stevens commented to Hemingway's sister that he didn't think much of her brother's work. Upset almost to tears, she made a quick call to Papa. He stormed

Papa Hemingway wrote some of his classic works at his Key West home.
Scribners Publishing

into the party, called Stevens outside, and broke his jaw with a single right hook.

In 1940, Hemingway left Key West for Havana. Although he owned the house until his suicide in Idaho in 1961, he was only an absentee owner and sometime visitor of the city that has embraced him.

"The moon was up now," Hemingway wrote of Key West in *To Have and Have Not*, "and the trees were dark against it, and he passed the frame houses with their narrow yards, light coming from the shuttered windows; the unpaved alleys, with their double rows of houses; Conch town, where all was starched, well-shuttered, virtue, failure, grits and boiled grunts, undernourishment, culture, prejudice, righteousness, interbreeding, and the comforts of religion . . ."

The Hemingway Home and Museum is at 907 Whitehead St., Key West 33040. Call (305) 294-1136. Follow U.S. 1 west, then right on Whitehead. Open 9 A.M. to 5 P.M. every day of the year. Admission: adults $11, kids 6 to 12, $6, 5 and under free. Website: www.hemingwayhome.com

Key West Chamber of Commerce: 402 Wall St., Key West 33040. Call (305) 294-2587. Website: www.keywestchamber.com

Florida Keys and Key West Visitors Bureau: 1201 White Street, Key West 33040. Call (800) FLA-KEYS (352-5397). Website: www.fla-keys.com

Read More About It

McClendon, James. *Papa: Hemingway in Key West.* 1972, Miami, Seemann Publishing.

McIver, Stuart. *Hemingway's Key West.* 1993, Sarasota, Pineapple Press.

Fort Jefferson

Dry Tortugas

The ordeal of Dr. Mudd

This outpost in the Gulf of Mexico stands as a symbol of outdated might, government folly, and the tragedy of injustice. The 17-acre fort, on a 23-acre island 68 miles west of Key West, was designed as the Gibraltar of the Gulf, part of a chain of forts defending the coast from the pre-airplane era's greatest threat: a sea-borne invasion. The six-sided fort, surrounded by a three-foot-deep moat, boasts 45-foot high, eight-foot-thick walls designed for 420 guns and a force of 1,500 soldiers. Thirty years of construction were hampered by weather, disease, and lack of supplies.

The fort was built to guard the strategic island, a supply depot for friendly ships and a dangerous staging area were it to fall into the hands of an enemy wanting to blockade shipping lanes or invade the Gulf Coast. At the same time, it served as a federal prison — America's Devil's Island.

Its most infamous prisoner was Dr. Samuel Mudd. One early morning in April 1865, the 31-year-old Maryland physician set the leg of a man he either knew at the time or later learned was John Wilkes Booth, assassin of President Lincoln. Mudd was caught up in a grieving nation's hunt for scapegoats. A quick trial ended in his conviction; soon he was on his way to serve a life sentence on the barren island of despair. Already there when he arrived, a scrawl leading to his cell that paraphrased Dante's warning at the entrance to the Inferno in *The Divine Comedy*, "Whoever enters here, leave all hope behind."

Mudd, reviled as a participant in the Lincoln assassination

Fort Jefferson was America's "Devil's Island." *Fort Jefferson*

conspiracy, was shackled after he tried to escape. Four years of imprisonment and exile was ended by, of all things, an attack of yellow fever that swept through the fort, striking 270 of its 400 occupants and killing 38. Among the first victims was the Army doctor. Mudd helped save lives. When the crisis passed, he returned to his cell. A year and a half later, in 1869, President Andrew Johnson gave him a pardon. Mudd, himself suffering from yellow fever along with a broken heart, returned to Maryland, where he died at age 49.

His grandson, Dr. Richard Mudd, who died at 102 in 2002, spent his entire life clearing his grandfather's name. Others have argued Dr. Mudd might have been guilty. The family's best shot came in 1992 when an Army panel concluded the government was wrong to try Mudd in a military court. But an Army official rejected the finding, saying the country was effectively under martial law at the time. Mudd's family appealed.

The fort was abandoned by the army in 1874 and later served as a quarantine station. It was used off and on during the Spanish-American war and both world wars. President Franklin Roosevelt rescued it from oblivion in 1935 by naming it a federal monument. It is the jewel of seven keys and part of the Dry Tortugas National Park, more than 100 square miles of ocean, popular for boating, fishing, and diving.

Park rangers who live at the fort provide tours. A visitor center features an introductory video, a bookstore, and exhibits. There's a self-guiding trail and a fee-based campground with picnic tables and grills. It's available first come, first served. Groups of ten need reservations and a permit. It has only composting toilets and no showers or fresh water.

Fort Jefferson is open daylight hours only. Daily transportation is available from Key West via charter boat (about two hours each way) or seaplane (about 1 hour roundtrip). $5.00 entrance fee. $3.00 camping fee per person per day. Florida salt water fishing license required. Visitors need to provide their own food and water. Website: www.fortjefferson.com

Everglades National Park: 40001 S. R. 9336, Homestead 33034. Call (305) 242-7700. Website: www.nps.gov/ever/

Florida Keys and Key West Visitors Bureau: 1201 White Street, Key West 33040. Call (800) FLA-KEYS (352-5397). Website: www.fla-keys.com

Read More About It
Summers, Robert K. *Dr. Samuel A. Mudd at Fort Jefferson, 1865-1869*. 2005, Arlington, Va., BookSurge Publishing.
Manucy, Albert. *Pages From the Past: A Pictorial History of Fort Jefferson*. 1999, Homestead, Florida, Florida National Parks and Monuments Association.
Landrum, L. Wayne. *Fort Jefferson and the Dry Tortugas National Park*. 2003, Big Pine Key, Florida, L.W. Landrum.

Sites By Type and Era

BY TYPE

Town/Resort Area
Cedar Key
DeFuniak Springs
Eatonville
Fernandina Beach
Historic Pensacola
Micanopy
Mount Dora
St. Augustine
Tarpon Springs
Ybor City

Hotel/Lodge
Biltmore
Boca Raton Resort & Club
Clewiston Inn
Don Cesar
Kenilworth Hotel
Wakulla Springs

Attraction
Bok Tower
Cypress Gardens
Hialeah Race Track
Historic Spanish Point

Event
Kennedy Space Center
Orange Bowl
Sebring International Raceway

Park
Cape Florida Lighthouse
DeSoto Memorial
Everglades National Park
Florida Caverns State Park
Indian Key
Jonathan Dickinson State Park
Jupiter Lighthouse
Koreshan
Lake Kissimmee Cow Camp

Paynes Prairie
Torreya State Park

Marker/Monument
Lone Cypress
Monument to the "Labor Day
   Storm"
Union Monument
Wreck of San Pedro

Museum
Batista Museum
Gilbert's Bar House of Refuge
John Gorrie Museum

Government Building
Freedom Tower
Miami City Hall
Old Capitol

Homestead
Barker House
Barnacle
Bulow Plantation
Cross Creek
Edison and Ford Homes
Gamble Mansion
Hemingway Home
Kingsley Plantation
Ringling Museum
Stranahan House
Vizcaya
Whitehall
Yulee Sugar Mill

School
Florida Southern College
University of Florida
University of Tampa

Cemetery
Grave of Charles Dummett
Port Mayaca Cemetery

Roadway
Alligator Alley

Battlefield/Fort
Castillo de San Marcos
Dade Battlefield

Fort Caroline
Fort Christmas
Fort Clinch
Fort Jefferson
Fort Pickens
Natural Bridge Battlefield
Negro Fort
Olustee Battlefield
San Luís de Talimali

BY ERA
(site's most significant historic period)

Age of Exploration (to 1776)
Cape Florida Lighthouse
Castillo de San Marcos
De Soto National Memorial
Fort Caroline
Historic Pensacola
Historic Spanish Point
Indian Key
Jonathan Dickinson State Park
Jupiter Lighthouse
Micanopy
Paynes Prairie
St. Augustine
San Luís de Talimali
Wreck of the San Pedro

Redcoats to Rebellion (1776–1861)
Bulow Plantation
Dade Battlefield Fernandina
    Beach
Florida Caverns State Park
Fort Christmas
Grave of Charles Dummett
John Gorrie Museum
Kingsley Plantation
Negro Fort
Old Capitol

Civil War in Florida (1861–1865)
Cedar Key
Fort Clinch

Fort Jefferson
Fort Pickens
Gamble Mansion
Natural Bridge Battlefield
Olustee Battlefield
Torreya State Park
Union Monument
Yulee Sugar Mill

Coming of Age (1865–1920)
Barnacle
DeFuniak Springs
Eatonville
Edison and Ford Homes
Gilbert's Bar House of Refuge
Koreshan
Lake Kissimmee Cow Camp
Lone Cypress
Stranahan House
Tarpon Springs
University of Florida
University of Tampa
Vizcaya
Whitehall
Ybor City

Boom, Bust, and War (1920–1945)
Barker House
Biltmore
Boca Raton Resort & Club
Bok Tower
Clewiston Inn
Cross Creek
Cypress Gardens

Don CeSar
Florida Southern College
Freedom Tower
Hemingway Home
Hialeah Race Track
Kenilworth Hotel
Miami City Hall
Monument to "Labor Day
    Storm"
Orange Bowl
Port Mayaca Cemetery
Ringling Museum

Modern Florida (since 1945)
Alligator Alley
Batista Collection
Everglades National Park
Kennedy Space Center
Mount Dora
Sebring International Raceway
Wakulla Springs

Bibliography

Here's a list of agencies and literature to assist your travels or just help you learn more about Florida:

AGENCIES

Florida State Parks: Tallahassee, FL. (850) 245-2157. www.dep.state.fl.us/parks/

Florida Department of State: 500 Bronough St., Tallahassee, FL 32399-0250

Office of Cultural and Historical Programs: (850) 245-6300. www.dos.state.fl.us

Office of Historic Preservation (850) 245-6333

Museum of Florida History: (850) 245-6400. www.dhr.dos.state.fl.us/museum/

Florida Historical Society: 435 Brevard Avenue, Cocoa FL 32922. Call 321-690-1971. www.florida-historical-soc.org/

BOOKS

American Automobile Association. *Florida Tourbook.* Published annually, Heathrow, FL, American Automobile Association. www.aaa.com.

Bicentennial Commission of Florida. *The Florida Bicentennial Trail: A Heritage Revisited.* 1976, Tallahassee, State of Florida.

Boone, Floyd E. *Florida Historical Markers and Sites.* 1989, Houston, TX, Gulf Publishing Company.

Burnett, Gene. *Florida's Past: People and Events that Shaped the State,* Volumes 1-3. 1986, 1988, 1991, Sarasota, Pineapple Press.

Federal Writers' Project. *Florida: A Guide to the Southernmost State.* 1939, New York, Oxford University Press.

Gannon, Michael. *A Short History of Florida* (Revised Ed.). 2003, Gainesville, University of Florida Press.

Kleinberg, Howard. *Miami, The Way We Were.* 1989, Tampa, Surfside Publishing.

McCarthy, Kevin M., ed. *The Book Lover's Guide to Florida.* 1992, Sarasota, Pineapple Press.

McGovern, Bernie, ed. *The Florida Almanac*. Published biennially. Gretna, La., Pelican Publishing Company.

McIver, Stuart. *The Florida Chronicles,* Volumes 1-3. 1994, 1995, 2001, Sarasota, Pineapple Press.

McIver, Stuart. *Glimpses of South Florida History*. 1988, Miami, Florida Flair Books.

Morris, Allen. *The Florida Handbook*. Published biennially. Tallahassee, Peninsular Publishing Company.

Reilly, Benjamin. *Tropical Surge: A History of Ambition and Disaster on the Florida Shore*. 2005, Sarasota, Pineapple Press.

Shofner, Jerrell. *Florida Portrait: A Pictorial History of Florida*. 1990, Sarasota, Pineapple Press.

Tebeau, Charlton W. *A History of Florida*. 1971, Coral Gables, University of Miami Press.

Tebeau, Charlton W. and Ruby Leach Carson. *Florida: From Indian Trail to Space Age*. 1965, Delray Beach, Southern Publishing.

Waitley, Douglas. *Florida History from the Highways*. 2005, Sarasota, Pineapple Press.

Index

*Items in **bold** indicate illustrations.*

If you enjoyed reading this book, here are some other Pineapple Press titles you might enjoy as well. To request our complete catalog or to place an order, write to Pineapple Press, P.O. Box 3889, Sarasota, Florida 34230, or call 1-800-PINEAPL (746-3275). Or visit our website at www.pineapplepress.com.

200 Quick Looks at Florida History by James Clark. Florida has a long and complex history, but few of us have time to read it in depth. So here are 200 quick looks at Florida's 10,000 years of history from the arrival of the first natives to the present, packed with unusual and little-known facts and stories. (pb)

Best Backroads of Florida by Douglas Waitley. Each volume in this series offers several well-planned day trips through some of Florida's least-known towns and little-traveled byways. You will glimpse a gentler Florida and learn lots about its history. **Volume 1** The Heartland (south of Jacksonville to north of Tampa) (pb). **Volume 2** Coasts, Glades, and Groves (South Florida) (pb). **Volume 3** Beaches and Hills (North and Northwest Florida) (pb).

Classic Cracker by Ronald W. Haase. A study of Florida's wood-frame vernacular architecture that traces the historical development of the regional building style as well as the life and times of the people who employed it. (pb)

Easygoing Guide to Natural Florida, Volume 1: South Florida by Douglas Waitley. This book is for those of us who like to enjoy nature with minimum effort. This is the first of three volumes that will cover the entire state. Here in southern Florida we visit east coast beaches, the Indian River Lagoon, the St. Johns Marsh, the Kissimmee Prairie and the interior scrub. Then we head farther south to the Corkscrew Swamp and Fakahatchee Strand, west coast beaches, the Ten Thousand Islands, the Everglades, and the Keys. (pb)

The Florida Chronicles by Stuart B. McIver. A series offering true-life sagas of the notable and notorious characters throughout history who have given Florida its distinctive flavor. **Volume 1** *Dreamers, Schemers and Scalawags* (pb); **Volume 2** *Murder in the Tropics* (hb); **Volume 3** *Touched by the Sun* (hb)

Florida Fun Facts, 2nd Edition by Eliot Kleinberg. From theme parks to ballparks, the quirky to the educational, Miami to Tallahassee—every city and county in Florida are covered in this newly expanded edition. It's everything you need to know about Florida and more! (pb)

Florida History from the Highways by Douglas Waitley. Discover Florida, with its unique geography and exciting history—from ancient gold to modern real estate speculation—by journeying along its highways. You'll travel through changing times and landscapes and emerge filled with new appreciation for what has made Florida the colorful place it is today. (pb)

The Florida Keys by John Viele. The trials and successes of the Keys pioneers are brought to life in this series, which recounts tales of early pioneer life and life at sea. **Volume 1** *A History of the Pioneers* (hb); **Volume 2** *True Stories of the Perilous Straits* (hb); **Volume 3** The Wreckers (hb)

Florida Place Names by Allen Morris. This book paints a rich historical portrait of the state and reveals the dreams, memories, and sense of humor of the people who have called Florida home over the years. (hb)

Florida's Finest Inns and Bed & Breakfasts by Bruce Hunt. From warm and cozy country bed & breakfasts to elegant and historic hotels, author Bruce Hunt has composed the definitive guide to Florida's most quaint, romantic, and often eclectic lodgings. With photos and charming pen-and-ink drawings by the author. (pb)

Florida's Past by Gene Burnett. Collected essays from Burnett's "Florida's Past" columns in *Florida Trend* magazine, plus some original writings not found elsewhere. Burnett's easygoing style and his sometimes surprising choice of topics make history good reading. **Volume 1** (pb); **Volume 2** (pb); **Volume 3** (pb)

Historic Homes of Florida by Laura Stewart and Susanne Hupp. Seventy-four notable dwellings throughout the state—all open to the public—tell the human side of history. Each is illustrated by H. Patrick Reed or Nan E. Wilson. (pb)

Houses of Key West by Alex Caemmerer. Eyebrow houses, shotgun houses, Conch Victorians, and many more styles illustrated with lavish color photographs and complemented by anecdotes about old Key West. (pb)

Houses of St. Augustine by David Nolan. A history of the city told through its buildings, from the earliest coquina structures, through the Colonial and Victorian times, to the modern era. Color photographs and original watercolors. (hb, pb)

The Sunshine State Almanac and Book of Florida-Related Stuff by Phil Philcox and Beverly Boe. Chock-full of statistics, recipes, and photos, this handy reference is a veritable cornucopia of helpful and just plain fascinating stuff! Includes a long list of what's going on around Florida every month of the year. (pb)

Visiting Small-Town Florida Revised Edition by Bruce Hunt. Now covers the whole state in one volume. From Carrabelle to Bokeelia, Two Egg to Fernandina, these out-of-the-way but fascinating destinations are well worth a side trip or weekend excursion. (pb)